D0126012

Also by Joanna Faber and Julie King

How to Talk So Little Kids Will Listen:
A Survival Guide to Life with Children Ages 2-7.

How to Talk: Parenting Tips in Your Pocket, a companion app
to *How to Talk So Little Kids Will Listen,* providing an interactive set
of tools that parents can use in the moment
for instant tips and advice.

Parenting Hero, an interactive app that provides
an animated introduction to the *How To Talk* approach.

How to Talk When Kids Won't Listen

Whining, Fighting, Meltdowns,
Defiance, and Other Challenges
of Childhood

Joanna Faber & Julie King

Illustrated by Emily Wimberly

SCRIBNER
New York   London   Toronto   Sydney   New Delhi

Scribner
An Imprint of Simon & Schuster, Inc.
1230 Avenue of the Americas
New York, NY 10020

Copyright © 2021 by Joanna Faber and Julie King

All rights reserved, including the right to reproduce this book or portions thereof
in any form whatsoever. For information, address Scribner Subsidiary Rights
Department, 1230 Avenue of the Americas, New York, NY 10020.

First Scribner trade paperback edition August 2021

SCRIBNER and design are registered trademarks of The Gale Group, Inc.,
used under license by Simon & Schuster, Inc., the publisher of this work.

For information about special discounts for bulk purchases,
please contact Simon & Schuster Special Sales at 1-866-506-1949
or business@simonandschuster.com.

The Simon & Schuster Speakers Bureau can bring authors to your live event.
For more information or to book an event, contact the Simon & Schuster Speakers
Bureau at 1-866-248-3049 or visit our website at www.simonspeakers.com.

1 3 5 7 9 10 8 6 4 2

Library of Congress Cataloging-in-Publication Data has been applied for.

ISBN 978-1-9821-3415-0
ISBN 978-1-9821-3414-3 (pbk)
ISBN 978-1-9821-3416-7 (ebook)

"Before I became a parent,
I didn't know I could ruin
someone's day by asking
them to put pants on."

—Anonymous

Contents

In which we tackle tough topics requested by readers and
workshop participants, and share their stories.

Contents

Contents

Contents

Introduction

Welcome to our book, dear readers. Here is a tour of the territory. Part One is an illustrated overview of the essential tools you'll need to survive life with kids, from toddlers to early teens. We included activities at the end of each chapter so you can practice your skills if you're in the mood. In Part Two you'll find popular topics requested by our readers. We also share stories sent to us by parents and teachers, and we answer questions about some of their toughest kid-wrangling challenges.

As always, we love to hear from you. We invite you to share your stories and questions with us at info@how-to-talk.com or visit our website, how-to-talk.com. Maybe your topic will be in our next book!

Note: Names and other identifying details have sometimes been changed to protect the frazzled (although occasionally we've used real names upon request). We've attempted to choose aliases that faithfully represent the cultural or ethnic identities of the storytellers.*

---

*Some of the letters from parents included in this book are composites of questions that more than one correspondent have asked.

PART ONE

THE BASIC COMMUNICATION TOOLS

If you've ever come across advice about how to survive life with kids, you're probably familiar with the following admonitions: be kind but firm, consistent but flexible, supportive but not hovering, and establish clear limits. And don't forget to give unconditional love, stay connected, show empathy, and while you're at it, be sure to *keep calm*!

Who could argue with this commonsensical wisdom? It sounds like it could be doable. Especially before there are actual kids in your life!

Of course, those of us who have taken the leap into life with flesh and blood children soon find ourselves in situations where the theory does not seem to apply. When your two-year-old is screaming like a banshee because you gave him the wrong color cup; your five-year-old is having an epic meltdown over his homework assignment to draw an object that begins with *B* (and he refuses to just draw a ball); your fashion-conscious twelve-year-old is ranting because you are the *only* parent in the *world* who won't let her buy those ultra-expensive designer sneakers; your newly-licensed sixteen-year-old ignores your prohibition on driving in bad weather in order to go to a party during a blizzard . . . you're in the middle of a battle and you don't find yourself feeling that loving connection.

So what do I do now?

If you've ever asked yourself this question, we're glad you're here! Over the last few decades, we've been teaching parents, educators, and other adults who live or work with children how to get through the really tough times—all those everyday pull-your-hair-out moments—without losing sight of the bigger picture. (Okay, well, occasionally losing sight, but only temporarily!) In this book, you'll find the tools you need to deal with the inevitable conflicts between adults and children.

Chapter 1

Dealing with Feelings

Why Can't They Just Be Happy?

When you thought about life with children—before you had any in your life—we're guessing you imagined good times.

By now you may have discovered that the reality of life with kids often looks different from the fantasy.

4

When faced with conflict or misery, we want to get back to the happy scene we have in our heads. But our most valiant and well-meaning efforts to be helpful, or to fix a problem, can end up making things worse.

Why is it that when we try to calm kids down, they sometimes get more worked up? Our intention is to be soothing. To teach them that this tiny bump in the road of life can be driven over without crashing the entire vehicle into a ditch. *It will be OKAY!* But the message they hear is a different one: "You can't have what you want and I don't care, because your feelings are not important enough to bother about." Now the distress is doubled—added to the original disappointment over the missing granola bar is that lonely feeling you get when you realize nobody cares that you're sad.

It's true that for adults a granola bar ranks way down on the scale of global disasters. But for a disappointed kid, that missing treat is just as upsetting as any of the petty disasters that befall us grown-ups during the day. Your annoying coworker constantly uses your pens and doesn't replace them? *Stop complaining. It's not a big deal!* Your friend shared your personal health problems with the whole neighborhood? *You're overreacting. Don't be so sensitive.* The mechanic overcharged you to repair your transmission and it broke down again a week later and he wouldn't give you a refund? *Hey, that's life! No use getting upset about it.*

Don't get mad at *us*. We're just trying to help you by *explaining* why you're wrong to feel bad.

It's pretty infuriating when our own disappointments, admittedly insignificant in the grand scheme of things, are summarily dismissed. When someone tries to calm us down by minimizing our troubles, we end up feeling worse—and we may even direct a fresh wave of irritation at the person who was trying to help. Our kids are no different.

Even trained professionals can unintentionally aggravate an aggrieved child:

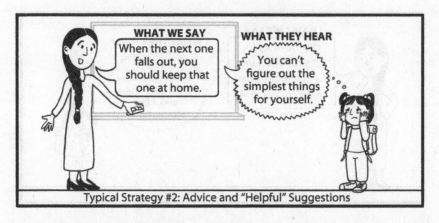

Typical Strategy #2: Advice and "Helpful" Suggestions

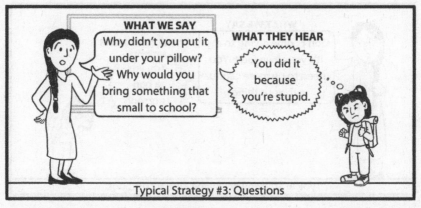

Typical Strategy #3: Questions

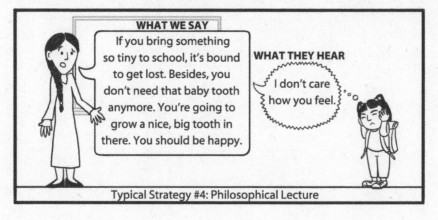

Typical Strategy #4: Philosophical Lecture

We desperately want to give kids some perspective. They can't go through life falling apart over every little thing. It's part of our job to help them learn what's important and what's not, isn't it? But the timing is wrong. When you're upset because your new shoes were stolen at the gym, that's not the moment you want your friend to remind you to be grateful you have feet. And when you lose your feet to gangrene, you don't want your friend coming over the day after the amputation to remind you that you're lucky because there are people who don't have legs. No doubt that will be a helpful perspective at some point in the future, but for right now you'd probably appreciate a little sympathy instead of a pep talk.

We may understand intellectually that we shouldn't try to talk people out of their misery in their moment of distress. But we still have a powerful urge to minimize or dismiss negative feelings, both for our kid's sake and for our own. When kids relate their tales of woe, we naturally try to convince them it's not that bad. They respond by dialing up the intensity to convince us that it is indeed *that bad*. We react with frustration, and before you know it everyone involved is sucked into an escalating spiral of irritation. The more we try to douse the flames, the hotter they get. It turns out we're pouring gasoline on the fire instead of water.

WHAT TO DO

Okay fine, so it's not helpful to try to get kids to look at the bright side, or to tell them that they should suck it up and stop whining because their problems aren't so bad. Now what? Sit on the couch with noise-canceling headphones? Is there literally NOTHING we can say or do that will not make things worse?

We're glad you asked! We present to you a set of tools you can grab when a child is in emotional distress.

Tool #1: Acknowledge feelings with words

Instead of arguing that the child is foolish, or wrong, or rude, or overreacting, stop and ask yourself: what is this child feeling? Is she frustrated, disappointed, angry, annoyed, sad, worried, scared?

Got it?

Now show your child you get it.

What we're looking for is the kind of thing you'd say with genuine emotion to a friend with whom you truly empathize. *That sounds scary. Oh, how disappointing! What a frustrating situation! It sounds like you're really annoyed with your _____ (brother/ teacher/friend) right now.*

11

Tool #2: Acknowledge feelings with writing

There's something about the written word that makes a kid feel like she's being taken seriously. Even children who are too young to read are often delighted to have their thoughts written down and read back to them. The writing may take the form of a list—a wish list, a shopping list, a list of worries or grievances.

Tool #3: Acknowledge feelings with art

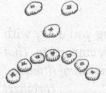

Art can be a powerful tool when strong emotions are in play. And the good news is, you don't have to be an artist. Stick figures will do just fine! Sometimes children will want to jump in and show you their sad or angry feelings with the help of a pencil, chalk, or crayons. Even Cheerios have been employed to create a sad face that lets kids know we understand how they feel.

Tool #4: Give in fantasy
what you cannot give in reality

When a child wants something that's impossible to have, our temptation is to repeatedly explain to them *why* they cannot have it. *"I already told you, we can't go swimming now, honey, the pool is closed for the day. There's no use crying about it."* These kinds of exercises in logic seldom persuade a youngster to accept reality. She'll cheer up more quickly if you say, *"Oh, I wish the pool would stay open all night. We could go swimming in the moonlight!"*

Next time you find yourself wanting to jump in with a dose of cold, hard reality, take a moment for whimsy instead. Tell your child you wish you had a magic wand to make a bathtub full of ice cream appear, you need some robots to help with cleanup, it would be great to have a clock that freezes time so you could have a hundred more hours to play.

Tool #5: Acknowledge feelings with
(almost) silent attention

Sometimes just a sympathetic sound is enough. Resist the urge to lecture, ask questions or give advice. Instead, simply listen with *oh's*, *ugh's*, *mmm's*, and *ah's*!

Yeah, but . . .

Sometimes it's obvious that a kid is feeling bad. A cookie falls from her hand, breaks to pieces on the floor, and is eaten by the alert dog. And it was the last cookie. The box is empty! Having just studied the section on acknowledging feelings, we leap to the emotional rescue. We resist the temptation to growl, "Sorry, kid, that's *literally* the way the cookie crumbles! You might as well learn it early." Instead we groan sympathetically, "Oh, gee, you were looking forward to eating that cookie! You didn't want Speedy to get it. He was so fast! He knew it was *chew it or lose it* time. I wish I had a magic wand to make another box of cookies appear instantly! What should we do now? Do you want to help me write COOKIES on our shopping list? Let's write it big so we can see it from across the room."

Hey, that was some champion-level kid wrangling. You just averted a cookie crisis. And your child is practicing fine motor coordination and learning to spell.

But sometimes figuring out feelings can be tricky. Kids get upset, or angry, and we didn't see it coming. We think we're having a nice, reasonable conversation, and the next thing we know we're caught in a drama of histrionic proportions. What the heck just happened?

Well, dear reader, for your convenience we have compiled below a list of typical interactions that can go from calm to conflict in a flash. The trick is to notice when children are expressing strong feelings even when they don't make it obvious.

Non-Obvious Expressions of Feelings

1. When a child *seems* to be asking a question

"Why don't you give the baby back?"

"Do I *have* to wear pants?"

"How am I supposed to do this assignment?"

A direct question deserves a direct answer . . . doesn't it?

"Because he's part of the family!"

"I just told you, it's 20 degrees out!"

"Well, you need to start by making an outline."

But somehow those answers get kids more agitated. Even though a child may not know the definition of the phrase "rhetorical questions," he is surely posing them here. It's more helpful to start the conversation by *acknowledging the feeling behind the question*.

> "Babies take a lot of attention! Sometimes you miss being the only one."

> "Ohh, I wish it was warmer out! You really feel more comfortable in shorts!"

> "It sounds like this assignment is overwhelming. There are so many parts to it, it's hard to know where to start."

Accepting the feeling behind the question may be enough to defuse the conflict and help a child accept disappointment or conquer anxiety. Or it might not be enough. That's why we wrote chapters two and three about engaging cooperation and problem-solving. But before you are tempted to skip ahead, remember it all starts here! We need goodwill to resolve conflicts without combat, and acknowledging feelings creates that goodwill.

2. When a child *seems* to be asking for advice

I don't know if I should join the team.

It feels like we've just been presented with a golden opportunity to share our hard-earned wisdom.

Of course you should join! You'll get exercise, you'll make friends, and it will look good on your college application!

Why did he storm off like that and slam his door?

Resist the temptation to offer instant advice. Consider that this child is actually expressing a feeling, and the most helpful response is to start by acknowledging it. But what *is* the feeling? Let's do a little respectful guessing.

17

You may have noticed that the parent* in this conversation made a suggestion. If you spend a generous amount of time accepting feelings, your child may be receptive to a respectfully offered suggestion. It's all in the timing! If we start the conversation by saying "Why don't you just give it a try?" a kid is more likely to argue or storm off. They need to feel understood before they're ready to consider solutions.

3. When a child makes a dramatic overstatement

"He's such a baby. He always cries when he doesn't get his way."

"I hate my teacher!"

"You never let me do anything fun!"

Our instinct tells us to correct course and provide a dose of reality:

"You have to be more patient with your brother. When you were his age, you were that way too."

"You don't hate your teacher. You know you're lucky to have him."

"Don't be ridiculous. You're just missing one party. There'll be plenty of others."

And yet somehow all of these responses ratchet up their rage rather than calm them down. Let's take a shot at acknowledging the feelings behind the overstatements. Here are some conversation starters that will turn down the heat and allow for a more civilized discussion:

* The parent in this conversation was Joanna, and her son did end up sticking with the cross-country team throughout his four years of high school. It turned out the bigger kids were less scary than they looked.

"It's not always easy having a little brother around. He likes to grab your stuff, and he screams when he gets frustrated."

"It sounds like your teacher did something that *really* annoyed you today!"

"It sounds like this party is really important to you. I wish we could be in two places at once."

Not *every* situation calls for acknowledging feelings!

It sounds like you're saying that absolutely everything is a feeling. This is exhausting! How are we supposed to get through the day?

You have a point there! We know that when strong emotions are involved, we can often avoid conflict and save energy if we address those feelings first. But there will be plenty of times when you can just live your life without emotional drama.

When a child asks a question that she actually wants an answer to:

You don't need to respond, "Sounds like you're feeling frustrated and unsure of how to pronounce that strange and confusing collection of letters." You can simply say "enough."

If your student asks:

You don't have to plumb the subtext, "Hmm, the indoor lighting can really make a person feel depressed, especially with all these fluorescent bulbs."

You can simply say, "Yes!"

When a child wonders:

Do real tigers live around here?

You don't *necessarily* need to explore feelings. "Oh gosh, that's a scary thought."

Feel free to give information. "Nope. Just in the zoo!" Or, if there are tigers roaming the neighborhood, "Why yes! If you see one, stay calm and back away slowly."

Many of our workshop participants have told us that when they're trying to accept children's feelings, it helps them to imagine what they would say to an adult friend. When we're talking to a peer, it often feels natural to empathize without denying their feelings, questioning, lecturing, or giving advice. But even with fellow adults our instincts sometimes fail us.

Joanna's story

A while back I got a call from a friend who was facing some medical tests. She told me, "The worst part is, I'm worried it's going to be cancer." Every instinct told me to dismiss her fear. *It's not that. Don't even think it!* There was an awkward silence as I corralled my thoughts. Finally I was able to reply, "That's a huge worry to be carrying around."

My friend let out an explosive, "YES! And do you know what people tell me? They tell me not to even *think* about it! Isn't that ridiculous? How can you not think about it?" I agreed that was as ludicrous as telling someone not to think about the pink elephant in the room. We both laughed a little bit. I didn't admit that I had been about to say those very same words as all the other "ridiculous" people.

When we accept the negative feelings of a person in distress, we're giving her a gift. At least one other person in the world understands what she's going through. She is not alone.

Acknowledging feelings is more than just a trick or a technique. It's a tool that can transform relationships. It doesn't guarantee that our kids will walk the dog, brush their teeth, or go to bed in a timely manner, but it creates an atmosphere of goodwill in which all things become easier and more pleasant. It also lays the foundation for kids to develop the capacity to care about other people and accept *their* feelings.

But you don't have to take our word for it. John Gottman, a prominent researcher in child psychology, published a study[1] in which he followed and compared parents with different communication styles over several years. The results showed that children whose feelings were identified and accepted had an enormous advantage, regardless of their IQ or their parents' social class, or educational level. They had longer attention spans; did better on their achievement tests; had fewer behavior problems; and got along better with teachers, parents, and peers. They were more resistant to infectious diseases and even had fewer stress hormones in their urine. So if we want children with superior urine (and who doesn't?) we should try acknowledging their feelings!

PRACTICE

In each situation, choose the response that best acknowledges the child's feelings with words, art, fantasy, or (almost) silent attention:

1. "Everybody hates me!"

    A. "That's just not true! Your parents love you, your grand-parents love you, your teacher loves you, and even your cat loves you!"

    B. "Well, what do you expect when you sulk and cry like that? Nobody wants to be around a whiner."

    C. "It sounds like you had a really rough day."

    D. "Don't be such a drama queen. You're always overreacting."

2. "My remote control car broke!"

    A. "Well you shouldn't have played with it so roughly. That's what happens when you drive it off the edge of your bed."

    B. "Oh no, that's disappointing. You really liked that car!"

    C. "Good thing you don't have a driver's license."

    D. "Don't cry. Daddy will buy you another one tomorrow."

3. "My teacher is so stupid!"

    A. "You sound pretty annoyed with her right now!"

    B. "Don't talk that way about your teacher. It's disrespectful."

    C. "I know! I found *three* typos in that permission slip she sent home last week. It was pathetic!"

    D. "I'm sure she had a good reason for what she did."

4. Your child sees a person walking a small dog. She starts to cry and climb up your leg.

    A. "Stop it! There's nothing to be afraid of. That little dog is not going to hurt you."

    B. "You can pet the nice doggie. Its fur is so soft."

    C. "Are you scared? Go run inside! I'll tell him to walk the dog on the other side of the street from now on."

    D. "Dogs can make a person nervous. You're not sure what it's going to do. Let's stand over here where you can see it but it won't be too close."

5. "I think I failed that math test."

    A. "Don't be so negative. You probably did just fine. And if you didn't, you should ask your teacher for a retest."

    B. "Well, you should have studied more. I've been telling you that all week, but you didn't listen."

    C. "Ugh, it's hard to wait for a test score when you're worried about how you did."

    D. "Nobody in this family is good at math. Sorry to tell you, you have bad math genes."

6. Your three-year-old won't stop crying because you told him he can't have the whole carton of ice cream for himself.

    A. "Do you want your teeth to rot? It's not healthy for you to eat that much sugar."

    B. "Don't be greedy. This ice cream is for everybody!"

    C. "You should be thanking me for buying dessert. If you keep complaining, you're not getting any ice cream at all!"

    D. "It's hard to share something delicious. You love ice cream so much you could eat a swimming pool full of it! Wait a second, let's draw it. Here you are diving into the ice cream. You can draw the chocolate chips."

7. "Tyler called me an idiot!"

A. "Don't let it bother you. Boys talk like that all the time. You two are such good friends, I'm sure he didn't mean it."
B. "That can be upsetting, to be called a name by a friend."
C. "That was a terrible thing for him to say! You should ignore him for the rest of the week. See how he likes that!"
D. "There must have been some reason for him to say that. What did you do to him?"

8. "Steven won the art contest again. I didn't even get fourth place."

A. "You can't expect to win 'em all. You should just try harder next time."
B. "That is so unfair. Your picture was much better. You couldn't even tell what his picture was supposed to be. He must be related to one of the judges."
C. "That's disappointing! You worked hard on that picture. It has so much detail in it—like this tiny bug in the grass, and the funny expression on the cat's face."
D. "Look, maybe you're not cut out to be an artist. Not everybody can draw. You're better at sports!"

9. "No fair! You're supposed to let *me* flush the toilet! I wanted to make it go down."

A. "Whoever told you life was fair? Anyway, you usually forget, and I didn't want the bathroom to stink."
B. "Stop fussing! You can do it next time."
C. "Just wait a minute. I'll drink a can of soda so I can go to the bathroom and then you can flush *my* pee."

D. "Oh . . . gosh. You really wanted to flush. Let's put a sign on the toilet so we'll both remember for next time."

> MOM
> DO NOT TOUCH
> MIKEY WILL FLUSH

10. "I can't fall asleep. I'm too worried."

A. "Lie down and try to relax. Things will look brighter in the morning."

B. "You think *you* have worries? Just wait till you grow up and have a mortgage!"

C. "Oh you poor thing. Maybe we should pull you out of that honors program. It's too much pressure."

D. "It's hard to get to sleep when you have worries on your mind. I'll get some paper to write them down."

---

1. Science project due next week. Too much work.

2. Bike chain is broken.

3. Need new battery for remote control plane.

4. Not enough money. Lost quarter under washing machine.

5. Messy closet. Need more space.

Answer Key:

1. C	6. D
2. B	7. B
3. A	8. C
4. D	9. D
5. C	10. D

REMINDER: DEALING WITH FEELINGS

1. Acknowledge feelings with words.

"It's not easy always having a little brother around."
"Sounds like this assignment is overwhelming. There are so many parts to it, it's hard to know where to start."

2. Acknowledge feelings with writing.

"You were looking forward to eating a granola bar. Let's write it on the shopping list."
"You have a lot on your mind. Tell me your worries and I'll write them down."

3. Acknowledge feelings with art.

"That can make a person feel sad. Do you want to draw the tears?"
"You really miss your mom. Let's draw a picture of her."

4. Give in fantasy what you cannot give in reality.

"I wish I had a magic wand. I'd make the sun come out right now."
"That party is really important to you. I wish we could be in two places at once."

5. Acknowledge feelings with almost silent attention.

"Oh . . . Ugh . . . Mmm . . . Ahh . . ."

Chapter 2

Cooperative Kids

The Impossible Dream? Why can't they just DO what we tell them to DO?

We can't just talk about feelings all day long. Sometimes we need to get kids to do things that they are *deeply* uninterested in doing.

How many kids care about not being late, washing their hands, keeping their rooms tidy, or changing their underwear?

It seems like the most efficient way to get kids to do things would be to tell them directly:

"Put the cat *down*, get your coat *on*. No, not later, NOW!"

The problem is that being on the receiving end of commands can inspire powerful feelings of irritation and defiance.

Imagine you come home from work and your partner says to you, "Oh good, you're home. Uh uh, don't touch the computer. Please go hang up your coat, wash your hands, and come set the table. Did I tell you to look at the mail? Put it down, now. Hurry up, dinner's going to be ready soon. Did you hear me? I said, *now!*"

Did you have the impulse to turn around and go right back out the door? After all, there is that Tuesday special at the pizza parlor.

When we order kids around (even when we do it politely by attaching a "please" to our command) we're working against ourselves. Orders and their close relations—threats, accusations, and warnings—do not inspire feelings of cooperation. And inspiring kids to *feel* cooperative is more than half the battle.

Let's look at some of the typical ineffective strategies that we adults use to get children to do things. And then, so as not to leave you hanging, we'll offer you the antidotes as well—alternatives that are much more likely to result in a cooperative kid!

Ineffective Strategy: Threats

Instead, **PUT THE CHILD IN CHARGE**.

When we find ourselves in a power struggle, it's more helpful to turn down the heat than to gear up for battle. A threat is often perceived as a challenge, which can only harden the resolve of a spirited child. Instead of trying for more control, try sharing the power. You may be pleasantly surprised!

Ineffective Strategy: Warnings

Instead, **DESCRIBE THE PROBLEM.**

When we warn kids about the disaster that is going to befall them, we're giving them the message that we don't trust them, they aren't acting responsibly, they can't trust *themselves* to figure out what to do or how to behave. Warnings (and the orders that go along with them) take away a sense of personal responsibility.

When we describe the problem, we do the opposite. We invite the child to become part of the solution. We give them a chance to tell themselves what to do.

If they don't come up with a solution, **TELL THEM WHAT THEY CAN DO INSTEAD OF WHAT THEY *CAN'T*.**

When children are driving us crazy, we naturally focus on what we *don't* want them to do. But kids can't just "not do"! It's much easier to redirect a child's energy than to stop it in its tracks.

Ineffective Strategy: Sarcasm

Instead, **WRITE A NOTE**.

We've all been there: repeating an instruction and being ignored over and over until it drives us mad. And then we erupt in frustration and say something truly mean and unhelpful. We need an antidote. How about a note?

The written word has many advantages. First, after expressing your irritation in your first draft, you can rewrite it and make it nicer. Second, it serves as a reminder to your child without you having to repeat yourself. Third, as one child put it, "Notes don't get louder." Fourth, there's just something about the written word, a magical quality that even pre-reading children find engaging.

Ineffective Strategy: Blaming and Accusing

Instead, **GIVE INFORMATION**.

What's obvious to us is not always obvious to a child. When we give information instead of hurling accusations, we're treating a child with respect. We assume that if she has the proper knowledge, she'll act responsibly.

It can help to think of the way we'd talk to an adult. It would be insulting to give a direct order: "Hey, stop tapping the fork on my table! You're making dents in the wood!" We naturally try to find a way to give them information: "That table's made of soft wood. Even a little tap from a fork can dent it." We let adults tell themselves what to do.

Ineffective Strategy: Rhetorical Questions

Instead, **DESCRIBE WHAT YOU SEE.**

When we're exasperated, it can be hard to resist asking rhetorical questions. The problem is, little kids don't get it and big kids get offended.

When we limit ourselves to describing what we see, we avoid the implied criticism and put the focus where it needs to be.

Ineffective Strategy: Lecturing and Moralizing

Instead, **SAY IT WITH A WORD**.

Many of us take great satisfaction in delivering a good old-fashioned rant, but nobody appreciates being on the receiving end. If kids haven't tuned out after the first few words (let's face it, they've heard it all before!) they're more likely to be consumed with feelings of irritation than to be infused with the spirit of cooperation. Even if they *were* planning to put those shoes away, after that annoying lecture, they don't want to do it anymore.

One alternative to the lecture is to use a single word.

The beauty of using the single word is that you're calling attention to the problem and letting your child tell him*self* what to do. The unspoken message is, "I'm sure you'll take care of this now that you're aware of it."

Caveat: Make sure your single word is a noun, not a verb. A noun can be heard as a respectful reminder. "Seat belt." A verb will be heard as an insufferable command. "Move!"

Ineffective Strategy: Name-Calling

Instead, **DESCRIBE HOW YOU FEEL.** (Use the word "I." Avoid the word "you.")

When we slap a disparaging label on a child, we're hoping to inspire her to act better. *Oh gosh, now that I realize I'm rude, I shall reform my ill-mannered ways.* Unfortunately, reality doesn't work that way. Kids are more likely to get angry or, even worse, to embrace the negative label. We have a better chance of getting a helpful response from children (and adults!) if we forgo the insult and describe our own feelings instead. It's important to use the word "I" instead of "you," when employing this tool. As soon as we say "you," a child will feel accused and defensive.

It can be a bit tricky. We often start out with the "I" and then within seconds the "you" sneaks its way in, destroying goodwill. "Hey, I don't like it when YOU poke me" will be less well received than "Hey, I don't like being poked."

Ineffective Strategy: Comparison

Instead, **OFFER A CHOICE**.

Inside every little person (and big people too) is a fierce desire for autonomy. By offering a choice, we engage the natural impulse to control one's own destiny. It also gives a child valuable practice in decision-making.

Ineffective Strategy: Orders and Commands

Instead, **BE PLAYFUL**. (Especially effective with little kids.)

WARNING: This tool is very powerful, but it cannot be operated when under the influence of irritation. You have to be in the mood!

Make an inanimate object talk: Kids don't like it when we tell them what to do, but little kids often find it irresistible when objects speak to them, even when it's glaringly obvious that the sounds are coming out of our mouths. Fortunately, you don't need to study ventriloquism to make this tool work! Just use a different voice for the object.

Play the incompetent fool: We adults are always in a position of power and authority. It strikes little kids as hilarious when we pretend to have no idea what we're doing, and they become the experts. We might as well enjoy the silly fun of this role reversal while we can. Soon enough our children will be more competent than us at . . . practically everything!

Pretend: Transitions are hard for kids. If we can make the transition itself a fun activity, we effectively eliminate the transition altogether.

Make it a game or a challenge: This is another way to make a transition enticing, instead of the end-of-all-fun.

How many big long steps will it take to get to the car? Let's count. OR Can you walk to the car backwards? OR I'll race you to the car. Ready... set... GO!

Use different accents or silly voices: Kids love the unexpected. Instead of a grim command, try talking like your child's favorite cartoon character, or a robot, or a sports announcer giving color commentary.

He's got fingers in the sleeve... now he's up to the wrist... now it's stuck on his elbow... no wait, it's coming through... we can see the tip of the fingers poking out the end... and GOAL! That's a big SCORE for his team! The crowd goes wild!

Do any of the unhelpful responses sound familiar? Unfortunately, our typical strategies tend to create hostile feelings in our children. And even when they do "work"—when a child does what we want him to do for fear of a threatened consequence—there can be other negative fallout. Every time we command, threaten, or accuse our kids, we're teaching them to command, threaten, and accuse others. It may seem reasonable when *we* say it, but when we hear the same kind of language coming out of our kids' mouths, it sounds pretty bad. (*"Well, if you don't let me play my video game, I'm not gonna do my homework!"*)

If we want our kids to be polite and respectful, it helps to model those qualities!

Of course there is no one-to-one correspondence between these tools and our unhelpful impulses to command, accuse, threaten, etc. You can mix and match. Give a choice instead of a command, give information instead of a lecture, describe how you feel instead of blaming. You get the idea. The above pairings are just serving suggestions to stimulate your creativity.

PRACTICE

For each scenario, fill in the blank with a response that uses the suggested tool for engaging cooperation.

1. Your child never wants to stop what he's doing when you ask him to wash his hands and come to dinner. You give him five-minute and one-minute warnings, but he still protests or completely ignores you.

Unhelpful Response:

Acknowledge Feelings:

Offer a Choice:

Put the Child in Charge:

Be Playful:

2. Your child hung her jacket on a doorknob and it slipped to the floor. You just tripped over it.

Unhelpful Response:

Say It with a Word:

Describe How You Feel (use "I" not "you"):

Describe What You See:

3. You see your child headed for the living room couch with a glass of juice and a bag of pretzels.

Unhelpful Response:

Give Information:

Note on Kitchen Doorway:

Describe the Problem:

Tell Her What She *Can* Do Instead of What She *Can't*:

4. You're ready to set the table for dinner but you discover it's covered with the remains of an abandoned art project. Scissors, markers, papers, tape, cardboard, glue, and string cover the entire surface.

Unhelpful Response:

Be Playful:

Describe the Problem:

Say It in a Word:

5. EXTRA CREDIT: See how long you can go without issuing a single command to your child(ren).

How long did you last?

A. 20 minutes
B. An hour and a half (but he was napping for the first hour)
C. The entire day
D. _____ (your answer here)

Did you notice a difference in your mood or your child's?

Answer Key (individual responses may vary!):

1.

Unhelpful Response: I just spent the last forty-five minutes making dinner. I'm tired of calling you. If you don't get your backside in that chair in the next thirty seconds, you can forget about dessert!

Acknowledge Feelings: It's not easy to tear yourself away when you're in the middle of . . .

Offer a Choice: Do you need one more minute . . . or five?
Do you want to use the liquid soap, or the dinosaur soap?
Do you want to wash my hands or should I wash yours?

Put the Child in Charge: Can you set the timer for five minutes and let everyone know when it's time to eat?

Be Playful:

Make the washcloth talk: I need some dirty hands to wash!
It - is - time - for - all - ro-bots - to - come - to - din-ner. Ro-bots - must - have - fu-el. Fol-low - ME.

2.

Unhelpful Response: How many times have I told you, you need to hang your jacket in the closet? It's going to get filthy! Don't be so lazy—it only takes an extra thirty seconds to hang your coat up properly. One of these days I'm going to break my neck tripping over it, and it's going to be your fault.

Say It with a Word: Jacket!

Describe How You Feel (use "I" not "you"): I don't like seeing a jacket getting dirty on the floor.

Describe What You See: The jacket fell on the floor.

3.

Unhelpful Response: Get back here right now! Don't you dare take food into the living room. You know the rules!

Give Information: Food belongs in the kitchen.

Note (on the kitchen doorway): No food or drink beyond this point! Please check pockets and shoes.

Describe the Problem: Oh, you wanted to hang out in the living room. The problem is, I don't want to have to worry about crumbs and spills on the couch.

Tell Her What She *Can* Do Instead of What She *Can't*: You can eat snacks in the kitchen and then come play in the living room.

4.

Unhelpful Response: Oh great . . . I can't set the table for dinner because it's covered with your mess. Why can't you do your projects in your room? That's what your brother does. It's called being considerate.

Be Playful: We need a fast clean-up. I'm gonna play [child's favorite music]. Do you think you can put everything away by the end of the song?

Describe the Problem: I need a clear table so I can put out dinner.

Say It in a Word: Joey, the table!

5. Extra Credit

    A. Nice start.
    B. You are on a roll.
    C. We stand in awe!
    D. Words fail us.

REMINDER: COOPERATIVE KIDS

1. Put the child in charge.

"Can you check the travel app and see when we have to leave to get there on time?"

2. Describe the problem.

"You have a lot of energy, and I'm worried about things getting broken. What should we do?"

3. Tell them what they *can* do instead of what they *can't*.

"Let's see how high you can jump."

4. Write a note.

"Dear Athlete, before you hit the streets, remember your cleats."

5. Give information.

"Spot doesn't like having his tail pulled."

6. Describe what you see.

"Oh, some milk spilled on the floor."

7. Say it with a word.

"Shoes."

8. Describe how you feel.

"I don't like being poked."

9. Offer a choice.

"Do you want to put away the leftovers or load the dishwasher?"

10. Be playful.

"I bet you can't beat me to the car. Ready, set, go . . . !"

Chapter 2 1/2

None of This Is Working!

The Problem with Chapter Two

You heavily implied that if I used these tools, my child would be cooperative. You lied!

What to do next? You may need to go in one of two different directions:

1. Take Action Without Insult

Sometimes you need to act immediately to avoid death or dismemberment (or to protect your furniture). There's no time for reflection!

> Your child is running recklessly for the road, heedless of your warnings? You're going to scoop her up, no matter how much she screams and protests, and take her inside, saying, "I can't let you run in the road. It's too dangerous!"

> Your child is using his paintbrush to spatter the couch, curtains, and cat instead of the canvas? You're going to grab the paint and brush and put them out of reach, saying, "It's too tempting to flick paint. I can't let you do that. It upsets me to see paint on the furniture!"

> Your child is about to slug his sibling in the stomach? You're going to drag him away, saying, "I can't let you hurt your brother!"

48

I can't let you hurt your brother!

Even when there's no imminent threat of property damage or bodily injury, you may find yourself losing patience when you've tried a few tools and your child doesn't respond. We're not suggesting you tamp down your rage and plow your way through the whole list. Take a breath. Think about something pleasant for a moment. Chocolate . . . kittens . . . long walks on the beach . . . and then take action without insult:

> Your child left an enormous mess from a cooking experiment (despite his earnest promise to clean up after himself), and now he expects a ride to his friend's house? You can take action by digging in your heels and saying, "I'm not willing to drive you until the mess is gone. I would feel very resentful if I had to clean it up myself before making dinner, and I don't want to feel that way toward you." (This is technically a *non-action*, but you get the idea. Sometimes a boycott can make a powerful statement!)

> Your child keeps jumping from one bench to another at the pizza parlor, even though you've described how people feel ("The jumping is disturbing other people in the restau-

49

rant.") and given her a choice ("You can sit inside, or jump outside."). You can take action by telling your child, "We're going home now. We need to let people eat in peace."

The principle is to *take action in order to protect people and property*, and sometimes to protect relationships as well. We're not claiming the kids won't wail and protest. But if we don't take action, children learn that they can ignore us because we don't mean what we say, and we will eventually give in out of exhaustion or exasperation.

The words we use when we take action are important. Notice that in all these examples we don't insult or attack the child. ("Don't be so lazy. Do you ever think about anybody's needs but your own?" "It's your own fault you're missing out. *You* broke your promise and left this big mess.") A child who is attacked will direct his energies to defending himself or counterattacking! ("No fair, I wasn't the only one who left things out. You always blame me for everything!") Instead we focus on our values, letting kids know our limits firmly but respectfully, while acknowledging their feelings, giving information, and describing our own feelings. If we can manage to resist the temptation to use insulting or accusatory language, our children will be more likely to absorb the message we want them to hear.

2. Ask Yourself "Why?"

When you do have time to reflect, ask yourself: What is going on in my child's head? Why is he so resistant to my "reasonable" expectations?

Common Problems that Interfere with Cooperation
(and what to do about them)

- Your child may have strong feelings that are making him uncooperative: **Acknowledge feelings.**

Remember way back in chapter one, all that stuff about acknowledging feelings? If your child is consistently refusing to cooperate with a specific request, try exploring feelings.

Do you have a massive battle every morning over leaving for school? If you start by accepting feelings, you may learn something useful.

Who knows how your child will respond? Maybe you'll find out he doesn't want to go to school because he's afraid to use the bathroom there. Maybe she's worried about a test. Maybe he thinks the baby will take apart his puzzle and chew on it while he's gone. Maybe it's very difficult to stop a video game in the middle of a level, and it's best to choose a different activity for morning play.

In any case, it's a safe bet that acknowledging feelings will help, and may even lead you to a creative resolution.

- Your child may be too hungry, tired, or overwhelmed to be cooperative: **Tend to basic needs—food, sleep, and recovery time.**

51

Does your child often melt down toward the end of the day? When a kid is tired or hungry, no amount of verbal skill will be as effective as a snack or a nap. This is especially true for little kids.

> We worked with one parent whose three-year-old, Nolan, became out of control every evening. He would scream, hit, kick, bite, throw things, dump water out of the tub, for no apparent reason. The parents had tried all kinds of different strategies, to no avail. Finally they figured it out. Nolan had recently stopped napping at preschool. By five o'clock, he was beyond all reason. His parents started getting him to bed much earlier, and the evening insanity ceased.

And it's true for older kids as well.

> In programs where teens were given free meals at school without the stigma of having to register as low-income students, and school start times were pushed forward so teens could get more sleep, student behavior and performance improved dramatically. Test scores went up, attendance rates went up, graduation rates went up, and disruptive behavior decreased. Two very simple solutions to a complicated problem. It's hard to concentrate on schoolwork and to behave calmly when you're hungry or overtired.[1]

If a child is feeling overwhelmed by sensory input or is emotionally exhausted, you'll want to find a way for her to recover before placing more demands on her or heading into a new activity. One mom shared this story with us:

> When my six-year-old, Amaya, gets home from school, her little sister, Kiana, gets very excited and can't wait to

play with her. I used to encourage Amaya to give Kiana attention, but it often backfired. She'd end up snapping at Kiana or shoving her. I finally realized that Amaya needs time alone to wind down after the stress of a school day. If I fend off Kiana for the first hour, Amaya will play with her very sweetly and patiently later on. I'm not saying that a day in first grade is major trauma, but there are a lot of things that are hard for my introverted daughter. Following all the rules, dealing with a large group of kids, worrying about being able to finish her work, worrying about getting the teacher's approval . . . it all adds up.

- Your child's developmental ability may not match your expectations: **Adjust expectations and manage the environment instead of the child.**

But he IS developmentally ready. He can do _____ when he wants to. He just did it this morning!

We tend to think that as soon as a child can do something once, they should be able to do it *consistently*. That is often not the case!

Just because she was able to use the potty in the morning after she woke up, doesn't mean she can get there in time when she's distracted by playing or eating. She may need gentle reminders, or she may be better off wearing a pull-up in the afternoon.

Just because he can play gently with the neighbor's kitten under supervision doesn't mean he's ready to take care of his own kitten—which would mean treating it gently even when he's excited or frustrated. It might be wiser to wait another year, despite his desperate pleading for a pet.

But at his age he should be able to . . . !

Individual development doesn't always perfectly follow the line on a chart.

> Just because *most* kindergarteners can sit in circle time for ten minutes without squirming doesn't mean this particular child can. He may need permission to get up and move around during story time.
>
> Maybe most of the fifth graders are ready to go on the three-day school camping trip, but yours is not. She may be too anxious at the thought of sleeping away from home.
>
> Perhaps some seventh graders can keep track of their assignments and do their homework independently in their room. Your particular child may need your help organizing his work and your company and support while he plows through it.

- Life has become all battles and no joy: **Take time to reconnect.**

It's easy to get caught up in this business of managing children and getting them to do things they have to do. Because, let's face it, that's a big part of the job description. But it's not enough to sustain a loving relationship.

Did you ever have a neighbor who only called you if there was a problem or a complaint? Even if that neighbor was very polite, didn't your heart just sink a little whenever you saw that number on caller ID? Weren't you a bit tempted not to answer the phone?

If we *always* approach children with the goal of correcting them or getting them to follow our agenda, at some point they're not going to see any reason to cooperate, or even interact with us at all. We may need to take some time to reconnect. To do something together "just for the fun of it."

Set aside your agenda, sit down with your kid, and read a story, build a block tower, give a piggyback ride, make a blanket cave, wrestle, poke raisin eyeballs into a lump of peanut butter, grab a hose and make a mud puddle, play a video game, listen to their favorite music . . . The idea is to follow the child's lead and do what they like to do. When the time is up, tell your kid, "I liked doing this with you. Let's do it again tomorrow when the baby's napping." It's nice to plan a specific time that your child can look forward to.

If none of these ideas are helping, you may have a more complicated problem, which calls for a more complicated solution. Move on to chapter three for ideas about how to tackle tougher conflicts.

PRACTICE

In each situation choose the appropriate response—either taking action, or acknowledging feelings, or adjusting expectations and tending to basic needs, or giving recovery time and reconnecting with the child.

1. Your child is being too rough with the kitten again. You've already warned her to be more gentle ten times in a single morning.

    A. Cats have nine lives. Distract yourself with a crossword puzzle.
    B. Ask her, "How would *you* feel if someone held *you* upside down by one leg?"
    C. Say, "I'm putting Fuzzball in my bedroom for now. She needs a break. You can play with your stuffed kitty." (Lock the bedroom door.)
    D. Tell her, "You don't deserve to have a pet! Say goodbye to Fuzzball, because I'm taking her back to the animal shelter tomorrow."

2. Your child keeps leaving his school papers, books, and sports equipment on the kitchen table. You've already described the problem ("I need to set the table for dinner") and let him know how you felt ("I don't like sports equipment on the table!"). Now you are out of patience!

    A. Sweep all of his belongings into a giant trash bag and loudly announce that you are throwing it in the garbage.
    B. Carefully stack his belongings into a teetering tower on one side of the table. Eat dinner while balancing your plate on the lacrosse stick.
    C. Hire a maid.
    D. Say, "I'm out of patience! I'm moving these things to

your bedroom!" Dump the items on the only clear spot, probably his bed.

3. Every evening your normally placid child transforms into a monster. She sobs tragically when the blue cup is not available, throws food off her plate, and screams when you try to get her into pajamas.

A. Lecture her about the importance of acting her age.
B. Consider a dramatically earlier bedtime, or reinstating a nap.
C. Tell her, "You have lost the privilege of having dessert! Children who throw food don't deserve ice cream."
D. Go online and order a dozen blue cups. Add a new pair of rainbow unicorn pajamas to the cart. Pay $43.65 extra for overnight delivery.

4. You don't want your child to leave his homework until the last minute. You give him time to relax and have a snack when he gets home from school, but when you urge him to get out his assignment book, he starts to cry.

A. Do his homework for him while he sits next to you watching videos on his tablet. (You may need to brush up on your long division.)
B. Explain how important math skills are in daily life. Warn him of the dangers of developing bad work habits and falling behind.
C. Don't expect him to dive right into homework after a whole day of rule following at school. Take some time to sit on the floor with him and add to the LEGO alien spaceship he's been working on all week.
D. Create a sticker chart. Tell him that if he gets ten stickers in a row for completing homework without complaining, you'll buy him a new remote control car.

5. You're planning to spend the weekend visiting your sister's family. Your child refuses to get ready, even though you've given her information ("We have to leave by ten o'clock"), given her a choice ("What snacks do you want to pack for the car ride?"), and described how you feel ("I'm worried about getting stuck in traffic if we leave late").

A. Tell her, "That's it, I'm leaving without you."

B. Start counting in a menacing way, "One, two, two and a half, two and three-quarters . . ."

C. Sigh tragically. Say, "I guess I just have to do everything myself."

D. Say, "It seems like you're not too excited about visiting your cousins." Spend the next five minutes listening attentively to her grievances and acknowledging her feelings. When you can't stand to delay any longer, say, "Let's continue the conversation in the car."

Answer Key:

1. C
2. D
3. B
4. C
5. D

NOTES:

1B. Ask her, "How would *you* feel if someone held *you* upside down by one leg?"

It's tempting to try to get your child to empathize with the kitten. The problem is, kids (and people in general) usually experience this type of question as a thinly veiled scolding. They are more likely to argue with you ("I would LOVE it if you held me upside down by one leg!"). Even if they can see why the kitten might not like it, they won't want to admit it to you.

Of course it's important to teach children to see things from the perspective of others, but if we want the message to get through, we can't do it in the context of a scolding. You can sit down with your child at another time and invite her to think about what scares the kitten and what makes her feel playful, and what makes her purr.

2D. Say, "I'm out of patience. I'm moving these things to your bedroom!" Dump the items on the only clear spot, probably his bed.

If this is a recurring conflict, you might want to follow up by problem-solving with your child. (See chapter three.)

4D. Create a sticker chart. Tell him that if he gets ten stickers in a row for completing homework without complaining, you'll buy him a new remote control car.

Research on motivation[2] confirms the experience of parents we work with. While sticker charts and rewards can inspire kids in the short term to do what we want, they have a tendency to backfire in the long run. For one thing, they are subject to inflation. Kids may decide they don't care about the reward and demand ever more valuable prizes for doing what you thought they should "just do" in the first place. For another, they may start demanding rewards for things they used to do for "free." *"You want me to clean up my room/set the table/shovel the driveway/walk the dog? What will you give me for it?"* Rewards also make children feel less intrinsically motivated to engage in the activity itself. Children who read books for rewards, for example, are far less likely to read for pleasure.

And finally, if a child fails to complete the task, the dangled reward becomes a punishment, with all the attendant resentment and ill will associated with that: *"Now you'll be deprived of this fantastic thing that you could have had if only you had made better choices!"* (Read more about the problem with punishment in chapter three.) Since rewards don't address the reason for the problem, a child may still have trouble starting his homework in spite of the promised prize. But now his misery will be compounded by loss of a reward.

REMINDER: WHEN THE COOPERATION TOOLS AREN'T WORKING

1. Take action without insult.

"I can't let you hurt your brother."

2. Ask yourself *why* **your child is resistant to your reasonable expectations. You may need to . . .**

a. Acknowledge feelings.

"You really don't want to leave. You're not in the mood for school."

b. Tend to basic needs: food, sleep, recovery time.

Does your child need an earlier bedtime? . . . a snack? . . . some downtime?

c. Adjust expectations: manage the environment instead of the child.

"Let's go back to pull-ups at night for now."

d. Take time to reconnect.

Spend time following the child's lead and doing something with them that they like to do—read a story, play a video game, bake cookies, build a block tower. . .

Chapter 3

The Problem with Punishment

and What to Do Instead

The Pros and Cons of Punishment

```
┌─────────────────────┬───────────────────┐
│   PROS              │   CONS            │
│                     │                   │
│ • it's traditional  │                   │
│                     │                   │
│ • it's popular      │                   │
│                     │  • doesn't work   │
│ • satisfies urge    │                   │
│   for revenge       │                   │
│                     │                   │
│ • opportunities for │                   │
│ creativity in       │                   │
│ dreaming up         │                   │
│ "logical            │                   │
│ consequences"       │                   │
│ abound              │                   │
│                     │                   │
│ • Gotta do          │                   │
│   SOMETHING!        │                   │
└─────────────────────┴───────────────────┘
```

The nice thing about punishment is that it appears to be a simple solution to the common problem of misbehaving kids. *"If you do this, I will do that to you. You will be so sorry, you'll learn not to repeat that behavior."* It's neat and uncomplicated. It can be made into a chart and laminated. Different levels of punishment can be listed and calculated for each anticipated infraction: Running into the street—*one hard smack on the bottom*; Lying—*ten minutes in the time-out chair*; Throwing food—*no dessert for you, kiddo!*; Biting your brother—*your parent will bite your arm* (not hard enough to draw blood, just hard enough so you know what it feels like); Stealing—*you just lost your smartphone for a month*; Failing math—*you're off the soccer team.* And so on.

The only problem with punishment is that *it doesn't work* in the long run. Study after study[1] has shown that children who are punished are likely to misbehave again.

- Punishment tends to inspire anger and resentment, rather than true remorse or a desire to do better in the future. A child who is spanked or put in the corner for pinching the baby is likely to feel even greater hostility toward the baby, and toward his parent as well. We'd love to imagine him reflecting constructively on his misdeeds: *Gee whiz, sitting in this chair in the corner I've had an epiphany! I should treat my dear brother more gently when he knocks down my block towers.* In actuality, he's more likely to be focused on himself: *How long do I have to sit here?* And consumed with indignation: *No fair, the baby never gets in trouble!* The punishment hasn't encouraged him to be gentle with this little intruder who is sucking up all his parent's attention. He may be inspired to become more sneaky in his attacks. Likewise, a teen who has her smartphone confiscated for not doing her homework is unlikely to suddenly develop a passion for algebra. She is more likely to become even more passionate in her hatred of math, stew with resentment against her parents, and find a devious way to access her social media accounts.

- Punishment fails to address the reason the child is misbehaving in the first place. It doesn't help children learn more acceptable ways to meet their needs. As one teacher put it, "The kids who get sent to the time-out corner are the same kids over and over again." Consider the child with poor impulse control who throws things when he gets upset. Being ostracized in the corner is not teaching him alternative strategies to handle frustration. The next time he's overwhelmed with emotion, objects will fly again. He'll be sent back to that corner. His sense of himself as a bad kid will be reinforced with each repetition. And there will probably be a lot of repetitions! When we assume punishment is the right course of action and it doesn't achieve results, the typical recourse is to use harsher punishment.

- When punishment is harsh it *can* extinguish an unwanted behavior. But there is bound to be collateral damage. Harsh punishment can result in loss of trust, fearfulness, aggressive behavior with peers, and a host of other psychological problems. The American Academy of Pediatrics cites overwhelming evidence[2] against the use of physical punishment (which includes spanking with an open hand) in their review of decades of studies. These studies found that physical punishment was associated with higher levels of aggression against parents, siblings, peers, and spouses, in addition to increased incidence of depression and anxiety, disruptions in parent–child attachment, increased use of drugs and alcohol, slower cognitive development, lower academic achievement, and higher levels of antisocial behavior. These effects are not just seen right after the punishment occurs. They last into the teen years and even adulthood.[3,4]

- And finally, when we punish our children we are modeling an approach to conflict that they will use with each other. When they don't like what someone is doing, they will think of a way to make them suffer instead of thinking of a way to solve the problem: *"If you don't let me use your light saber I'm not inviting you to my birthday party."* . . . *"If you don't stop singing in my ear, I'm going to punch you."* . . . *"Get out of my room now or I'll break your phone!"*

So with all that evidence against the practice of punishment, have we arrived at a gentler future in which every conflict is resolved with a shower of love, and unicorns, and a rainbow sparkling overhead? Does this mean that all we have to do is remember to be kind and reasonable with our children?

Have you ever MET a child?

The fact is, even when we start out trying to be kind and reasonable, we sometimes find ourselves faced with negativity and defiance from our kids. Before we know it, we've painted ourselves into a corner where it feels like punishment is the only option. How does this happen? Let's watch in slow-motion:*

*Based on a true story.

A command disguised as a question

An attempt to be nice

The Problem with Punishment

The unadorned command

A warning, with name-calling

A lecture

A threat of punishment

This parent started out with the best of intentions. He made a perfectly reasonable request, gave his daughter more than one opportunity to cooperate, and explained why she needed to clean up.

Sure there were a few missteps—commands, a lecture, a threat—but even if you do everything "right" you can still find yourself having to take action while your child furiously protests (possibly including, but not limited to, screaming and kicking and throwing of objects). You can't endlessly offer choices and acknowledge feelings while the baby stuffs handfuls of choking hazards in his mouth.

Even if we muddle our way through this time, the conflict is not over. The baby's going to take another nap tomorrow. Big sister will want to do another activity involving small pieces. Should Dad double down on his threat of no more art projects? That would be sure to increase ill will between father and daughter, and contribute to the daughter's growing resentment of the baby's very existence!

Or should Dad cave in and give his uncooperative daughter another chance? That may increase Dad's resentment, and give his child the message that he makes empty threats, which she is free to ignore.

Happily, there is a third way! When a situation goes sideways and leaves children feeling disgruntled and parents trying to remember why they had kids in the first place, the time is ripe to try problem-solving. This process helps put kids and parents back on the same team. By the end of a problem-solving session you'll no longer feel like your children are tireless enemy combatants. You'll have converted their boundless energy from a force for resisting authority into a force for finding solutions that respect the needs of all parties.

Problem-Solving

Step Zero: If tempers are flaring . . . wait! Problem-solving is not a tool to employ in the heat of battle, when you're angry. You'll need to find a peaceful moment, when you're feeling a modicum of patience.

Step One: Acknowledge your child's feelings

This first step is the most important. Don't rush it! Listen to your child and continue to accept her feelings. The more time you spend showing her you understand her point of view, the more willing she'll be to consider your point of view in step two.

Step Two: Describe the problem

This step needs to be short and sweet! Kids tune out long lectures. You'll get a better result if you resist the urge to go on and on, waxing eloquent about the problems she causes by leaving her art supplies in reach of the baby.

Step Three: Ask for ideas

You don't *have* to make a written list, but it can help. Kids will appreciate the fact that you take their ideas seriously enough to write them down and read them back. Try to let your child come up with the first idea, and write down *all* ideas, even the inappropriate ones. It can be especially satisfying for a child to see an outrageous suggestion in print!

Step Four: Decide which ideas you both like

The Problem with Punishment

Here's where either of you get to veto the ideas that you're not comfortable with. (See, you didn't have to worry about locking the baby in the bathroom!)

Step Five: Try out your solutions

It may sound like a lot of effort just to move a kid from the floor to the table. Why not cut out all the negotiating and simply tell the child, "Go do your project on the table, where the baby can't reach"?

You could give it a try, but you might not get an enthusiastic response. When you invite your child to participate in solving a problem, the solutions you come up with together will work better for your child because she had a part in creating them. You'll have converted an opponent into a teammate! As an added bonus, you are teaching an invaluable life skill: how to resolve a conflict in a way that respects the needs of everyone involved.

What planet are you living on? Do you have any idea how many conflicts there are in my house per day . . . per hour? If I stopped to do this problem-solving rigamarole for every battle of wills between my kids and me, that's all we'd ever do.

Okay, okay, not every problem calls for a long, drawn-out process. You can save problem-solving for the thorniest conflicts that crop up repeatedly and resist resolution. For a quick fix, there are plenty of other tools you can choose from when those micro-conflicts pop up.

It's very tempting to attack a child's character when he does something we have *just* told him not to do. *"Look what you did! You never listen! And now you've made a big mess!"* Unfortunately that kind of talk makes children feel defensive and hostile. *"It's not my fault. You distracted me!"* If we can resist the urge to attack, and stick to describing our own feelings (using the word "*I*," avoiding the accusatory "*you*"), it's more likely that a child will be able to focus on what actually happened and feel remorse.

The theory behind punishment is that we need to make a child feel bad in order for him to learn to be good. Punishment *does* make kids feel bad about themselves and angry at the person who is punishing them. But it does *not* inspire them to be good.

One way for a child to learn to do better in the future is to give him an opportunity to do better in the present. Instead of thinking about what kind of punishment (or "consequence") we can come up with for a child who has misbehaved, our energy is better spent teaching him how to make amends.

Offering a choice can help him move on to a more acceptable activity. Now that we've told this kid what he *can't* do, let's tell him what he *can* do. Next time he has the urge to juggle, he'll have a way to do it without upsetting his mother (or breakable objects).

If your aspiring circus performer continues to ignore you, you may have to take action. Confiscate the abused fruit and hustle him out of the kitchen, letting him know that you don't appreciate the rotten spots that result from apples hitting the floor.

When we have a conflict with a child, we're not just putting out a fire in the moment. We're teaching them what to do when people are at odds with each other. We're modeling the behavior we want to see our children use in future conflicts. Whether they're having a quarrel with their spouse, or a disagreement with their boss, they'll have the tools to resolve the conflict while preserving the relationship.

PRACTICE

Part A: Find the missing pieces in this problem-solving puzzle.

> **Mom:** Noah, our morning routine is not working. I'm tired of being late to work every day. We need ideas for how to get out of the house on time.
> **Noah:** Well I'm tired of you yelling at me every day. Anyway, why do we have to talk about this now? I'm trying to answer Tyler's text about the math homework.

1. Why is Mom getting such a hostile response? Which two vital steps of problem-solving did she forget to do?

If she had remembered these steps, what might she have said?

Let's continue with this same scenario:

> **Mom:** We need ideas for how we can leave on time in the morning without ending up mad at each other. I think the first thing we should do is set your alarm a half hour earlier.
> **Noah:** Well, you can forget that. I'm not waking up any earlier.

2. What principle of problem-solving was left by the wayside?

What might Mom do so her son will feel more engaged?

Back to our scenario:

> **Noah:** Why don't you drive me to school, instead of making me take the bus? That way we could leave later, and I'd have more time.
>
> **Mom:** No, we can't do that. I'd be late to work. And besides, it's better for the environment when all the kids take the bus.
>
> **Noah:** (rolls eyes)
>
> **Mom:** I don't want to see that attitude!

3. What principle of problem-solving was left out this time?

How else could Mom have responded to an inappropriate suggestion?

Back to our scenario:

> **Mom:** Okay, we both agree that you'll get yourself ready without reminders. But if that doesn't work, you're taking a taxi and it's coming out of your allowance.
>
> **Noah:** No it won't. I'll just skip school!

4. Why did the problem-solving session go sour?

What could Mom have said instead, to preserve the spirit of cooperation?

Back to the scenario (a few weeks later):

> **Mom:** Please, please, PLEASE would you *hurry*! I am begging you! You're going to get me fired and then we'll all be out on the street. Is that what you want??

5. What can this parent do if her child continues to miss the bus?

Answer Key:

1. The mom forgot to find a peaceful time to talk, and she forgot to start by acknowledging her son's feelings. Her son will be more open to considering his mom's needs if she opens the conversation like this:

> **Mom:** I've been thinking about the problem of getting out the door on time in the morning. Is this a good time to talk?

Once they sit down together, the conversation might go something like this:

> **Mom:** I noticed we're getting into a lot of fights in the morning. It annoys you when I yell at you to hurry.
> **Noah:** Yeah and you also yell "FOCUS!" I hate that. I don't need you to tell me what to do.
> **Mom:** Oh, so that word is particularly irritating to you.
> **Noah:** Yeah!

2. It's usually a good policy to let your child come up with the first idea. When we jump in too quickly, we send the message that we don't really care about including them in the process of finding solutions. By waiting quietly, we demonstrate our respect for their ability to think through a problem.

> **Mom:** We need ideas for how we can get out the door on time without ending up mad at each other. Let's see what we can come up with. I'll write down our ideas.

Wait . . . Wait . . . Count to five . . . Wait some more . . . Count to five again . . . If your child doesn't seem like he's ever going to respond, make your first idea something whimsical. "We could get a transporter beam, so you could skip the bus and instantly materialize at school."

3. When you're brainstorming with your child, it's important to write down *all* ideas without evaluating. Even if you are definitely *not* willing to act as a personal chauffeur for your son (*"Never gonna happen!"*), you can acknowledge that he would *like* for it to happen. This can be painlessly achieved by writing it on the list. If you shoot down his ideas as they come out of his mouth, your child will see no point in continuing to brainstorm.

It might go something like this:

Mom: Oh, you'd like me to drive you, so you can have some extra time in the morning. Let me write that: "Drive Noah to school." Okay, what else . . . ?

Writing it down shows respect for your child's ideas. Don't worry—just because you write it doesn't mean you have to do it! In step four you'll have your opportunity to say, "I wouldn't be happy with this idea. When I have to drive you to school first, it makes me late to work."

4. It's important to end a problem-solving session with feelings of goodwill and optimism. If you end it with a threat, you're undermining your efforts. How would you feel if you were presented with a threat after solving a problem with a partner or coworker? Would it make you more or less likely to be enthusiastic about using your solution?

Mom could have said, "Okay, we have a plan! Let's try it and see how we like it!"

There will be plenty of opportunities to take action if the solution you both agree to ends up not working.

5. If your plan doesn't work, you may want to sit down again and look for some fresh ideas with your child.

Mom: I'm not happy about this! We made a plan, and it worked for a while. Now we're back to the same problem. We need new ideas.

Or you may feel that it's time to take action:

Mom: I can't be late to work anymore. From now on when you miss the bus, you can ride your bike or pay for a taxi (or whatever else may be appropriate for the area you live in).

Part B: Handle these situations without punishing the perpetrators.

Situation 1: Your six-year-old is taking great pleasure in riding his scooter into the wall, even though you've warned him not to do that.

    1. Express your feelings strongly:

    2. Give your child an opportunity to make amends:

    3. Offer a choice:

    4. Take action without insult:

Situation 2: Your teenager borrows your nicest pair of boots to go to a party at her friend's house. You only agreed after she begged and begged and promised to return them in perfect condition. She comes home with no boots! Apparently she took them off when her feet started to hurt, borrowed a pair of flip-flops from her friend, and then promptly forgot all about your boots.

1. **Express your feelings strongly:**

2. **Give your child an opportunity to make amends:**

3. **The next time she asks to borrow something from you, take action without insult (protect people or property):**

4. **Offer a choice:**

Answer Key:

Situation 1:

Answer 1. Hey, I don't like it when the scooter bangs into the wall! It makes marks on the paint.

Answer 2. Here's a scrubby and some soap to clean off the marks.

Answer 3. You can ride your scooter in a circle around the cones, or if you're in a crashing mood you can crash it into the beanbag chair.

Answer 4. I'm putting the scooter away for now. You're in a crashing mood and I don't want marks on the wall. Let's find something else to do.

Situation 2:

Answer 1. I'm really upset! Those are my nicest boots, and now I'm worried that they're lost.

Answer 2. I'd feel better if you call your friend now, ask her to find the boots, and arrange to pick them up tomorrow.

Answer 3. I'm not going to lend my clothes for a while. I don't want to have to worry about whether they'll be returned.

Answer 4. You can find something in your own closet or you can use your allowance to buy what you want.

REMINDER: ALTERNATIVES TO PUNISHMENT

1. Try problem-solving.

Step Zero: Find a peaceful moment when you're not feeling angry or impatient.

Step One: Acknowledge feelings.

"It's hard to stop when you're in the middle of a project."

Step Two: Describe the problem. (Be brief.)

"The problem is, I worry about the baby choking on small pieces."

Step Three: Ask for ideas.

"We need ideas. How can we make it safe for the baby while you do your art projects?"

Step Four: Decide which ideas you both like.

"I'll put everything on the kitchen table."

Step Five: Try out your solutions.

"Let's get some newspaper to protect the table."

When you don't have time for problem-solving:

2. Express your feelings strongly, without attacking the child.

"It upsets me to see bruised fruit and broken glasses."

3. Give your child an opportunity to make amends.

"This needs to be cleaned up. Here's a container for the broken glass."

4. Offer a choice.

"Next time you want to juggle you can use scarves or beanbags."

Chapter 4

Praise and Its Pitfalls

Why Do They Act So Bad
When We Tell Them They're Good?

Everyone knows that kids (and people in general) thrive with positive feedback. If all we do is criticize, pointing out mistakes and failures, we run the risk of discouraging children so thoroughly that they lose the will to keep trying.

So we praise and praise. And then we worry . . . Are we praising enough? Should we be laying it on thicker to raise their self-esteem? Or are we praising too much? Are we going overboard and giving them an unrealistic view of themselves? Will all this praise cause them to crash and burn when they realize they're not so great after all? At what exact rate should we be doling out these encouraging words?

Maybe these aren't the most helpful questions. Recent research suggests that it's the *kind* of praise we use, rather than the amount, that makes the difference. When we want to encourage, motivate, and inspire, the words we choose are important! Words of praise that judge or evaluate don't always achieve the effect we intend.

Sometimes we praise kids because we want to let them know their strengths so they'll aspire to greater achievements.

What went wrong here? *Evaluative praise*—for example, calling a child talented, brilliant, perfect—can interfere with a child's learning process and actually inhibit her willingness to take chances. Children who are slathered with evaluative praise often lose confidence when faced with new challenges. They may decide it's safer to quit while they're ahead than to stick with a difficult task and reveal their incompetence.

Researchers[1] have found that many children who are told they're "talented" have a harder time than "non-talented" children when finally, and inevitably, they come up against a problem they can't easily solve. It's not hard to imagine why. The "talented" kids are taking a strong blow to their self-image when the answers don't come quickly. Some kids will become anxious and want to quit. Others may act bored or defiant rather than risk not living up to the evaluation of their parents and teachers.

So how *can* we respond to our kids in a way that will bring out the best in them—that will demonstrate our pleasure in their accomplishments and also increase their confidence and willingness to take on greater challenges?

One way to inspire a child is to **describe effort**. When a child's effort is noticed and appreciated, it gives them the message that they can triumph in the face of adversity. Struggle is not an indication of weakness or lack of talent, but rather a point of pride, and a reflection of their growing abilities.

When we focus on effort, children learn that their ability is not a fixed trait, but something that grows when they work at it. Children with this mindset are more likely to keep trying when faced with new and difficult challenges.

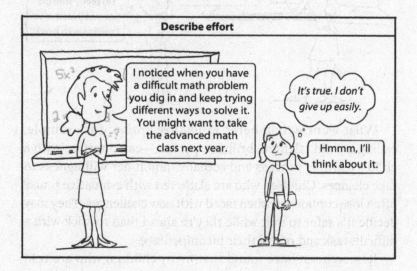

Sometimes we praise kids when they're feeling demoralized or overwhelmed. We want to give them a dose of confidence.

It's hard for a child to accept superlatives like "great" and "excellent," when they don't match his own perception. Often such praise causes him to focus on his weaknesses instead of his strengths. And if a child does accept our proud parental pronouncements at face value, it might cause other problems down the line. We're not giving him a realistic picture of his abilities. Where can you go from "great" and "excellent"? Why would you put in the hard work to improve?

We need an alternative to the unsupported superlative!

One way to give kids feedback that is both supportive and realistic is to **describe progress**:

87

Sometimes we praise kids in order to get them to repeat their behavior. They're finally doing what we want, and we want them to do it again!

When we use *global praise* (*you are a good brother, a great writer, a perfect parent*) it can be experienced as manipulation. It may cause a person to doubt the sincerity or judgment of the praiser. This child knows that he's not "such a good brother." His mom is lying or delusional. Either way, he will set her straight!

And the final twist, "when you try" is a criticism disguised as praise. *You're just not trying most of the time!* Would you appreciate it if your partner praised you by saying, "See, I knew you could get dinner ready on time if you tried!"?

Is it starting to sound like it's dangerous to open your mouth? Never fear, the solution in this case is simple. Instead of offering insincere flattery, **describe the effect of the child's actions on others**. The child can then draw his own conclusions about himself.

And finally, sometimes we praise kids because they crave attention from their special people (*"Look ma, no hands!"*) and we want to satisfy their urge to connect with us and to be seen and appreciated.

Great! Perfect! Fantastic! Beautiful! Good job! This kind of praise is strangely too much and too little at the same time. *Too much* because these superlatives don't come across as authentic. *Too little* because they can feel generic and dismissive. Did Dad really look at it? Does he like it or is he just saying that? It's easier to say

89

"good job" than it is to pay close attention to something a child is showing us. Often kids will respond, "But do you really like it?"

What can a parent or teacher do instead that will satisfy a child's need for recognition? You can take an extra minute to **describe what you see**. If you have another minute to spare, you can even **ask a question** to show your interest and give your child an opportunity to elaborate. It can be enormously gratifying to a child when an adult takes the time and effort to notice the details of her accomplishment. It can even inspire her to greater heights.

Notice that these adults are not overpraising. They aren't exaggerating the children's accomplishments to give a false impression of excellence. Instead, they are providing useful feedback that gives children an accurate picture of their achievements.

You did a very good job reading this chapter. You get a gold star for making it to the end. We knew you could do it if you tried. (See how annoying it is to be praised in a judgy way?) Now you can go experiment on your children using descriptive praise and see what happens.

PRACTICE

For each scenario choose the response that avoids evaluative praise, and instead describes effort, progress, effect on others, or what you see; or ask a question that shows your interest.

1. You and your child are in the checkout line at the grocery store. She's helping you load items onto the conveyor belt instead of grabbing for the candy and gum on the display stand as she usually does. You want to encourage this behavior!

   A. Good girl! You are Mommy's little helper.
   B. I like it when you act like a big girl, instead of grabbing candy like a baby.
   C. You stacked all those cans on the belt. That's a big help!
   D. You've been so well behaved, you deserve an ice cream cone.

2. Your child is struggling to learn a difficult piece on the piano and says, "This is too hard." You want to encourage him to keep trying.

   A. No it's not. It sounds beautiful. You're a very talented musician.
   B. Those dotted eighth notes in the second section are really tricky. It sounds like you're starting to get it when you practice it without the chords in the left hand.
   C. Don't give up! I know you'll get it if you keep trying. You've just got to put in the effort.
   D. The intro sounds good, but you need to spend more time on the second section. Those are dotted eighth notes, not quarter notes. And you're slowing down the tempo. You should be using a metronome.

3. Your child shoveled the whole driveway after a snowstorm. She proudly shows you her accomplishment.

   A. See what you can do when you try? It's nice to see you helping out instead of sitting around staring at your phone.

   B. The driveway looks good, but you didn't finish the walkway from the house to the car. That's the most important part.

   C. Good job!

   D. Wow, you moved a lot of heavy snow! That was an enormous job. And you didn't stop until you got all the way to the street.

4. Your child has a homework assignment to draw something that begins with the letter *D*. He just crumpled up his picture of a dinosaur and threw it on the floor, saying, "I can't do this! The face isn't coming out right!"

   A. Just do your best. That's all that counts.

   B. Oh no, honey, don't crumple it, let me see . . . This is really good!

   C. Oh, I see a purple dinosaur with green stripes and very big scary teeth. But you're not happy with the face. You want it to be different.

   D. Oh for Pete's sake, stop whining and just draw a picture of a donut and be done with it!

5. Your child cleaned up her room and organized her shelves all by herself.

   A. Your room looks fantastic! Good for you!

   B. What a big girl you are. This room looks great. I wish your brother would learn to clean up like this. His room is a pigsty.

C. Don't you feel better having your room so clean? Now let's see how long you can keep it this way.

D. Wow, look at all this hard work you did. You've got the whole desktop clear. You put your dirty clothes in the hamper. And you organized all the bins on your shelf.

6. Your teen shows you a computer animation he created.

A. Wow, how did you figure out how to get the movement to look so realistic?

B. Very nice, honey. Have you started your homework yet?

C. Excellent! I'll bet there isn't one other kid in your class who could do anything half as good.

D. You're always so creative!

7. Think of something your child has done in the last week that you'd like to praise.

What did s/he do?

What could you say to him/her that describes effort, progress, effect on others, what you see, or asks a question that shows interest?

Answer Key:

1. C
2. B
3. D
4. C
5. D
6. A
7. Very good job filling in the blanks! (Just kidding.)

93

REWARDS

1D. You've been so well behaved, you deserve an ice cream cone.

It's tempting to give a child a reward for behaving the way we want. The problem is, children who are rewarded lose internal motivation. Studies consistently find that, compared to children who are not rewarded in the first place, children who are rewarded are actually *less* likely to repeat a behavior they have been rewarded for, once the reward is removed. Next time your child helps out at the checkout counter, she'll expect another ice cream cone (or two—inflation!), and she may refuse to participate if ice cream is not on offer.[2]

DESCRIBE EFFORT

2C. Don't give up! I know you'll get it if you keep trying. You've just got to put in the effort.

C is a trick answer! Demanding effort is not the same as describing effort.

CRITICISM

2D. The intro sounds good, but you need to spend more time on the second section. Those are dotted eighth notes, not quarter notes. And you're slowing down the tempo. You should be using a metronome.

Even when criticism is valid, it can be very discouraging to a struggling child to be presented with a list of what he's doing wrong. Pointing out one positive thing can inspire a child to work harder than pointing out ten negatives. If we have to draw attention to something in need of improvement, we'll get a better reception if we first describe with appreciation what he's accomplished so far, and then limit ourselves to one criticism at a time.

ACKNOWLEDGING FEELINGS

4C. Oh, I see a purple dinosaur with green stripes and very big scary teeth. But you're not happy with the face. You want it to be different.

When a child is frustrated, it's more important to acknowledge feelings than to offer praise that contradicts the child's perception.

QUESTIONABLE QUESTIONS

3A. See what you can do when you try? It's nice to see you helping out instead of sitting around staring at your phone.

5C. Don't you feel better having your room so clean? Now let's see how long you can keep it this way.

3A and 5C are trick answers. The parents are asking questions, but they are not questions that show interest. They are actually implied criticisms.

COMPARISONS

5B. What a big girl you are. This room looks great. I wish your brother would learn to clean up like this. His room is a pigsty.

6C. Excellent! I'll bet there isn't one other kid in your class who could do anything half as good.

It's tempting to use comparison when we praise, but it often ends badly. We don't want our kids to resent each other or be threatened by each other's accomplishments. A child should not feel that our approval is based on the failure or inadequacy of another person. We want them to feel good about helping a younger sibling or collaborating with a classmate.

REMINDER: HELPFUL WAYS TO PRAISE

1. Describe effort.

"I notice when you had those difficult math problems, you dug in and kept trying different ways to solve them."

2. Describe progress.

"You're blocking a lot more shots than at the beginning of the season."

3. Describe the effect on others.

"Your brother really enjoyed the building project. He was excited to play with you."

4. Describe what you see.

"Ooh, you painted noodles bright green . . . and added gold glitter . . . and you got a string through those tiny holes."

5. Ask a question.

"How did you think of using pasta for a necklace?"

PART TWO

TROUBLE IN PARADISE

In which we tackle tough topics requested
by readers and workshop participants,
and share their stories.

Since our first book, *How to Talk So Little Kids Will Listen*, was
published, we have received over a thousand letters from readers
all over the world. Many of you asked questions about how to
handle difficult situations, or shared your own stories of using the
communication tools with your children (or students, spouses,
coworkers, and in-laws). You'll find answers to questions from
both our readers and our workshop participants, as well as some
of their stories, in this part of the book. This time around we've
included scenarios with older children as well, for those of you
who are now facing the challenges of parenting tweens and young
teenagers.

This section of our book is not intended to be read sequen-
tially. Feel free to jump directly to whichever chapter you'd like.

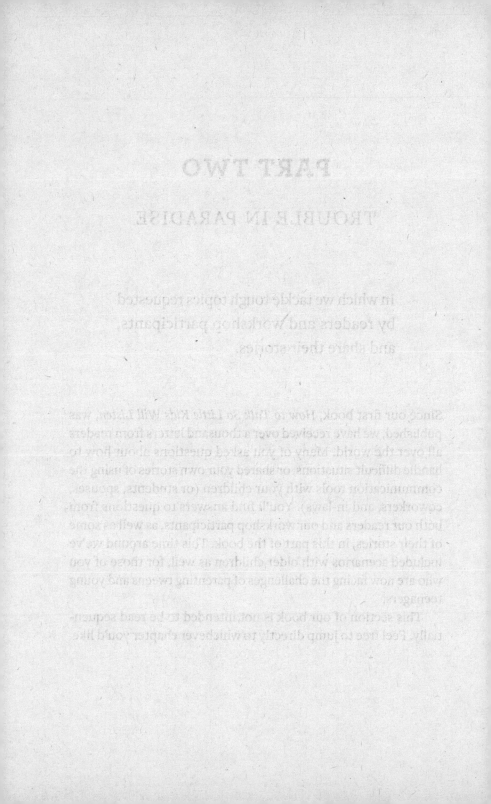

Section I

Getting Through the Day

1

Enough Already!
When Kids Are Completely Unreasonable

We've heard from many parents and teachers that the tools for accepting feelings have made a profound difference in their relationships with children. But we also have a stack of stories that could be filed under the theme: *Enough Already!*

Some feelings just don't seem worthy of our sympathy. It's pretty hard to accept a feeling when we can't see even the *slightest* justification for it.

Here are some examples expressed by real life, frustrated parents in our workshops:

Popping Mad

Last weekend we went to a birthday party. The kids all got helium balloons and I made *sure* that we got the same size and color for the twins. But of course Jenna started complaining as soon as we got home. Her balloon wasn't good enough. She wanted Ella's balloon. I was like, "Oh my gosh, just stop, you're being ridiculous! The balloons are exactly the same!" She whined and sulked for the rest of the evening. I felt like going into their room with a pin and popping both balloons just to get it over with. You have to admit that sometimes kids complain over nothing, just to get attention. I don't want to encourage that.

Stick Fight

My kids fight over sticks. One finds a stick, the other one wants *that* stick, no matter how much I point out that the yard is full of sticks. It's not even a situation where there are limited resources. I tell my son, "There's nothing special about that stick your sister has! Go get your own. There are hundreds of sticks out there, buddy." You can guess how well *that* works.

Little Big Spender

It's hard to accept feelings when my daughter is not respecting the values we've taught her. Mariana, my twelve-year-old, finds things on the internet that she wants. She showed me a pair of sneakers online that cost $229. She insisted that she *needed* them because that's what her friends have. I'm not going to acknowledge *those* feelings! That's the last thing I want to encourage—competitive fashion spending in a twelve-year-old. I'm going to nip that in the bud!

These are the times that put us to the test! If we can find a way to acknowledge children's feelings *even when they seem unjustifiable*, it actually makes it easier for kids to move on. But what might that sound like?

"This balloon doesn't seem as good to you. Even though to me they look the same, there's something about your sister's balloon that you like better."

When she responds, you can continue to acknowledge feelings, "Oh, you don't like the way your balloon floats crooked because of the knot. And it's not as round."

We're not suggesting you run to the party store and get her another balloon. Just your acceptance alone will help her calm down. Or not. She may *need* to cry. It's not always about the balloon. We think a birthday party is one long, joyful experience, but to a four-year-old who didn't get to swing at the piñata because it broke just before her turn, got her foot stepped on in the tug of war, didn't get the prize she wanted (and also the one she got broke in the car on the way home), and her stomach hurts from all the cake and ice cream . . . she may get home and cry over a balloon. A kid's day is often full of small frustrations, worries, and disappointments. There's a cumulative effect. We can give our kids comfort by accepting feelings without challenging their logic at that moment. (*"Ohh, you wish your balloon was different! You are not at all happy with this balloon!"*) When kids complain over nothing, just to get attention, we can just give them attention, because that's what they need—emotional comfort from us.

But how about those sticks? What can you say to a child surrounded by sticks that are inferior to his sister's stick? (A truly sticky situation!)

"To you *that* stick is special! Even though there are lots of sticks in the yard, you really like that one. Something about it appeals to you."

We wouldn't expect that to end the discussion. No doubt your child will argue that this particular stick is microscopically straighter than the other one.

You don't have to argue back. Admittedly, there's a powerful temptation to claim that neither stick is straighter. We can try that strategy. The problem is, even if you win the argument, you lose, because you still have to live with the "loser."

Instead, you can continue to acknowledge feelings. "Oh, so *you* like a stick that is super-duper straight! Straight as an arrow! Do you want help looking for more super-straight sticks, or do you want to look by yourself?" (Notice how we're helping the child move on with a friendly choice.)

But what about the shoes? Are we in danger of creating overin-dulged, materialistic children if we commiserate about ridiculously overpriced footwear?

We'll have more success teaching a child to become a wise consumer by accepting her feelings than by scolding her for her desires. This is the perfect moment to give wishes in fantasy. "You really like those sneakers with the zigzag pattern on the bottom. I wish they weren't so expensive. It would be nice if they suddenly went on sale for 90 percent off." Let her have the pleasure of describing what she likes about the sneakers to a sympathetic listener. When she's had her say, you can tell her, "Here's the problem. We have $___.___ [fill in your number here] to spend on new sneakers. Should we go to the store and see if we can find something you like, or would you rather look online to see what you can find for $___.___ or less?"

Look at all the tools we just used: acknowledging feelings, giving wishes in fantasy, offering a choice, and putting the child in charge by assigning a research job.

But what if your child has a longer attention span for misery than you do, and you just can't listen to it anymore? How long can a human parent without superpowers of empathy stand to hear a child wail over a balloon, or a stick, or an expensive pair of shoes?

For as long as you can stand it, and no longer. Once you've let your child know you hear their grief, you can abandon ship. But do it sympathetically, not insultingly! Mind your parting words. Don't say, "Oh for Pete's sake, get over yourself, life is only going to get harder. If you can't put up with a crooked balloon, you're doomed."

Instead, you can let your child know you are on their side, even if you're not *by* their side. You can frankly describe your own feelings. "I can't listen to more about balloons right now.

I'm going to the kitchen to start dinner. When you feel ready, you can come help me wash the lettuce and spin it dry." Or you might offer a choice to help her move on. "Do you want to draw a face on the balloon to make it better, or would you rather leave it plain?"

Back in the 1600s, a philosopher named Blaise Pascal noted, "The heart has its reasons of which reason knows nothing." Even thousands of years ago, the ancient Greeks were probably pining for sandals they couldn't afford. You know, the ones with the golden tassels?

You can't convince kids, or adults for that matter, not to want the thing they want, whether it's a balloon or a stick or a shoe. No doubt every single person reading these words can think of something they have yearned for that would break the budget (a Lamborghini, a beach house, a 70-inch flatscreen with surround sound, a full-time nanny). Acknowledging feelings doesn't mean we're agreeing with them. It doesn't mean we're spoiling kids by giving in to their whims. Accepting kids' feelings, even when those feelings seem irrational or unjustifiable, makes it easier for kids to accept reality.

Stories from the Front Lines

The Thin Green Line

Rahul, almost four, has a little notebook that he loves scribbling in with a pen. He filled up an entire page with his "writing."

The next thing I know, he's crying because there's a green line on the page.

Me: What's wrong?

Rahul: The whole page is ruined. There's a green line on my writing.

Normally this is where I'd say things like, *It's not such a big deal. You can turn the page and write on the next page. Besides, YOU made the green line!*

Not that *that* would help.

This time I tried acknowledging his feelings.

Me: Oh no, that's not what you want.

Rahul: No!

Me: You wanted a clean page of writing in pen.

Rahul: Yeah!

Me: Now the whole thing is ruined.

Rahul stopped crying, but he was still upset.

Me: What can we do? It won't erase.

My two-year-old was listening this whole time. He picked up a piece from a board game (we have board game pieces all over the house, there's no way anyone can ever play these games for real anymore), put it on top of the green line, and said, "Tape it!" Rahul really likes tape, so he was enthusiastic about this idea. My two-year-old ran to get another board piece (like I said, they're all over the place) and taped it on top of the green line. Rahul was very satisfied with this solution. It was an amazing save.

Ice Is Nice

Last week we were late for preschool as usual. I had finally gotten Isabel in her car seat, and then I had to get out and scrape ice off the car windows. I didn't have gloves and my fingers were freezing. I was not happy! When I started scraping Isabel's window, there was her little face, bawling. I opened the door and asked her what was wrong. She screamed, *"I DIDN'T WANT YOU TO TAKE OFF THE ICE!"* Before this workshop I would have said, "Well, I'm sorry, but I have to see out the window." I mean, how unreasonable can you get? But this time I said, "Oh, you didn't want the ice scraped away!"

She sobbed, "I wanted to watch it melt!"

I said, "Ohhh, you wanted to watch it melt. That's disappointing!" Then I said, "The problem is, I can't back out of the driveway without seeing through this window. I would crash into other cars. Maybe we could leave the ice on the window across from you and you could watch that one melt."

She said she wanted ice on her *own* window.

I kept acknowledging her feelings, "Oh, you wanted it on the window right *next* to you! Well . . . do you want me to leave some on the other window?" She agreed, and the ride was actually pleasant.

Thomas the Conductor

I took Tommy and his little sister to the Thomas the Train Christmas exhibit at the botanical gardens. The kids got to go up front and talk into the microphone, to pretend they were engineers. Tommy loved it and went up three times. He was so excited. After all, the train is his namesake! His little sister got to do it only once. On the way home, Tommy started complaining that he didn't get enough turns. I was pretty annoyed. I really wanted to say that he got *more* than his share—he should be grateful!

But I didn't. I told him, "Wow, you really, really loved being the engineer. I'll bet you wish you could have had a hundred turns." And then I couldn't resist adding, "And even though you had three turns and your sister had only one, it wasn't enough."

He was happy with that response. He said, yeah, he wanted to be an engineer when he grew up and he would take his whole family on train rides. That was the end of it. But I noticed he was feeling very generous about including the family after I acknowledged his feelings.

Waffling Over Waffles

Emma asked for waffles for breakfast, but once they were on the table she desperately wanted pancakes. If we hadn't just had this group I definitely would've told her she was being unreasonable, even though I know it would have enraged her. Instead, here's how the conversation went:

Emma: I don't want waffles! I want pancakes!

Me: Gosh, that's frustrating to get waffles when you really want pancakes! That could be upsetting.

Emma: I AM upset! . . . Oh look, a squirrel!

She started eating her waffles.

I was this close to making a big deal out of how she had to eat them because she asked for them. Good thing I didn't bother getting into *that* fight.

Self-Centered Teen

There was a bad winter storm and we had a town-wide blackout. It was predicted that the power outage would last for more than a week. Since my ninety-year-old mother was living with us and I didn't want her to get chilled, I booked a hotel for our family. When I told my fifteen-year-old daughter we had to pack, she threw a fit.

"It's not fair . . . I don't want to go to a hotel . . . You can't make me . . . School is closed and all my friends are going to hang out together . . . You're ruining it!"

She flounced off to sulk on her bed.

A thousand things to say to her ran through my head:

"How can you be so selfish? Do you want your grandmother to get sick? Why don't you take this opportunity to spend some quality time with her? She might not even be alive this time next year. Your friends are not going to be hanging out with no electricity. That means no TV, no computers, no showers, no opening the refrigerator every five minutes. Do you realize people are actually suffering in this storm? It's not all about you!"

After allowing myself the satisfaction of all these thoughts, I was able to go into her room and say sincerely, "I can see how disappointing this is for you. You were really looking forward to staying here and hanging out with your friends." Then I left the room.

Five minutes later she came into the kitchen and cheerfully helped us pack. It was like I had waved a magic wand.

The Wrong Water Bottle
(conversation in a workshop)

Mom #1: We were driving back from Sacramento after a long, good day at a theme park. We were five minutes from home when my son started complaining that he wanted water in a *different* water bottle. I tried to explain we were almost home and Daddy's driving as fast as he's allowed, but my son started wailing. So there I am, trying to pour water from one bottle into the other, and I hand it to him, and he whines that it's not enough water . . . and he's SOOOO thirsty . . . but he's not drinking any of the water I gave him! At this point we were two minutes from home, and I just couldn't get myself to say anything understanding. I knew I should "accept his feelings" but I was so DONE, I didn't even want to *try* to figure out what his feelings were. I couldn't bring myself to say anything helpful. How do you get yourself to do this?

Mom #2: I know what you mean. It's so hard to think of what to say when you're in the thick of it. I'm sitting here, and it's easy for me to think, *Oh, you should tell him* "I WISH *the water was in the right water bottle! I wish it had just the right amount of water.*"

Mom #1: Yeah, that might've been good if I could've thought of that. Maybe next time.

REMINDER: WHEN KIDS ARE
COMPLETELY UNREASONABLE

1. Acknowledge feelings, even when they seem unjustified.

"To you that stick is special! Even though there are lots of sticks in the yard, you really like that one. Something about it appeals to you."

2. Give in fantasy what you can't give in reality.

"Wouldn't it be great if those shoes suddenly went on sale for 90 percent off?"

Then, to help them move on, you can:

3. Offer a choice.

"Do you want to draw a face on your balloon or leave it plain?"

4. Put the child in charge.

"Your mission is to find a pair of shoes you like for under $____.____."

Taping Your Phone Calls

I find it extremely challenging to get through a phone call at home without at least one of my kids having a major meltdown. It's like they can't stand the idea that I'm right there but not paying attention to them.

I usually hiss, "Stop it!" "Be quiet!" "Can't you see I'm on the phone?" (Yes, they can definitely see that.) When they don't stop (which is always), I mute the phone and warn them, "If you don't be quiet for the next five minutes while I finish this call, you will be sorry!" (At this point I haven't figured out what I will do to make them sorry, but hey, I am *trying* to focus on my phone call!) They whine, "But you're *always* on the phone." I say, "That's ridiculous! I'm hardly ever on the phone."

I decided to try *telling them what they can do instead of what they can't.* I needed a special activity that they'd be allowed to do *only* when I was on the phone. I told them I was going to have to make a call, and they were going to have "tape time." I gave them a roll of painter's tape (which doesn't mark the wall) and told them they could make tape pictures on the wall.

It's working better than expected and now we have a new routine. They're like little cavemen tapping into their ancient cave drawing genes. Sometimes they actually ask me to make a phone call just so they can use the wall tape.

Outfit Impasse—Mini Shirt Saves the Day

I've been using drawing to help when my daughter can't get
what she wants. She has a favorite shirt and begs to wear
it most days. I decided to draw, laminate (with tape!), and
cut out her "shirt." I told her that when she can't wear her
actual shirt, she can carry one of her mini shirts around. It
worked! She also became less fixated on wearing the real
shirt—big win!

2

How to *Listen* When Kids Won't *Talk*

"How was your day?" *Good.*
"What'd you do?" *Nothing.*

The art of interrogating a child

It's frustrating when our kids venture out into the world, leaving us to wonder how they're faring. And the more we pry, the tighter they clam up. It's hard to accept that our kids won't always want to share the details of their lives. But accept it we must! Kids need to be able to go out and experience life without constant parental debriefing sessions. Still, there are strategies that will help keep the lines of communication open. We can't expect or demand, but we can extend an invitation.

1. Model the behavior you'd like to see

Out the Window (Julie's story)

When Asher started kindergarten, I was dying to know about his day. Did he like school? Was he making friends? I couldn't get any useful information out of him. Our conversations always followed the same script: "How was your day?" "*Fine.*" "What did you do?" "*I dunno.*"

It occurred to me that maybe I needed to show him how it's done. So the next time I picked him up from school I asked him,

"Do you want to know about *my* day?"

He looked surprised and a little confused, as if he were thinking, "You have a day? You exist without me?"

I made a point of telling him stories that included feelings ("I was worried that I lost my car keys. I was so happy when I found them in the laundry basket!") Then I asked him, "Is there anything you want me to know about *your* day?"

After a few afternoons of this routine, Asher answered that question with an emphatic, "Yes! Liam climbed up on the bookshelf, and then he climbed through the window. And then he fell out!"

"What? That sounds scary! Is he okay?"

"The teacher said he was lucky he fell in the bushes, so he didn't get hurt."

As soon as I got home, I called Liam's mom. "I heard what happened. Is Liam okay?"

She replied with exasperation, "How come *you* know? I had to hear it from the school. My kid doesn't tell me anything!"

2. Acknowledge feelings instead of interrogating

What about when my child comes home from school looking upset? When I ask, "What's the matter?" he doesn't tell me.

When a child is in distress, the last thing he needs to hear is a barrage of questions. "What's wrong?" "What happened?" "Why are you so upset?" will almost always elicit responses along the lines of *"Nothing"* and *"I don't know."*

Questions can be threatening. A child may not be able to explain exactly what's bothering him. He may feel unable to justify his distress. Maybe he's worried his parent will respond, "Oh, that's not so bad. That's nothing to be upset about!"

It's infinitely more helpful and

114

comforting to a child when the parent simply acknowledges the feeling without requiring an answer.

Instead of, "What's wrong?" Try, "You seem sad."

Instead of, "Why are you so upset?" Try, "It looks like you had a rough day."

Instead of, "What happened?" Try, "Something happened."

These responses don't put a kid on the defensive. A child will feel free to talk if he needs to, or to simply take comfort in your sympathetic words and a hug.

Date Dread

When my normally cheerful twelve-year-old was moping around the house one day, I asked him several times what was wrong. Each time he answered, "Nothing." Finally I remembered your advice: Don't ask questions, just name the feeling.

"Jayden, you seem down today."

Immediately he gave a big sigh and revealed that he had been asked on a date by a girl. (*Oh, the horror.* I had to suppress the urge to say, "*That's* what you're upset about?") He was worried. What would he talk about? It could be awkward!

"Oh, no wonder you look glum. That sounds like an uncomfortable situation."

He talked some more and decided a movie date was the safest because there wouldn't be much talking. He walked away smiling. The cloud had lifted.

Don't Ask! (Joanna's story)

When I entered the main office of PS 161, I saw a small crowd of teachers and secretaries surrounding a crying girl. They were all asking her, "What's wrong? What happened?

Are you okay??" in concerned tones. The more urgently the adults questioned her, the harder she sobbed. She was a sixth grader, not one of my students, but I had twenty minutes before my first class, so I volunteered to sit with her.

I walked her over to some chairs and sat with her as she cried. After a minute or so I said, "Something really upset you."

She took a few gulping breaths and choked out, "I heard a loud sound in front of the school and I thought they were shooting at me."

"Oh, that's so scary!"

"Yeah, someone got shot on my street yesterday." Her breathing steadied. She leaned into me a little.

If I had any doubt about the power of accepting feelings without interrogation, it was dispelled a moment later. Seeing that the girl was now calm, two of the adults approached and began asking questions again. "Did you find out what happened? Is she okay? What was the matter?"

Under this well-meaning onslaught, the girl began her panicked sobbing again. I told them, "She got scared, she's going to be okay," and they backed off.

We sat for another five minutes, and then I told her I had to go to my class. I offered to take her to the guidance counselor's office, but she said she was ready to go to class, and we parted ways.

We don't always need to find out what "the matter" is in order to give comfort. But I think in this case she needed to tell, and I was glad I knew how to make that easier. If I weren't in possession of that counterintuitive bit of knowledge, I would've been doing the exact same thing everyone else was doing, frantically trying to pry out the information so I could figure out a way to help.

3. Put the child in charge

But what about when my child isn't in distress? I just want to have a conversation. I want to know about her day. Can't I show interest? I tried modeling and that didn't work for me. It seems uncaring not to ask anything at all.

Imagine that you get a phone call shortly after you arrive home from vacation. You've been traveling all day, a long flight and on top of that a long ride through heavy traffic on the way home from the airport. You haven't unpacked or eaten yet. There was just that tiny pack of almonds and bad coffee on the plane. Your limbs are still getting used to being unfolded after being squished into various vehicles for so many hours.

It's your mother! She wants to know, "How was your vacation? Did you have a good time? Where did you go? Did you get a chance to visit that museum I told you about? Who were you with? Did you make any new friends?"

She's only asking because she cares! But perhaps you'd prefer: "Oh you're back from your vacation. I'd love to hear about it when you're in the mood to tell."

Our children are not so different from ourselves. When they come home after a long day at school, they don't appreciate being met with a barrage of questions: "How was your class trip?" "Did the teacher like your presentation on hurricanes that we spent all week preparing?" "How did you do on that math test you were so worried about?" They'd rather hear, "Welcome home, honey. Have a snack!"

So how can you show interest in their lives? *Offer an invitation instead of a demand for information:*

"I'd love to hear about your class trip when you're in the mood to talk about it."

It's very likely that minutes (or sometimes hours) later, you'll feel a tap on the shoulder. "Mom, do you want to hear about my trip now?"

The key words here are "... when you're ready" or "... when you're in the mood." Those words let children know that we respect their feelings, and that they're in charge. By removing the pressure we're more likely to get a fuller picture of our child's experience, rather than the scraps they'll toss us to get us off their back.

4. Be playful: make it a game

Tall Tales at the Table (Julie's story)

In our family we had a game that we played at dinnertime for years. It was called *A Truth and a Lie*. We went around the table and each person got a turn to tell about their day. One story was true and the other was not. The job of the listeners was to guess which of the stories really happened.

The kids had a lot of fun making up outlandish tales, and I got to learn something about their day. (I learned some interesting things about my husband's day as well!) As a bonus, they all learned to listen very carefully to each other, in order to tease out fact from fiction.

I've heard of other families playing different versions of this game in which each person tells a good thing and a bad thing that happened in their day (or funny or sad, or surprising or boring ... you get the idea).

I've even done this kind of thing with dinner guests, going around the table and sharing a "highlight of the week." I really like it because I get to hear interesting stories from people who wouldn't otherwise muscle into the conversation. It makes a space for each person—shy and bold, adult and child.

REMINDER: HOW TO *LISTEN* WHEN KIDS WON'T *TALK*

1. Model the behavior you want to see.

"Do you want to hear about *my* day? I was worried that I lost my car keys . . ."

2. Acknowledge feelings instead of interrogating.

"It looks like you had a rough day."

3. Put the child in charge: Offer an invitation instead of a demand for information.

"I'd love to hear about your class trip when you're in the mood to talk about it."

4. Be playful: Make it a game.

Play *A Truth and a Lie* at dinner.

Are We There Yet? Crisis in the Car

The whole family was headed home in the car, a ten-minute drive. Our five-year-old son, Rishi, was thirsty, but we had no water.

We tried some of our usual tactics: "You'll have to just deal with thirst for ten minutes." "You're not actually dehydrated! You need to learn how to wait!" His frustration was mounting.

My husband handed me his phone with the *How To Talk* app and I tapped on the first option in the menu: *I need help with difficult feelings.* Another menu popped up to select the feeling your child is experiencing. So I asked Rishi, "Are you angry, disappointed, or frustrated?" He said, "I'm frustrated!" I tapped on *frustrated* and another menu popped up with a list of things to say to acknowledge the feeling.

I literally read aloud the three text statements listed in the app, substituting our scenario for the one in the example, and it really worked! He started to calm down and asked if we could tell him about a time when *we* were frustrated. My husband shared a very funny story about a time when he wanted to buy chips but his mother said, "No!" He decided, "If we aren't getting chips, we aren't getting anything," and began putting all the groceries from the conveyor belt back into the cart. But by mistake he removed groceries belonging to the next person in line! There were lots of giggles from the back of the car.

I shared a story of when I was a kid and we had gone for a hike but my brother gulped all the water early on. I was irritated that there was no water for me, and even more frustrated that my father told me to "just get over it."

We were out of the woods until our seven-year-old said, "Well, let's not remind Rishi about the *WATER* because it seems like he's moved past it." Unfortunately, this led us back to the original problem because Rishi was now reminded of his thirst!

I looked down at the app and there was one option that said *That helped, but it didn't completely solve the problem.* I tapped on it and up popped a menu of additional tools. I opted for using fantasy and offered to make him "fairy water" with my magic fairy dust. I rolled up a piece of paper and started chanting spells. By this time we were pulling up to the house. I asked him, "Rishi, do you want real water or fairy water, since we're home now?" He said, "Fairy water!"

I whispered to his sister to bring a cup of water from the house. I chanted fairy magic spells. When she returned, we slipped the cup of water into the center of the paper vessel and said, "Abracadabra Poof!" Water appeared in a cup in the center of the paper vessel!. He smiled and quickly gulped it down.

"Lost" Car

I gave the kids a five-minute warning before we had to leave the park, but I could see they were having too much fun. There was going to be a battle. I told them, "I don't know where the car is!" They said, "We'll show you!" and led me to the car.

3

Homework Hassles

Is my kid the only one weeping over the worksheet?

It's hard to think of a single issue that has caused more kids to melt down and more parents to tear out their hair in frustration than homework.

Back in the good old days, when these two authors were in kindergarten (Together! In Mrs. Deaner's class!) homework didn't exist. We went to school to use finger paints, play with blocks, and figure out how to zip our own jackets when it was cold out. There was a daily spurt of academic activity when we briefly sat in a circle to sing about the days of the week and the months of the year. That was a very confusing part of the day: June . . . October . . . March . . . there was some kind of mysterious order involved . . . whatever.

Homework was barely introduced in second grade with the occasional invitation to "bring something in to share for show and tell *if you would like to.*"

By the time we grew up and sent our own kids to school, the world had changed. Our kids came home from kindergarten with nightly assignments such as *Write the letter B ten times and then draw four objects that begin with B.*

Joanna Reminisces

I remember watching my five-year-old son Dan tearing through the paper with his eraser as he struggled to depict the bicycle that existed in his head. There was no way I could convince my sobbing son to "Please, *just draw a ball*," instead of an infernally complicated two-wheeler. That was just the second day of kindergarten! In grade school, it got worse. Pages of long division problems, five-paragraph persuasive essays, science webquests, all designed to bring a parent with a tired child to the edge of insanity.

Every parent imagines that his or her child is the only one having such trouble. Surely the other children are happily scribbling cute little drawings of bubbles, balloons, and boxes, while your own is becoming unhinged. Some children may handle homework with relatively little stress, but we haven't met many. There's no simple solution to the homework dilemma. We need to tackle the problem from all angles.

According to research, there's no evidence that homework in the early grades is necessary for academic success, or even beneficial for students.[1] Yet almost all parents will be faced with the nightly misery of tired (sometimes weeping) kids, who are melting down over "packets" of homework.

Conversation with a Mom

"My kid doesn't ever want to do homework. It's a battle every single night."

"What do you tell him?"

"I tell him, 'You just gotta do it!'"

"How does that go over?"

"Not very well."

Let's indulge in a little thought experiment. Imagine that you come home from a long day at work and say to your partner, "I can't believe how unreasonable my boss is! I've been slaving away at this report all day, and now he's insisting that I finish it tonight. I'm exhausted. It's going to take me hours. I don't think I have it in me. I'm not being paid for this! When do I get to relax and do what *I* want to do? This is so stressful. I don't have a life!"

Your partner replies, "Well, you just have to do it. Better stop complaining and get started!"

(We believe this relationship is in trouble. Start googling marriage counselors.)

You *know* you have to finish the report. You can't afford to lose your job, just as your child may not be able to get away with skipping out on all that counter-indicated-by-research homework. The teacher may keep him in from recess, or he may get enough homework zeroes to fail the class.

So here we are between the rock and the hard place. What will help?

We have to start by **meeting basic needs** before pushing kids to produce. Kids need downtime. Even adults get irritable when they haven't had time to relax, eat, move their bodies, reconnect with loved ones, let their minds wander instead of having to focus on what somebody else wants them to do. A steady routine of no downtime will take its toll on the best of us. Adults can push through (sometimes!), but we can't expect the same of children. If you're thinking your kid can go to school, then an after-school program, then dance/karate/piano/soccer, and then come home and have a quick snack before plunging into homework, your expectations may be . . . optimistic.

But even a kid who's had his basic needs met is not likely to say, "Whoa Daddy, I feel refreshed and ready for homework! Bring it on!" If you have that child, you can skip the rest of this chapter. For everyone else, we need more tools to help our kids face the odious task of schoolwork at home. So what can we do next?

Acknowledge feelings! Be on your child's side. In the same way that adults appreciate a partner who is willing to commiserate over an unjustifiable (yet unavoidable) workload, kids appreciate emotional support from their parents over the homework load.

Instead of chirping, "The sooner you start, the sooner you'll be finished!" Try out some of these more helpful (and less enraging) responses:

> "Ugh, homework!"
>
> "That sounds like a lot!"
>
> "The last thing you want to do after a whole day at school is sit down and do more schoolwork."
>
> "If *you* were the teacher, you wouldn't torture your students with a ton of homework!"

Obviously the first two comments are keepers, and will withstand a lot of repetition as long as you put your heart into it and say it like you mean it. But you can't just recycle the last two comments every day. You'll have to get creative and change it up a bit. Maybe by the end of the week you could be wishing for a clone to do the homework, or envisioning an elaborate excuse involving spaceships and aliens.

Homework Mountain (Julie's story)

Rashi came home from school, collapsed on the couch, and started complaining. "I have *so much* homework! I have to write a draft of my essay for English, and I have a science lab to write up, I have a long problem set for math, and there's a chapter in the history textbook I'm supposed to read . . ." As he was talking *my* anxiety was rising: *OMG, how is he ever going to get all this done. This is going to be a disaster. He's never going to finish, and then he won't want to go to school tomorrow.*

I wanted to say, "Just *stop talking* and *start working*! Do the math first—that's your best subject, you can get that over with the fastest—and then tackle the other subjects."

But I didn't, because I'd tried this tactic in the past

and it *never worked*! What *should* I say? My mind was frozen.

"Rashi, hold on a sec." I walked to the kitchen and pretended to fiddle with the oven while I tried to jumpstart my brain. What would I tell a parent in my workshop to do? Oh yeah, *acknowledge feelings!*

I went back and said, "Wow, that's an overwhelming amount of homework for one afternoon. It's hard to know where to start with a list that long."

He sighed. "Yeah." Then he got up and walked to his room, saying, "I think I'll start with the math."

Commiserating with the kids about homework won't necessarily solve your problem so easily. But it's an important start. We want our kids to know we're not the opponent. We're on the same team.

The next strategy could be to **offer choices**.

"What's the least painful way to get it done?"

"Do you want to get it over with right away and have the evening free, or do you want to ride your bike (or play with LEGOs, or shoot some hoops . . .) first and start your homework at 5:30?"

"Do you want to do your homework with snacks, or with music? (Or both?)"

"Do you want to work alone in your room or in the kitchen while I'm cooking dinner? Do you want to work at the kitchen table or *under* the kitchen table?"

"Do you want me to quiz you for the test, or do you want to quiz me?" Hint: When your child quizzes you, be sure to give plenty of wrong answers so they can correct you. For a younger child, you can pretend not to know; for an older child, there will be plenty that you don't know without even trying! You probably won't have to pretend you remember that quadratic equation, or all the causes of World War I.

When the homework is particularly oppressive, the best strategy may be to **adjust expectations**. A homework assignment that is reasonable for some of the class may not be appropriate for the developmental ability of your child. Kids develop at different rates (whether they have a diagnosed disability or not). You may need to communicate with the school to advocate for your child.

Talking to the teacher about their child's homework woes is not the first thing that occurs to most parents. But we've found that many teachers appreciate respectful feedback and suggestions. Their aim is not to create havoc in the home. You may find that your child's teacher is willing to modify assignments so that they work for your child and your family.

One parent, whose child was consistently overwhelmed by the homework load and was becoming increasingly stressed and miserable about school, wrote this letter to the teacher.

> *Dear Ms. Strictler,*
>
> *Thank you for alerting me to the problem of the missing homework assignments. I discussed your concerns with Jeremy. Our new plan is to put a time limit on the homework so it doesn't feel so overwhelming to him. We agreed to stick to the school expectation of 30 minutes a night of homework for third graders. Our plan is to have Jeremy set the timer and work steadily until it goes off.*
>
> *I promised Jeremy that he will not be required to work beyond the 30 minutes, even if the entire assignment is not completed. Jeremy is relieved and encouraged. I feel this is the best way to get him back on the right track, and I expect that you will see an improvement in his homework. Thanks so much for your support!*
>
> *Jane Goodberry*

Another parent decided to opt out of the reading homework entirely, once she realized the negative effect it was having on her child.

Mom Pushes Back

Partway through third grade Sonia's teacher added a reading log to the daily homework assignment. Students were required to record the title and author, time spent, and number of pages read each day. Until then, Sonia had enjoyed reading—in fact I often had to drag her away from a book to get her to come to dinner—but now she started to dread it. She could no longer just pick up a book that looked interesting and start reading. She had to go find her log, laboriously record the title and author, look at the clock and write down the time, and stay aware of how many pages and how many minutes she spent working. It sucked all the joy out of reading! I wouldn't enjoy reading either if I had to watch the clock and count pages.

I was afraid if I didn't do something quickly, Sonia would be turned off to reading entirely, so I arranged a meeting with the teacher. I told her I appreciate that she wants all the children to develop a love of reading. The problem is that the reading log is stopping Sonia from picking up a book for pleasure. It might work for some families, but for us it's having the opposite effect. I said I wanted to relieve her of the obligation to get Sonia to read. I'd take over that responsibility.

Surprisingly, the teacher agreed to my proposal! Sonia was very relieved to be freed from the reading log. It actually took several weeks before I saw her pick up a book for pleasure.

If you've tried some of these tools and still face a nightly battle, you may need to sit down with your child in a calm moment and tackle the issue by **problem-solving** together.

Homework Horror

Logan started sixth grade this year. There's so much homework, and it takes him so long to do it, that he's given up. He has difficulty with his handwriting, so it's very slow and tedious for him to write out assignments. We have massive fights about it every night.

I've taken away playdates because he won't finish his homework first, and I know he won't do it afterward. I've taken away his Xbox and TV privileges. I've yelled at him until I'm hoarse. One night I followed him up the stairs saying, "Logan, you *have* to do this homework. It's very important!"

Logan snatched the sheet from my hand and said, "No . . . I . . . don't!" as he ripped it into little pieces and threw them down the stairs.

The school called me in for a conference with his teachers and the guidance counselor. They told me that Logan was in danger of repeating the grade. Every time he misses a homework assignment, he gets a zero. Even if he passes all his tests, he may still fail. I was too upset to say much. I just told them I'd talk to my son and get back to them.

The more I thought about it, the more I realized that for an active kid like Logan, sitting down to do homework after a long day at school really does feel like torture. I needed to stop trying to convince him that homework is "good for him" or "not really such a big deal if he'd only get down to it."

I decided to try problem-solving. I started by telling him I needed his help. "We both hate having this battle about homework every night. You hate being yelled at and I hate getting all angry and frustrated. I don't want us to do that anymore."

Then I spent a long time acknowledging his feelings. I said things like, "It's a really difficult problem. You come home after six-and-a-half long hours at school, and then you're supposed to sit down and do even more schoolwork. That stinks! You'd rather watch TV and relax, or run around, or play video games, or eat . . . *anything* but more schoolwork."

Logan looked suspicious at first, but then he got more enthusiastic, nodding his head as I went on. Then I said, "The problem is, the school can really give you a hard time if you don't do your homework, and I don't want that to happen. So we have to find the *least* painful way to get through this. We need ideas!" I got a piece of paper and I wrote "Horrible Homework Ideas" at the top.

I thought it might help to start with some outrageous ideas to lighten the mood. I wrote, "Tell them the dog peed on it." Logan said, "Yeah!" Then he suggested, "Say Emily (his little sister) peed on it!" I wrote it down. Then he offered, "Use a mind-wipe laser like in *Men in Black,* so they'll forget they assigned it." I added, "Pray for a snowstorm on heavy homework nights." Logan said, "Pray for a blackout if it's too warm for snow." I decided the mood was right for a few more realistic ideas.

Me: Have a snack to give you energy before homework.
Logan: Have snacks *while* doing homework.
Logan: Eat ice cream while doing homework. (He knows he's not allowed to have ice cream before dinner, but I wrote it down anyway.)
Me: Do five jumping jacks after each math problem. (Current scientific research strongly supports this solution!)*
Logan: Do homework while watching TV.

---

* "The more neuroscientists discover about [learning] the clearer it becomes that exercise provides an unparalleled stimulus, creating an environment in which the brain is ready, willing and able to learn. Aerobic activity has a dramatic effect on adaptation, regulating systems that might be out of balance, and optimizing those that are not—it's an indispensable tool."[2]

Me: Do it while listening to music.

Me: Set the timer and stop when it rings.

Me: Write the longer assignments on the computer? (Logan said that wasn't allowed, but I said we had to put down *all* the ideas, so we left it in with a question mark.)

We looked over our list. Logan laughed heartily at the first few ideas, and said, "I think we need something a little bit more *practical*, Mom." So I crossed them out. I also crossed out the TV idea because I knew that wouldn't work.

Logan liked the idea of using a timer. I think he resists starting homework because he feels like it lasts forever (or at least until bedtime) . . . which it often does, because he finds so many ways to distract himself when he's supposed to be working. The school says the standard is sixty minutes a night for a sixth grader, so we decided that we would set the timer for twenty minutes of math, then twenty minutes of English, and twenty minutes of reading, which we would do together. If the timer went off before he was finished I'd write a note to the teacher *if* he had worked steadily. He also liked the idea of the jumping jacks, working to music, and having snacks while working.

Here are the results:

I no longer ask him about homework as soon as he gets off the bus. When I start dinner, I call him inside for homework. Then I say things like, "Ten vocabulary words to look up? That's a lot! Twenty math problems? Ugh!"

He chooses his music playlist, and sets out his snacks. Then we start the timer. It really helps him to know that there's an end to the ordeal. He sometimes surprises me by going beyond the time to finish up his work. "Just two more sentences, Ma. I can do it!" A few times he quit when the timer rang, but then finished up in the morning before the bus came. I never would have thought of leaving homework until the last minute as a good idea, but I'm impressed by how much more efficiently he can work after a night's sleep.

I wrote a letter to his teachers explaining our new plan about using the timer, and also letting them know that we're going to have Logan use the computer if he has more than one writing assignment in the same night. That way Logan can practice handwriting on shorter assignments, like spelling words, and have the benefit of using the computer for longer assignments where normally he would fall apart because his hand starts to hurt.

The teachers agreed! I guess the way I put it was hard to resist. This has made our lives so much more *livable*!

REMINDER: HOMEWORK HASSLES

1. Meet basic needs first.

Provide downtime, food, opportunity for physical movement and relaxation.

2. Acknowledge feelings. Be on your child's side.

"Ugh, homework!"
"That sounds like a lot!"

3. Offer choices.

"Do you want to do your homework with snacks, or with music? Or both?"
"Do you want to work alone in your room or in the kitchen while I'm cooking dinner?"

4. Adjust expectations. Advocate for your child.

Call or write the teacher to let her know what is going on and respectfully suggest solutions, such as using time limits and reducing the length of some assignments.

5. Try problem-solving.

"What is the least painful way to get homework done? We need ideas!"

Second Grade Is Too Hard!

Samantha just started second grade, and it's been a rough transition. She came home from school saying, "I hate school! I'm not good at math. And there's too much homework! And no one likes me." I wasn't sure what to say, so I just sort of repeated back what she was saying: "Math feels hard!" "Second grade has a lot more homework." She was still upset and ran into her room crying.

I sat down next to her on the bed and said, "School sounds really rough!" She said "Yeah!" And then she started telling me about how the teacher yelled at her because she lost one of her worksheets, and her friend was mad at her because she didn't sit with her on the bus. It turns out that what was really upsetting her were those two specific things. I don't think she would've told me about the problem with the teacher and the friend if I had argued with her as I usually do. ("You *are* good at math, and of *course* people like you!") After she shared those two sorrows, she seemed to relax.

4

All Wound Up and They Won't Calm Down

Dear J & J,

I have a nearly five-year-old son and a two-year-old daughter. I need help with my son's boisterous and sometimes just plain violent behaviour. He adapted amazingly well to becoming a big brother and for the most part shows unbelievable kindness and patience to his baby sister. But he can get really wound up. Sometimes he'll zoom past his sister and push her down, or he'll run past me and whack me in the leg (or on the back of my head if I'm sitting down). He gets even wilder when we have friends over, which is frustrating because then they don't see his wonderful, loving side. They only see this crazy boy who is completely out of control—loud and charging around and hurting people. He shouts, screams, pushes, and kicks. He tries to trip people like it's a game, which makes my husband and me really mad.

I'm at a loss as to how to tackle the problem. I've tried explaining the feelings of the person he hurts. I've tried acknowledging his feelings that he's so excited and that he didn't mean to hurt someone. I've tried coming up with a plan before a friend comes over for what to do if he feels too excited and needs to calm down. I've tried exercising him well before playdates like you might a dog, to physically drain his energy. None of it has helped. I want to be able to have friends round and I want my child to be able to play with others in a somewhat civilised way. Please help.

—Mom of Berserk Kid in the UK

Dear MOBKUK,

You are bringing back memories. And not particularly good ones! I (Joanna) had many of the same thoughts and feelings you are experiencing when my son, Dan, was that age. I distinctly remember thinking I should tire him out like a dog, so he would be calm in the house. There was one particular friend who he adored, and I liked the mom too. But I dreaded their playdates. Dan would get so wired that he'd run around and wrestle with this boy, crashing into people and the few breakable objects left in the house, including light fixtures and wallboard. I really struggled to get him to act "human," which he was capable of doing most of the time, especially when nobody was there to witness! I remember one time when we had guests over, I begged him to stop running wildly in circles in the kitchen, and he yelled, "I AM NOT RUNNING IN CIRCLES! I AM RUNNING IN OVALS!!" Well, at least he had good geometry skills.

It may be comforting to know that time will help. My son and this other "wild child" are still very good friends, and they enjoy each other's company without destroying their surroundings or hurting each other. But you need a solution for the present, not ten years from now.

What you can do ahead of time

When there's an impending social occasion that you know will get your son wired, plan ahead. This is a good time for **problem-solving**. Sit down with him and say, "Last time we had Henry over, things got too wild for me. We need ideas for projects and activities to do when Henry's here." Make a list together and gather whatever supplies you'll need. This kind of planning can help a kid channel his excitement into an acceptable activity rather than into generalized mayhem.

To prime the pump, here are some of our favorite activities for surviving the challenge presented by wild whippersnappers when you're stuck indoors.

Jumping game: In Joanna's house the game was usually called lava, or quicksand or alligators. Kids would leap from a low, sturdy child's craft table to cushions or beanbag chairs on the floor. They had to leap from pad to pad to survive. Sometimes they "fell in" and succumbed dramatically to the hazards. In Julie's house the game was called crash pad. Julie  sewed two old sheets together and stuffed them with scraps of foam. Kids would repeatedly leap from an old couch onto the crash pad with great glee.

Obstacle course: Set up some Hula-Hoops, a tunnel, a few sticks to jump over, a couple of cones to run figure eights around. A homemade tunnel can be created with a blanket over chairs. Kids will soon learn to set up their own course. Kids can use a stopwatch to time each other and then they can try to beat their own times. (Don't have them try to beat each other's times. You don't want to add competition and cause a fight!)

Here comes the train: The two of us used to play this game at Julie's house. Her mom played the piano while we ran around in "ovals" through the kitchen and back into the living room. When she played fast train music, we ran fast; then she played slow train music and we chugged along in slow motion; fast again, faster FASTER and then CRASH!! She hit all the keys at once and we would fall to the floor in a dramatic train crash heap. Then repeat. It was our favorite game. If you don't have a piano player you'll have to improvise (perhaps a drum to set the pace and two pot lids for the crash?).

A counterintuitive idea is to give kids a fine motor activity. This redirects a child's energy from running and crashing, to the effort it takes to focus on a task that will challenge their small muscle strength and dexterity. Here are some ideas to get you started:

Make your own play dough: Mixing flour, salt, and water, and squeezing and pounding dough can be surprisingly physical and satisfying, and can also redirect running, crashing energy into a sit-down task. If you're feeling bold, add food dye for different-colored dough.

Ooze (aka Oobleck): Have kids mix cornstarch and water in a pie tin. This crazy concoction has some very strange properties. If you touch it gently your hand will sink through the liquid to the bottom of the tin. If you slap or punch it, it's hard and solid. If you squeeze a handful, it remains in your hand like a lump of dough. If you relax your fingers it flows through like water. This can be *very* messy, so don't say we didn't warn you!

Sewing project: A favorite at both of our houses was to have the kids sew beanbags and then play toss-the-beanbag-in-the-bucket after they finish their creations. Let them pick their material from your rag bag, cut out a rectangle, fold in half, hand-sew three and a half sides, and pour the beans in when there is just an inch or so left to be sewn. Kids can decorate with googly eyes or permanent markers if they want.

Paint: Cover your dining table with a plastic cloth, set out watercolors or finger paints, and let kids go at it. Next time you have adult visitors they will marvel at the exquisite modern art, which you have framed and hung in your bathroom.

Let it fly!: Grab a stack of paper and teach the kids how to fold paper airplanes. Get them working on the folds and then encourage them to see how far their creations will soar. Give them crayons to decorate the wings.

And finally, as part of your plan, consider keeping playdates shorter so it's easier for your child to keep up his best sociable behavior for the duration.

What you can do in the moment

What if your kid still goes off the rails, whether on a playdate or at home with a sibling? It's time to **take action without insult**. Don't feel bad about removing your child from the scene if he starts to hurt people or make them feel uncomfortable.

It might work to simply tell him, "I need you to come sit with me for a few minutes. You can go back when you're ready to play a more gentle game." If he says he's ready, you can ask him what game he wants to play, to make it clear that he is "going back in" with a plan.

If he's really wound up, you may need to physically walk him out of the room. The words you use still matter. He'll have a harder time cooperating if he's feeling bad about himself. You don't want him to get stuck in the role of "the rough and wild child." Resist the urge to lecture, "Now you're getting too wild. We talked about this! You're going to hurt somebody. Think about how bad it feels to be hit like that!"

Instead, describe the problem in more neutral terms. "You're full of energy right now. You're like a rocket zooming to the moon. I can't let you crash into people."

If he needs more help calming down, **tell him what he *can* do instead of what he can't**. You can send him to the chin-up bar, direct him to do ten jumping jacks, toss him in the hammock swing . . . whatever works best for your child.

What you can do when an overtired child gets wild

Sometimes kids get wound up when they aren't getting enough sleep. We don't always make this connection, because it seems like they're bursting with energy when in fact they're running on fumes. The answer may lie in **tending to basic needs**, which in this case could mean helping a child get to sleep earlier or adding a nap.

Music's Hypnotic Charms (Julie's story)

When my son Asher was three years old he'd get very crabby without a nap, but he'd often get so wound up he couldn't fall asleep. And he wasn't willing to try! I complained to Joanna about it. A week later I found a package from Joanna in my mailbox with a homemade cassette tape inside labeled *Asher's Dance & Rest Tape*. (Nowadays you'd probably email a playlist, but this was back in the stone age.) The first piece was "Batonga," a very rhythmic, percussive song by Angélique Kidjo that had Asher jumping up and down like a punk rocker on a pogo stick. I danced with him to get him started. There were a few other upbeat tunes, then a piece called "Airplane" by the Indigo Girls, a more gentle song that had Asher swooping around the room with his arms out like an airplane. The end of the tape had Gregorian chants by the monks of the Benedictine Abbey. By this time Asher was content to lie down on the floor and let the music lull him to sleep. Asher used that tape until he grew out of needing a nap. It was an essential part of his daily routine.

Reply from MOBKUK

Dear J&J,

I have an update for you. We had a playdate at our house last week with my son's "wild child" friend, which I'd been dreading. I have to say it was a roaring success!

I decided my tactic would be to have a combination of free play and some planned activities spread out over the playdate so they weren't left to their own devices for too long.

We got in from school and I gave them a snack. Then I left them to it for about half an hour. We then made the oozey slime stuff, which created the most mess I've ever seen. But they both loved it and it totally captured their attention. They then went outside to run around and play soccer for a bit while I tackled the mess and did some kitchen prep.

When they came in we made homemade pizza for dinner (another fine-motor activity!). They had a bit more free play while the pizza cooked. That was probably the hairiest time as we were two hours in and they were getting hungry and there was a bit of rough play, but not too bad, no tears or injuries, and then the pizza was ready, phew! They sat and ate their pizza and I then convinced them to take on a more peaceful activity of building a marble run together. Before we knew it, his dad was at the door ready to take him home. Success!

Thanks for all your tips. I think going into playdates with a few activities planned might be the key for us moving forward.
—Mom of Calm(er) Kid in UK

REMINDER: ALL WOUND UP

What you can do ahead of time

1. Try problem-solving.

"Last time we had Henry over, things got too wild for me. We need ideas for projects and activities to do when Henry's here."

What you can do in the moment

2. Take action without insult.

"I need you to come sit with me for a few minutes. You can go back when you're ready to play a more gentle game."

Physically walk him out of the room. "You're full of energy right now. I can't let you crash into people."

3. Tell them what they *can* do, instead of what they *can't*.

"Let's go to the chin-up bar and get out some of your energy. How many chin-ups do you think you can do?"

What you can do when an overtired child gets wild

4. Tend to basic needs.

Experiment with creating routines that help a child get to sleep.*

---

* For more ideas on how to help a child who has a hard time getting to sleep at night, see chapter 13 in *How to Talk So Little Kids Will Listen*.

Let the Sun Shine—Cure for a Rainy Day

Emotions ran high yesterday when the sun decided not to come out, *yet again*. Instead of getting into an explanation of the weather patterns (as I would have done in the past) I asked my almost three-year-old Meera, "What can we do when the sun just won't come out?" The response: "Can we make our own sun?"

So, I present: our sun!

Daddy Gets Schooled—Tot Teaches Pop Problem-Solving

Meera is becoming an expert on problem-solving. Last week she had a problem-solving session with her dad. As he started debating the "rightness" of a solution she had come up with, she reminded him, "Daddy, you just write and draw. Don't judge. We'll review when we are done!"

Section II

Unnecessary Roughness

5

HELP! My Kids Are Fighting!
Peacekeeping on the Home Front

The first question we have for you is: How desperate is the situation?

Are they physically pummeling and throttling each other *right now*??

Put down the book (gently, don't throw it at the combatants) and go separate them. Oh but wait, before you abandon the book, here's a quick dialogue for you, in case you need some helpful words to go along with your actions:

> "*HEY!!!* [You probably have to yell to get their attention.] I can't let you hurt each other!" Physically grab a kid if necessary. "You, to the couch. And you, to the chair."
>
> Once they are safely simmering in their separate corners you can say, "Something happened! You guys are really mad at each other!"

Take a moment—just a split second—to notice how skillful you were, protecting your kids from harm, stating your values without attacking their character, and accepting their feelings in the heat of battle!

But what's next? You're probably tempted to launch into an enlightening lecture about the downside of using physical violence

145

to resolve differences. You're ready to present an airtight case supporting the argument that "you should be more patient with your brother because he's younger than you," or that you kids are "making a big deal over nothing," or that "it's not nice to pinch. You wouldn't like it if someone did that to you!" We empathize. We've been there, and we can tell you (having been there) that your kid is extremely unlikely to respond, "Oh gee, thanks for the words of wisdom. Now that you've *explained* to me that my problem is unimportant and my reaction was inconsistent with family policy, I regret my behavior, and I'm determined, going forward, to treat my sibling with patience and loving kindness."

So now we know what *not* to say. What *would* be helpful?

1. **Start by acknowledging each child's feelings in turn.** Avoid taking sides!

> **"You really didn't like it when** . . . she turned off the music you were listening to."

> **"And you weren't in the mood for** . . . loud music with a lot of drum solos."

> **"And you got mad when** . . . she grabbed the remote control out of your hand."

> **"It hurt a lot when he** . . . bent back your fingers and pinched your arm."

> **"And it doesn't seem fair to you that** . . . she gets to listen to her music and you don't get to listen to yours."

> **"Oh, so both of you wanted to** . . . listen to music, but two different styles."

And so on . . .

Sometimes that will be enough. When children feel heard, they calm down. They can think more clearly and may be able to come up with a solution on their own.

What if they don't calm down, and instead they start calling each other names?

You can **express your feelings strongly**: "Hey! I don't like to hear name-calling! That makes people angrier."

Then help them express their feelings without insults: "You can tell your brother: 'I don't like loud music when I'm reading. It really bothers me!'"

If they haven't wandered peacefully away by now, you can continue to help them by moving on to step two.

2. **Describe the problem** without minimizing it.

"One person is in the mood for loud rock music, and the other person is not. This is a tough problem."

This may be enough to inspire your young adversaries to resolve the conflict on their own.

But if not, don't worry. Have you noticed that we've already made it through the first two steps of **problem-solving**? You've seen how this process works between adult and child in chapter three, *The Problem with Punishment*. This is your chance to take it to the next level and teach your children to use problem-solving *with each other*. Think of it as a golden opportunity for your kids to practice the problem-solving process that they will one day internalize, enabling you to go have a cup of coffee while they work out their own problems. Here's your next step:

3. **Brainstorm ideas**.

"What can we do that will work for both of you? We need ideas."

Don't reject ideas while brainstorming. (Not, "Oh, so you want to spend $30,000 to create a soundproof studio? That's not happening!")

It can help to write down all of the ideas. You might have to bite your tongue so you don't immediately burst out with your own brilliant ideas ("Why don't you just . . . ?"). Keep in mind that any solution they come up with on their own is likely to be more effective, and every minute that you wait quietly conveys the message, "I trust you to be able to think of solutions."

4. **Review your list of ideas and choose the ones that everybody likes.** You can circle them, X them out, add check marks, smiley and frowny faces, whatever tickles your fancy.

	Nia	Marcus	Mom
-create soundproof studio	☺	☺	☹
-use headphones for music	☺	☺	
-use earplugs for quiet	☹	☺	
-Listen in different rooms	☺	☺	
-Max Volume 5	☹	☹	☺
-Take turns choosing one song each	☺	☹	
-create a playlist that both agree to	☹	☺	

Grab a magnet, stick your list of mutually agreeable solutions on the fridge, and lie in wait for an opportunity to use them.

What if the solution doesn't work? Or it only works once? Now what??

Now you figured out what doesn't work. You're closer to a good solution. Problem-solve again. You can tell your kids, "Well, we gave that idea a try, but it didn't turn out as well as we hoped. Let's see what else we can come up with." Console yourself with the knowledge that even though it's a whole lot more work than just telling kids what to do, it's worth the effort. The ability to resolve conflict with mutual respect is the prelude to world peace. Imagine life with children who can solve their own problems without your intervention! It's a lofty goal!

Are you kidding? I don't have the time or energy for this. My kids can't agree on anything. You're exhausting me!

If it's been one of those days and you or your kids don't have the patience for loftiness . . .
Briefly sum up each child's point of view and take action. If necessary, remove the assailants from each other's vicinity, or remove the object of contention. Return to problem-solving when you have the patience for it.

> "Marcus wants to listen to his favorite music, and Nia doesn't want to hear it while she's reading. She'd rather have a different kind of music, without drums or vocals. For now *I'm* going to decide, even though it might not make everybody happy. I'm going to let Marcus finish listening to this one song and then I'm turning off the stereo and putting away the remote control. We can sit down together later and figure out a solution that works for everyone."

But what if one kid is continually attacking another, either physically or verbally, and all this talking does nothing? Shouldn't that kid be punished?

We adults do have to take responsibility for limiting unacceptable behavior and protecting the children in our charge. The question is, does punishment achieve that goal?

The problem with punishment is that it doesn't teach the "aggressor" how to manage a similar conflict in the future, it doesn't repair the relationship, and it will not make the victim safer.

And punishment doesn't address the underlying reason for the fighting. There can be many: jealousy over a new baby, anxiety about a new school routine, conflict over a possession, or frustration that has nothing to do with the victim. We can be most helpful when we tailor our response to the underlying feeling or need.

Stories from the Front Lines

You're a Baby!

I've read that when one kid is being mean to another, you should give attention to the victim, not the instigator. But in my family that wasn't working. The teasing was becoming an endless cycle.

This time, Lev (age eleven) was tormenting Avi (age eight) by telling him that he was "acting like a baby." Avi was trying to mount a defense, but Lev kept needling him, "What you just said *proves* you're a baby!"

I demanded that they separate. My head was telling me not to punish, but my gut was screaming, "Lock him up and throw away the key!" I was in such a boiling rage that I shut myself in the closet, where I could vent without the boys hearing me.

Ughhhhh! I hate this! Avi just wants a tiny bit of attention and approval. How can Lev be so nasty to his brother? I gave birth to a horrible person!

I actually lead How To Talk workshops, so I thought to myself, *What would I tell a parent in my workshop to do? . . . I'd tell them to try to see it from Lev's perspective and acknowledge his feelings. . . . But I don't care how he's feeling! He's a monster!*

Eventually I calmed down enough to leave the closet

and talk privately to Lev in his room. "I know that you can be a kind and understanding person. There must be something that made you really mad to say those things to Avi."

The floodgates opened. He had a long list of complaints. "Every time we're going to a baseball game, Avi lies down on the floor and says he's tired and he makes us late, so I always miss the beginning of the game . . . and when we do family clean-up and we're all supposed to help, he says he's too tired and he doesn't help, and that's not fair! . . . and he makes us late every day for school because he has to go to the bathroom exactly when it's time to leave . . ."

The complaints kept flowing. From Lev's point of view, Avi *was* acting like a baby! He couldn't control his energy level. He couldn't control his bladder. It must have been very frustrating for an older brother.

I didn't argue with him, or try to explain. I just listened. (I shouldn't say "just," because it wasn't easy to hear it all.) Then I said, "Wow, no wonder you're so mad at him. He did a lot of things that you really resent. I think Avi needs to hear from you that some of the things he does are making you mad. The problem is, it's a long list, and I think it would be too much for him to hear all those bad things at once. How about you pick one thing to talk to him about?"

Lev chose to tell Avi how resentful he felt when Avi didn't help with cleaning up. Avi replied that he wanted to help, but sometimes he really *was* too tired. I asked, "What can we do so the cleaner-uppers don't feel resentful, and Avi doesn't feel forced when he's too tired?" We came up with chores Avi could do on his own schedule, when he *did* have energy—taking out the garbage and recycling. Avi made sure to tell his brother when he did these chores. He wanted to redeem himself!

That discussion made a big difference in their relationship. Sure, they continued to have conflicts, but without the constant mean teasing. Lev knew he could talk to me and to Avi when he got resentful, and we could figure out a solution to the problem instead of letting his anger fester.

When Avi was diagnosed with severe sleep apnea a year later, the first thing he said was, "Let's tell Lev!" He wanted his brother to know there was finally an explanation for all that irritating tiredness!

Sometimes the best way to reduce the fighting is to give each kid a little extra attention, as the parent in the next story did:

The Floor Solution

My kids' bickering was really getting to me, and I was starting to notice a pattern. It happened predictably as soon as I got them home from the after-school program. We'd walk in the door, and in the minute it took me to race to the kitchen and get a pot of water on the stove, they were at each other, arguing over toys, or who breathed on who. I'd run back in to stop them from hurting each other, and everyone always ended up angry and irritated—especially me!

Last week I started a new routine. As soon as we walk in the door, I dump my coat and bags on the couch and sit in the middle of the living room floor. I'm like a magnet for the kids. Miriam (age five) climbs into my lap, Joseph (age seven) shows me what he's brought home, and Rachel (age nine) tells me about the latest drama from her social group. I ignore the phone and the dinner that needs cooking, and I don't even sneak a glance at my email, for at least five minutes straight. That's all it seems to take, and then I can say, "Hold on, I've gotta go start dinner." They manage to find something to occupy themselves, or they come "help" me in the kitchen. I never would've guessed that a five-minute investment could buy so much peace.

Can I Have Your Attention, Please?

My four-year-old, Trang, has been throwing toys at his eight-year-old sister Mai. She gets very upset. I acknowledge her feelings ("You don't like being hit by toys!"), and confiscate his projectiles ("Toys are not for throwing at sisters!"). But that only stops the behavior in the moment. There's always a next time.

It occurred to me that I didn't know why he was doing it. I knew it wouldn't help to ask him a direct question, so this time I said, "Something made you mad enough to throw that block at Mai. I wonder what it was . . ."

He told me that he wanted his sister and me to come to his puppet show, and nobody was listening to him. It was true. I'd heard him calling us over, and we had ignored him. When he realized we weren't coming, he started throwing things to get our attention. It made me feel more sympathetic. I told him, "I can't allow throwing, but I'll try harder to notice when you call me, and I'll let you know if I can't come instead of ignoring you." That satisfied him.

So far there hasn't been another hurling incident. It's been a week without flying objects.

Sometimes there's a surprisingly simple solution to a conflict:

Please Fence Me In

I have two boys. Dom is four and a half and Rocco is one. Ever since Rocco became mobile, he's been getting into Dom's stuff, and Dom has become increasingly violent toward his little brother. The other day, Dom was building a castle with LEGOs, and Rocco knocked it over and destroyed it. Dom screamed and hit Rocco in the face.

I was almost overwhelmed by my impulse to hit Dom. The thing that stopped me was the thought of telling him, "No hitting!" while hitting him. So I screamed *"NO HIT-TING,"* took Rocco into my bedroom to comfort him, and locked the door to keep Dom out. Dom was utterly distraught—sobbing and screaming outside the door. When everyone finally calmed down, I couldn't bring myself to talk with them about it. I was wrung out! I needed some moments of peace before I could think straight.

That night, when I was putting Dom to bed, we were both calm enough to try problem-solving. I said I knew it was hard to have a little brother grabbing your things and wrecking them. I asked him for ideas of what to do so his LEGO creations wouldn't get destroyed and Rocco wouldn't get hurt. I suggested he play with LEGOs in his room, but he doesn't like to be alone, so he rejected that idea. His idea was to put Rocco in the playpen, but I rejected that because Rocco hates to be penned in, now that he's learned to walk. Then we had the idea of making it a *LEGO* playpen instead of a *baby* playpen. Dom could build LEGOs in the playpen and Rocco wouldn't be able to get in to grab them. We tried it and it's been working brilliantly! Dom gets to be in the middle of the living room with all the family, and his creations are safe.

I've also noticed that we didn't just solve the LEGO problem. Since the "playpen solution," Dom has generally been much better about con-trolling his temper around his brother. Even though he still has his moments!

Some conflicts have no easy answers. But they can still be approached with respect for feelings and an open mind:

Musical Discord

I have twin ten-year-old girls, Samantha and Jennifer, and a six-year-old son, Tyler. Samantha loves songs from musicals, and she's always singing around the house. She heard about a singing teacher from her friend and got excited about the idea of taking singing lessons herself. Her sister immediately chimed in that she wanted singing lessons too. I said they could both take lessons, but Samantha got really upset and said it was *her* idea, and if her sister did it too, "That ruins everything!" She stomped off in angry tears.

My mother-in-law told me to let Samantha be the only one to have the lessons, because she asked first. Her sister's just engaging in me-too-ism. But I wasn't sure. On the one hand, I understood how Samantha felt. It's not always easy to be an identical twin. She wanted to have this one activity be her own thing. On the other hand, how could I deny music to one kid and give it to the other? That seemed wrong!

I talked to a friend of mine who is actually a professional singer. She had a very strong reaction. She told me that in her family, she was the one who got the music lessons and her sisters didn't, because she was "the talented one." To this day her sisters resent her for it. They don't want to hear anything about her career, and they don't come to her shows.

That gave me a chill. But I still had the same problem. If I insisted that both of them have the right to take singing lessons, it would ruin it for Samantha. She's trying so hard to carve out a separate identity and find something unique she can do.

155

Ultimately I decided to tell them how I felt, talk about their feelings, and cross my fingers and hope for a good outcome! Here's what I said:

"This is a very, very tough problem. Samantha wants to take singing lessons. She does a lot of things with her sister, but she wants this one thing to be a special activity that she tries by herself. She feels so strongly about it that if she can't do it alone, she doesn't want to do it at all.

"Jennifer likes to sing too. She doesn't want to be told she's not allowed to have lessons just because she didn't think of it first.

"I don't know what we should do! I don't want to tell Jennifer she isn't allowed to take singing lessons. Music isn't just for one person. But I want Samantha to be able to have her special thing. I can see how much it means to her."

Jennifer said, "Well, I don't really want to take lessons. I just want to be able to borrow the sheet music so I can sing the songs too."

Samantha said, "I don't mind if you borrow the sheet music. I can make you copies."

Now Tyler jumped in. "But I want singing lessons too!" (Of course! It couldn't be *that* easy.)

My husband suggested that he could start teaching Tyler chords on our ukulele and then we could have a sibling band. It took some convincing, but Tyler finally agreed.

This felt so right. It was a relief to be honest with my kids. I'm really glad I didn't make the decision for them one way or the other, and leave one of them feeling bitter and resentful.

We expect children to learn to use words instead of fists. But we sometimes forget to acknowledge what a difficult challenge that can be for them:

Bedding Battle (Joanna's story)

Sam and Dan were fighting over the blankets, *again*! The game always started with giggling—five-year-old Sam yanking down the blanket from seven-year-old Dan's top bunk bed. Dan always retaliated by pulling Sam's blanket up to his territory. At one point Sam realizes he's out-muscled by his larger, stronger brother, and in danger of losing the game. He starts to pull back his own blanket with an earnest ferocity. His face turns red. He yells, "STOP IT!" Dan keeps on pulling, oblivious to the change in mood. He hangs upside down from his perch and grabs Sam's sheets and pillow to add to his upper-story pile of loot.

Sam is beside himself. He starts to swing at Dan. Dan is outraged. "He's hitting me! There's no hitting allowed!" He hits back at Sam. I run in to break up the now-very-physical fight.

As I separate them, each to his own bed, and redistribute the bedding to the rightful owners, I deliver my standard speech. "I can't let you hurt each other. There's no hitting allowed. Tell him with words not fists." They've heard it all before. Why hasn't it sunk in?

It strikes me that it's *hard* not to hit. What's a younger brother supposed to do when his older brother won't listen to his words? And what's an older brother to do when his little brother is landing some pretty big, rage-fueled punches?

So I alter the script. "It's hard not to hit when you get mad! Even a lot of grown-ups have trouble with that."

I sense a change in the atmosphere. The kids are actually paying attention to me. Dan says, "What do you mean? Grown-ups don't hit each other."

"Well, sometimes they do when they get really mad. The angry feeling goes into your body and makes you want to hit. (I made a fist and shook it.) It's actually against the law for grown-ups to hit each other, because they're big and strong and they could hurt each other very badly. So they have to learn to control that feeling and let it out in words, or they could get put in jail."

Now the kids were riveted! I thought I'd better say something reassuring. I wasn't trying to frighten them.

"Kids don't go to jail, because kids are still learning not to hit. But it's not easy! One way to help each other learn is to listen to each other's words. So if your brother says, 'Stop!' and you stop, you're helping to teach him that he doesn't have to hit."

Dan was miffed, "But he started it. And he was laughing a minute ago!"

Sam: "Was not!"

Dan: "Was too!"

I broke in. "So it's pretty confusing when someone starts a game and they're laughing, and then they suddenly get mad and want to stop."

Dan: "Yeah!"

"That makes it tricky to play rough games. So another thing you have to do is keep looking at the other person's face to make sure they're still enjoying it. And if you're getting mad enough to hit, what can you do to stop yourself?"

They both gave me a blank look.

"Well, if it happens again, you can call me. Yell, 'EMERGENCY!' And I'll come running in to help you get what you need without hitting."

I remember their sense of awe over the idea that grown-ups themselves have to struggle with anger, and control the urge to hit. It validated the challenge they faced, which made them more inspired to conquer it. I noticed a change in their conflicts after that. They were less likely to hit, and more likely to listen to each other. And I could remind them to "look at the other person's face" when I saw roughhousing getting too intense, which turned out to be a very useful instruction!

It's hard for any child to see a conflict from another person's perspective, and it can be especially challenging for kids on the autism spectrum, like Noah in the following story:

Computer War

Noah (age nine) paused his computer game to go to the bathroom. David (age twelve) closed out Noah's game and started his own. When Noah returned he yelled at David to get off the computer, and it quickly escalated into loud shouting and name-calling.

I ordered them into the living room, away from the computer. "You both sound furious! I want to know what happened, but I can't understand when you're both talking at once." Noah seemed the most unhinged of the two, so I said, "Noah, why don't you go first. David, you'll have your turn when he's finished."

Noah spluttered, "David *knew* I was in the middle of my game. He closed me out! He made me lose my points. He's not allowed to do that! It was my turn."

David was itching to jump in, but I first acknowledged Noah's perspective. "Oh, so you weren't finished but you had to go to the bathroom. You thought David should know you'd be right back. You're mad because you lost all your points." Noah said, "Yeah!"

"David, your turn."

"I didn't know he was in the middle of playing. He never closes out his games when he's finished."

Noah interrupted, "You KNEW I was in the bathroom, you just wanted to take over the computer!"

"Noah, it's David's turn to talk. You can have a turn again when he's finished."

David continued, "How am I supposed to know he's in the bathroom?!"

I summarized. "So David thought the computer was available, and Noah thought David should know he was in the middle of a game and he'd be right back. We need to figure out a system for using the computer, because this could happen again." I pulled out a pad of paper and asked for ideas. Here's how the conversation went.

Noah: "David should have to check to see if I'm finished using the computer before he closes out a game." (I wrote it down.)

David: "No way! I shouldn't have to go look all over the house before I use the computer."

Me: "We're writing down *all* our ideas. Later we'll decide which ones we like."

David: "We should have a rule that when you leave the computer, your turn is over."

(Noah often becomes so engrossed in a game that he doesn't notice his bladder is full until it's too late. He's only recently started making progress on getting to the bathroom in time. This idea would be a disaster! But I'd just told David to hold off on criticisms and I figured I'd better follow my own rule. I wrote his idea down.)

Noah: "But what if I have to go to the bathroom?"

David: "Okay, so then you have to put a note on the computer that you're still playing." (I wrote it down.)

Noah: "I don't have time to write a note."

Me: "What if you write a sign ahead of time that says, 'Noah is using the computer,' and put it on the keyboard if you go to the bathroom."

Noah: "Okay . . ."

David: "And if there's no sign, I'm allowed to close out your game and use the computer."

I never had to read through all the ideas. They agreed that Noah would make a sign, and he'd leave it on the keyboard if he went to the bathroom in the middle of a game.

Interestingly, Noah never actually made the sign, *and* he and David never had this fight over the computer again. When Noah needed to go to the bathroom during a computer session, he would yell to David, "I'm still on the computer." And David would check to see where Noah was before closing out a game. The process of expressing their viewpoints and negotiating solutions made them more sensitive to each other's perspectives. For a child on the autism spectrum, being able to guess what someone else is thinking or feeling can be challenging. I think problem-solving is helping him develop that ability.

REMINDER: HELP! MY KIDS ARE FIGHTING!

1. **Take action without insult.** Physically separate the combatants.
   "HEY! I can't let you hurt each other!"

2. **Acknowledge feelings** without taking sides.
   "You didn't like it when she turned off the music you were listening to."
   "And you got mad when he grabbed the remote control out of your hand."

3. **Describe the problem** without minimizing it.
   "This is a tough problem. One person is in the mood for loud music and the other person isn't."

If that's not enough:

4. **Continue with problem-solving:**
   - **Ask for ideas.**
     "What can we do that will work for both of you?"
   - **Choose the ideas everybody likes.**
     "Let's circle these and put them up on the refrigerator."

Quick fix (if time or patience are in short supply):

5. **Briefly sum up each child's point of view** and **take action.**
   "*You* want to listen to your favorite music, and *you* don't want to hear it while you're reading. For now *I'm* going to decide, even though it might not make everybody happy."

KFC versus McDonald's

I picked up my kids after work and told them we were going to grab dinner on the way home. My son said, "Let's go to McDonald's!" His sister said, "No, we're going to KFC. It's my turn to choose and I want the mashed potatoes." He kicked the back of her seat. *"I want McDonald's!"*

I said, "You sound angry!"

"I'm not angry. I just want McDonald's!"

I said, "Well, it is your sister's turn, so it's KFC this time. It sounds like you really wish we could go to McDonald's. What will you get to eat at McDonald's when it's your turn to choose?"

"Chicken."

"Hey, we can get chicken at KFC!"

"Oh, okay!"

I guess he doesn't know what the C stands for in KFC!

6

HELP! My Kid Is Hitting Me!

The Art of Self-Defense Against Small Combatants

Dear J&J,

My husband and I have been doing a lot of acknowledging feelings and problem-solving with our four-year-old son, Max, and he is becoming quite good at thinking of solutions. Our new challenge is that Max will fly off the handle very quickly and start screaming, kicking, and punching. I barely have time to realize he is getting upset before he explodes.

Any little thing can set him off. For example, during bath time we were spelling words with foam letters on the tile, and I accidently knocked a letter into the water. He climbed out of the tub and started attacking me. I had to hold his arms and legs down to protect myself.

I've tried expressing my feelings strongly:

"That hurts me!"

"I don't like that!"

"No hitting!"

And finally . . . "STOP HITTING ME!"

If he hits me before bedtime I tell him:

"I can't lie down with you tonight. I'm too scared of getting hit. Maybe we can try again tomorrow."

So far nothing has helped. It stinks to feel like I'm trying so hard and continuing to come up short.

—Not a Punching Bag

Dear NPB,

You're doing all the right things in the moment. You're letting him know your feelings strongly, and you're taking action to protect yourself—all without attacking him.

Once he's calm (later in the evening or the next day), you can say something like, "Last night when you were taking a bath you were so mad when the letters got knocked down. And I was really mad, too. I didn't like getting hit. We were *furious* with each other. That wasn't fun! I don't even want to use letters in the bath if I'm gonna get hit if they fall down. Let's make a plan for next time so you can let me know when you're mad, without hitting. Should we make up a special word, like "BLARGH!!"? Or a special signal, like thumbs down?"

If the plan works, and he uses the special word or signal, you can respond by acknowledging his feelings dramatically. "Oh no! You didn't want the letters to fall down! They should stay UP! That is *so* annoying!"

Here's what we want him to learn: When you hit and kick people they get very mad at you. They don't want to play with you anymore. Not because they want to punish you, but because they need to protect themselves. And we want him to learn what he can do instead—how to express anger without causing physical damage.

It might also help to think about why Max has such a hair-trigger temper lately. It's common to see this kind of behavior after a major change or a stressful experience: a switch to a new school, a new baby (expected or arrived or newly mobile), a difficult day at school, a new nanny, a move to a new house, a death in the family, parents fighting, a health problem (for example, an ear infection or an oncoming cold), or even a disrupted sleep schedule. Any of these could result in a short fuse causing a child to "lose it" over the littlest thing.[1] The letter falling in the tub is not just a letter falling in the tub. It's the last straw!

Dear J&J,

I didn't make the connection until I read your list of stressful changes. Max's little brother, Finn, is about to turn one, and over the past couple of months he's started crawling. He's very interested in what his big brother is doing and he's all over Max's stuff. We took a few boxes of Max's old toys out of hibernation and gave them to Finn. Max gets upset when he sees Finn playing with his old toys. He once said with such sincerity and fear, "Finn is going to take all my toys!" while his eyes filled with tears.

I realized that Max is also getting upset because we've been scolding him for playing with Finn's toys, mostly because he either plays too roughly or snatches them out of Finn's hand. Yesterday he got into the playpen with Finn, which started out okay, but then he got rough and was told to get out. He hit his dad and said, "You're mean to me!"

After everyone cooled down my husband took Finn on a walk so I could sit down with Max. I got out the paper and crayons and started to write "Max feels so angry he hits when Mom and Dad don't let him play with Finn's things." (He prefers me to write it down and read it to him, instead of just saying it.) He asked, "How do you spell mad?" I told him and he wrote it on the paper. We talked about how he still likes his old toys even if they are for babies. I said that Mommy and Daddy still enjoy playing with some baby toys too! He said he doesn't like it when he's having fun with Finn and we tell him to stop. I said, "That sounds very frustrating! You don't like it when we stop you from playing with your brother." Then I wrote "IDEAS," which he recognizes now from so many problem-solving sessions. He came up with all of the ideas:

1. Max can play in Finn's playpen when Finn is napping.
2. Max can play with Finn's toys whenever Finn is not around.

3. Max can play with baby toys that Finn isn't holding.
4. Max isn't ready to give Robbie the Robot to Finn and he'd like it back. (I suggested he keep it in his room.)

We circled all the ideas because we liked them all. So far he's been doing well with it.

He did get angry and hit me once when he didn't want to stop playing to get dressed, but I said, "Whoa! Max is so angry, he's hitting! He must be very upset!" and we were able to solve the problem. We made up a hide-and-seek game where, instead of counting, the finder gets dressed while the hider hides. The faster you get dressed, the less time the hider has! Another successful game we came up with is to pretend to be spies, getting socks and shoes on silently, then surprising Dad that we are ready to go.

UPDATE:

The hitting is better but not gone. He has the urge to hit but I can tell he's working to fight it, which I think is pretty admirable for a four-year-old. He's getting better at managing it and letting out his anger in other ways (crumpling paper, squeezing fists, grunting loudly) while I acknowledge his feelings. He's doing better overall with his brother and I'm doing better at making special time, sometimes even just five or ten minutes, to do what Max wants to do—like playing LEGOs or reading his panda book.

I'm also trying to get better at recognizing when Max needs a break. If he's overtired or just done from a long week at school, I ease up on the expectations. I'll let him skip a bath, or watch a TV show. Sometimes I put up a barrier in the playroom and let him have a "big kid" side all to himself so he can play with his toys without worrying that Finn will grab them.

REMINDER: HELP! MY KID IS HITTING ME!

1. Express your feelings strongly.

"That hurts me! I don't like that!"

2. Acknowledge your child's feelings.

"You didn't want that to happen! That makes you so mad!"

3. Take action without insult.

"I can't lie down with you tonight. I don't want to get hit."

"I'm holding your arms. I won't let myself be hit."

4. Try problem-solving.

"You didn't like when the letters got knocked down, and I didn't like getting hit. Let's make a plan for next time, so you can let me know when you're mad without hitting."

 **TIP** It's common for kids to develop a hair-trigger temper after a major change or a stressful experience. You may have to manage the environment instead of the child.

Unchained*

When I was teaching elementary school in West Harlem, I was supposed to be helping students with learning disabilities improve their test scores in math and reading. But many of my students had hair-trigger tempers, and anyone who's ever taught knows that kids can't learn when they're angry or frustrated. So I spent a lot of time dealing with feelings. I helped them put their emotions into words ("That made you angry! You didn't like it when he grabbed your hood. Let's tell him, *no hood grabbing*."). I reminded them that roughhousing has to stop if someone is hurt or upset ("Look in the person's face. Is he crying? Does he look angry, or is he still having a good time?").

Luis was a small, wiry fifth-grader with a very short fuse and a fierce temper. He was creative and curious in the classroom, but formidable on the playground. One afternoon when I was on recess duty, I saw a clump of kids around the fence. One of the third-graders had kicked the fence where it was loose at the bottom. His foot was stuck under the chain link. The surrounding kids were laughing and jeering as this poor kid tried to free himself. Some of them were holding the fence down around his foot to prolong the

---

* Confession: This is actually a story from Joanna, not from a reader.

entertainment. As I moved toward the fence to assert my adult authority, I saw Luis dart in front of me. He snarled at the crowd to back off, and he lifted the fence, freeing the trapped child.

I asked Luis, "What made you do that?"

"Ms. Faber, I looked at his face like you told us, and he was definitely NOT having a good time!"

I was filled with pride for my student. He faced a mob, and he acted with courage and empathy for a younger child. He could have joined in, or walked on by, but he didn't. I couldn't take full credit for this young man's integrity, but I know that I had at least provided the language that helped him to think in an empathic way.

7

Animal Etiquette

Kids and Creatures

Dear J&J,

My neighbor's cat had kittens, and the kids begged and begged for one. I should never have given in. Now I have constant conflict on my hands.

Julian, who's two-and-a-half, loves to chase the kitten. I keep telling him he's scaring her, but that doesn't register at all. He laughs when Ally claws up the curtains to get away from him. His six-year-old brother Sebastian is even worse, because he uses more advanced tactics. He sneaks up and grabs her when she's eating, because he wants to carry her around (against her will). He's already gotten scratched, but he still does it.

I'm getting very frustrated with using the phrase, "We expect you to play gently with the cat!" and showing them ways to play properly. We have to tell them both multiple times a day and it's just not working.

Please help!

—Cat-astrophe in California

Dear J&J,

I could use some advice about kids and dogs. I don't have a problem with my own kids, because we've had our golden retriever since before they were born, and they know how to behave around animals. But I have trouble with other people's children.

My dog is pretty tolerant, but he's getting old, and he doesn't enjoy having his nostrils poked or his ears pulled, or worse yet, being sat on. I tell visiting children to leave Rocky alone, but some of them just don't listen, at least not for long. It really worries me. Even a dog that's good with kids has a breaking point. Sometimes I don't let my kids invite those friends to our house, and then I feel guilty.

Is there any way I can have kids over for a playdate without having to lock the poor dog in the bedroom for the whole time?

—Barking Up the Wrong Tree (so far)

Dear Cat-astrophe and Barking,

Children and animals look so good in the movies. And literature is full of the wonders of the bond between young humans and their creatures. But it doesn't always go as smoothly in real life. Even Lassie and Timmy must have had some bad moments that were edited out of the final cut.

A determined, animal-loving child will not be easily discouraged. You can forget about:

Commands and Accusations: "Stop it, you're not being gentle enough." "Leave the cat alone, you're scaring her!" "You're going to hurt the puppy."

Warnings and Threats: "You'll get scratched if you keep doing that." "You're going to get bitten and it'll be your own fault!"

Lecturing, Scolding, Appeals to Empathy: "Don't pull the doggy's ear. That's not nice. How would you like it if someone did that to you?"

It's important to keep in mind that the capacity for empathy is developmental. We can't count on young children to be gentle. Even if children have demonstrated this skill in some circumstances, you can't expect them to be consistent, especially when they're excited.

So what can we do to protect the animals, the children, and our sanity?

We've got to start by acknowledging feelings, then give simple information, and offer the child something he *can* do, instead of focusing on what he *can't*. It's easier to redirect a child's excitement than to turn it off.

Here's how it might go:

Acknowledge feelings

"It's exciting to chase the kitty."

"You really love pulling the dog's floppy ears!"

Give information

"Cats don't like being chased. That scares them."

"Dogs don't like having their ears pulled. It hurts them."

Tell them what they *can* do, instead of what they *can't*

"Do you know what cats like? They like chasing string with crumpled paper tied to it. Here's how we make a cat toy. You can try dragging it slowly along the floor in front of her."

"Cats like being scratched very gently behind the ears. You can do that while I hold her in my lap."

"Sometimes cats like to sneak inside paper bags. Can you find a bag for Ally?"

"Let's sit back here and watch the dog while he's drinking. Look at how his tongue scoops up the water."

"Do you know what my dog likes? He likes to fetch his tennis ball. Will you toss it for him?"

A CAT TOY

"You can pet him softly on his chest."

"Rocky likes to eat biscuits. You can toss one on the floor for him or hold it in your palm."

"You can hide the biscuit for him under this paper and we can watch him use his nose to sniff it out."

Give descriptive praise: describe the effect of the child's actions on your pet

"Look at how the kitty is jumping on that string. She's having fun with the toy you made."

"I can hear Ally purring. That means she likes how you're petting her!"

"Rocky likes it when you scratch him that way. He's wagging his tail."

"He's fetching the ball for you. You're giving him a good workout."

"Rocky found the biscuit. You're helping train him to find lost things!"

But what if none of that works?

What if a child is too excited to interact gently with a pet, or you have children who simply want to spend more time with your pet than your pet wants to spend with them? You need to protect your pet and the child from each other so that neither one gets hurt.

Acknowledge feelings and offer a choice

"You're in the mood for wild play right now. You can play with your stuffed kitty, or you can climb up on the sofa like a cat and jump to the rug like you're pouncing on a mouse."

"Looks like you're in the mood for kicking. We can't kick a dog. Do you want to kick a ball or a balloon?"

Tell them what they *can* do, instead of what they *can't*: redirect kids' energy into activities that don't involve touching the pet.

For Cats: Kids can make a bed for the cat out of a cardboard box with soft rags inside. They can draw designs on it with crayons. They can put out treats for her and watch her eat. They can look at picture books of cats. They can lie down on the floor to observe her, pretending they're scientists who are studying wild animals. They can pretend they are cats, stretching, crawling, jumping, and meowing to each other. If they're old enough to use a needle and thread, children can sew little pouches and put catnip inside.

For Dogs: Put kids to work poking kibble into empty plastic wide-mouth bottles to create a puzzle for the dog. They can watch while the dog paws the bottle to get the kibble to fall out. They can braid rope to make a tug toy, or find a plastic bottle in the recycling bin, stuff it into an old sock and knot the open end to make a fetch toy. Kids can pretend they are dogs: drinking water from a bowl without using their hands, crawling through a "dog obstacle course" of tunnels and Hula-Hoops. They can look at books and draw pictures of dogs.

Take Action Without Insult: Remove kid from pet, or pet from kid.

Temporarily: "I'm putting Ally in the bedroom with the door closed for now. She needs a break from being held."

Permanently: If you truly feel you made a mistake getting a pet when your children are too young, consider finding another home for that pet. There's no shame in respecting your own needs and the needs of your animals. Better to have safe children and a happy animal in two separate households, than to be constantly stressed and have your children and pet at risk from each other.

You may be noticing that it can be a lot of work to ride herd on young children in the presence of animals. We're not suggesting that young kids and pets don't mix. There are many joys to be had in a house where every sweater needs major work with a lint roller before being worn out in public.

But if the whole experience is giving you more misery than pleasure, you're not being fair to yourself or your pet. While you're figuring out if you can make it work, the simple rule is, *if you can't supervise young children and animals, they should be kept separate.* Don't rely on the good nature of a pet, or the good sense of children.

Stories from the Front Lines

Kitten Chaos

I told the kids your idea about making toys for the kitten. Sebastian wanted to sew something. He spent a long time going through the rag basket picking just the right materials. I bought catnip at the pet store to stuff into his little creations. He's so proud to watch Ally play with *his* toys. Julian was happy just to play with the pipe cleaners and feathers.

I also put Sebastian in charge of feeding the cat. He's the one who fills her bowl with kibble, and then he watches her eat. He drew a picture of a cat and taped it to the wall next to her food bowl so that she would "know" that was her special spot. Now that I've recruited Sebastian as a helper, he's transformed.

Julian still gets overexcited and grabby with Ally, no matter what I say. I try not to get worked up about it anymore. I just put her in my bedroom and close the door with a hook and eye lock that we added so that Julian can't open the door by himself. The first time I did it, he howled and beat on the door. We bought a stuffed toy cat he can play with when Ally is "not in the mood." He already has a name for it—Julian's Baby Ally Cat. Very original, no?

It was probably a mistake to get a kitten in the first place, but it is getting better. Last night Julian said "gentle" while he touched the cat. He brought his hand down v-e-r-y slowly, as if it took a huge amount of self-control to touch her softly. There is hope!

Paper Ticks

Emma saw me pulling a tick off our dog with tweezers. She wanted to do it too. She started going after Teddy. Can you imagine how a sensitive Pomeranian would react to a four-year-old jabbing at him with pointy metal tweezers? Not a pretty picture. I told her, "NO! Teddy wouldn't like that," but Emma was determined. She was very confident that she could do it.

I had a little brainwave. I told her there weren't any more ticks on Teddy, but I had a way for her to practice. I drew little ticks on a piece of paper and cut them out. I taped them onto her stuffed collie and set her to work picking them off with the tweezers. Emma was completely satisfied with this activity, and I'm sure Teddy was grateful too.

The Good Dog

My elderly black Lab is famously tolerant with children. Last week my friend was visiting with her one-year-old, Isabel, who was playing at our feet in the kitchen while my friend and I made snacks. Smudge was snoozing under the table. Isabel crawled under the table and on top of Smudge. Smudge must have been startled, or maybe Isabel put a knee in his ribs, because all of a sudden Isabel was sobbing. Her skin wasn't broken, but she had a bright red mark on her cheek, right near her eye.

Neither of us had ever considered the possibility that Smudge would bite. My friend and I were both pretty freaked out. We decided that if kids are on the floor, the dog would be in the crate or outside in the yard. We can't expect a dog to put up with whatever a little one might dish out.

Perils of the Park

Before I had kids, I had a little dog named Sparky. He was very fluffy and attractive to children, but he was scared of them. I was walking him in the park when a pack of little kids came running up asking if they could pet him. While they were asking, they were chasing him, and he was winding the leash around my legs, trying to get away from them. I told them my dog is shy, but it had no effect on them. Then I went into my teacher mode and yelled, "FREEZE!" The kids stopped. I said, "I can see you guys really like dogs. Do you want to help me train him?" They agreed enthusiastically.

I asked who would like to hide a sandal for Sparky to find. They were all eager so I let them take turns hiding a sandal behind a tree or bush, and then I sent Sparky to fetch it. The kids were thrilled. I let them take turns tossing him a ball, and tossing him biscuits (which I always carry when out with the dog). I thanked them all for helping me and waved good-bye. They all waved and yelled good-bye to Sparky. The interesting thing was that they hadn't touched him at all, but they were still satisfied and excited to have "played with him."

How Dogs Talk So Kids Will Listen:
Approaching a Stranger's Dog (Joanna's story)

I'm the last person to tell you to keep your children away from dogs. I was a dog lover from before I could walk. Family lore has it that when I was six months old, my parents left me napping on a blanket at the beach while they strolled toward the water's edge to cool their toes. Looking back they saw an enormous German shepherd bounding toward their helpless infant. Hearts in mouths, they ran to save their baby, but the powerful dog was faster. By the time they got to me, the shepherd was vigorously washing my face with his tongue and I was squealing with joy. Since then I've petted every dog I could get my hands on, and now, as a dog owner, I regularly invite strangers' children to pet and play with my own dogs. I pride myself in giving fearful children a positive experience with my "scary-looking" dogs. The sight of dogs and children together gives me inexplicable joy. So the following words aren't meant to discourage, but rather to keep children safe!

Most people know the rule: *You shouldn't touch a stranger's dog without asking first.* Imagine your child, coached by her responsible parent, has just popped the proper question. And she's thrilled by the reply.

"Sure you can pet him. He's friendly. He loves children!"

Even with an enthusiastic invitation from the owner, *you still need to supervise* your child's interaction with Fluffy. You don't know if you can rely on the owner to "read" her dog. Often dogs give subtle signals of distress that go unnoticed. The owner would like to believe that Fluffy harbors friendly feelings toward children, but she may not be familiar with the unpredictability of actual kids. Her dog might not be comfortable with a child lurching into his face, suddenly screeching, running at him from

behind, poking at his eye, grabbing at his ears or tail. Fearful
dogs often bite to protect themselves, and it can happen in the
blink of an eye.

So how should you proceed?

First, do not allow your child
to approach the dog. Instead, *invite the dog to approach the child.*
While standing a few feet away,
have your child pat his own leg and call the dog over in an inviting
voice. "Hello doggy, can I pet you?"[1]

If the dog doesn't approach, explain to your child, "The dog
doesn't want to say 'hi' today. Let's go." And then walk away.

If the dog is leaping at the end of his leash with excitement
and the owner can't calm him down, explain to your child, "This
dog is too excited for petting right now," then walk away.

If the dog calmly approaches, *show your child how to let the dog
sniff her hand, and how to pat the dog on the side of the neck or on the
chest.* No face kissing, no arm around the dog's neck, no hugging.

Dogs can feel threatened when a stranger reaches over their
head or grabs them around the neck. And even if this particular
dog doesn't mind, you have to think about what might happen
when your kid tries that move on somebody else's less tolerant
dog.

And finally, *don't follow the dog if he moves away.* Allow the dog
to determine the end of the "playdate."

These rules may seem overly strict. *Many* dogs are very tolerant and will put up with all kinds of shenanigans from young
humans. But teaching your child how to behave around dogs
(and supervising her while she practices) will help her to be
safe with *all* dogs.

REMINDER: ANIMAL ETIQUETTE

1. Acknowledge feelings.

"It's exciting to chase the kitty."
"You love to touch the dog's fluffy tail."

2. Give information.

"Chasing scares the cat."
"The dog doesn't like having his tail grabbed."

3. Tell them what they *can* do instead of what they *can't*.

"You can drag this string in front of Ally for her to pounce on."
"You can throw the ball for Rocky to fetch."

4. Use descriptive praise: Describe the effect of the child's actions on the pet.

"The kitty is having fun with the toy you made."
"The dog likes the gentle way you're petting him."

5. Offer a choice.

"I see you're in a kicking mood. Do you want to kick a balloon or your foam ball?"

6. Take action without insult.

"I'm putting the dog in the crate for now. He needs a quiet place to eat."
"The kitty is going in the bedroom with the door locked. She needs a break from being held."

Section III

Anxiety, Fears, and Meltdowns

8

Fears

Dinosaurs, Spiders, and Ants . . . Oh My!

Dear Reader, do you have a suspicion (or even a fear) that we're going to launch into a discussion about acknowledging feelings . . . *again*? Well, you're right. You already know this! It's just that in the case of childhood fears, it can be particularly challenging for us to acknowledge feelings. The urge to dismiss fearful feelings and to slather on reassurance is very powerful. We want so badly to protect our kids from the intense unpleasantness of fear. Especially when it's unnecessary fear!

It can help to put ourselves in the child's shoes by imagining something that frightens us as adults. Whether you have a fear of heights, hairy spiders, public speaking, or pandemics, you probably would not feel comforted if someone told you, "That's nothing to be scared about! Come on now, be brave! You're perfectly fine."

When someone talks to us this way, the message we hear is: *There's no justification for you to feel this way. You are a cowardly, unreasonable, wreck of a human being!* Now you feel scared and you also feel bad about yourself for *being* scared.

We can't talk children out of their fears using logic, but most of us have tried.

Dino Dread (Joanna's story)

Many years ago, my six-year-old was afraid to go to sleep after seeing an animated movie about dinosaurs. There were "bad guy" dinosaurs chasing the friendly dinosaurs, so yeah, maybe I shouldn't have picked that one if I wanted to avoid bedtime drama. "But Zach," I argued, "those dinosaurs aren't real. I mean, yes, dinosaurs existed, but they died out millions of years ago."

Zach was offended. "I *know* they're not real! That doesn't mean I'm not scared of them!"

Once I accepted that basic premise—"I know what you mean, Zach. Unreal things can still be very scary. Especially at night!"—Zach was able to calm down enough to take comfort from his standby *Things That Go* book and then drift off to a dinosaur-free sleep.

About eight years later I had cause to reflect on that conversation. My kids had enthusiastically encouraged me to watch the movie *Sweeney Todd* with them because their high school was putting on the play. I found it horrifying. I tried to defend my view. "They're showing people getting their throats slit and the blood gurgling out as they die gasping for breath! It's going to give me nightmares!"

Zach raised an eyebrow quizzically at me—a move he had perfected in the intervening years. "Mom, you know that's not *real*, don't you? They're actors. It's special effects!" I spluttered, "Just because it's not real doesn't mean it's not upsetting!"

So how do we help kids overcome their fears, if we can't reassure them? We have to start where we would want people to start with us. Not by belittling or dismissing our feelings, but by acknowledging them.

Say, for example, your child is nervous about staying overnight at Grandma's house because you won't be there with him.

Instead of: "You're going to be just fine sleeping at Grandma's house for one night. How can you be scared? Grandma loves you!"

Acknowledge feelings: "It's worrisome to sleep in a different house, and a different bed, without your parents. Even though you know Grandma really well, you don't feel comfortable about this sleepover."

Chances are you're going to hear a lot more about what worries your child, once you've acknowledged his feelings. We're not suggesting that you go beyond what your child expresses. Try not to accidentally add frightening possibilities that haven't occurred to him. ("Are you worried you'll have that nightmare about ghosts?") Just take your time and listen. You can even write down the worries on a list.

But if we coddle kids too much, how will they learn to face their fears? Accepting feelings may make him feel better in the moment, but I still need him to get over it. He has to stay at his grandmother's house because I'm going out of town!

Sometimes just acknowledging feelings will be enough to give a child the courage to face a fear. Other times we'll have to provide more support. A child whose feelings have been acknowledged is more likely to be open to considering suggestions. If we can find a way to **put the child in charge** and help them come up with solutions, they'll find it easier to manage their fears.

So for the anxious overnighter we might say:

"What can we do to make the sleepover less worrisome?
Let's make another list." And then write down his ideas.

> Ask Grandma to keep the hall light on
> Bring teddy bear and airplane book
> Tell Grandma no onions in the dinner
> Do a practice sleepover in our living room

Let's see what this approach might sound like in some other
typical scenarios.

Instead of: "You shouldn't be nervous about a recital. Just practice
your piece and do your best. That's all anyone can ask of you."

> **Acknowledge feelings:** "It's stressful to think about per-
> forming! You worry that you'll mess up in front of people."
>
> . . . and then, after giving your child ample opportunity to
> express her dread of recitals, you can **give information** or
> **offer a choice**: "Even famous musicians get really nervous
> before performing. One thing that can help is to practice in
> front of people. Do you want to call up your grandmother
> or your uncle and try playing your piece for them?"

Instead of: "A little ant crawling on your leg isn't going to hurt you.
Come on, you can't just stay inside all summer! That's ridiculous.
We're going to the park and that's that."

> **Acknowledge feelings:** "You do *not* like bugs crawling on
> you. Not even tiny little ones. Even if they don't bite, they
> can still be creepy!"
>
> . . . and then, after listening sympathetically to your child
> soliloquize on the horror of six-legged creatures, you can
> **offer a choice**: "Hmm, what should we do to protect you

from the ants? Do you want to wear long pants and bring shorts in case it gets really hot? Which towel do you want to bring to sit on? The blue one, or the one with the fish?"

Instead of: "The tornado is over. You're fine! You need to stop thinking about it!"

Acknowledge feelings: "That was really terrifying. The winds were so loud!"

. . . and then, after giving full due to her windy weather worries, you can **give information** and **put the child in charge:** "It's a good thing we have a basement. Even though the sounds of a tornado are really scary, we're safe down there. Can you think of some games and snacks we can store there? Let's carry some stuff down together. It makes me feel better to know that we're prepared."

Fears serve a protective function. They alert us to danger. Even if it worked to tell children to ignore their fears, we would not necessarily be happy with the result. One day those feelings may save their life, as long as they haven't been taught to ignore them. We want children to tune in to their feelings, and not brush them aside. We can help them the most by giving them some control over the scary situation and then respecting their pace.

Stories from the Front Lines

Alarm in South Africa

A little while back a technician came to repair our house alarm. He set off the alarm, which made an awfully loud noise in the house, and our two-year-old, Evan, got the fright of his life. It traumatized him to such an extent that he would no longer sleep in his own room. Also he would no longer play on his own and he refused to go anywhere in the house unescorted. This was driving us insane.

On many occasions during the day he would tell us the alarm story. He called the alarm "the bweep." Every time he told us about the bweep we'd brush it off, and say things like, "No, the bweep is gone" or "I don't want to hear about the bweep."

After about a week of this I went to bed and read the first chapter of *How to Talk So Kids Will Listen*. It blew my mind that we were doing the absolute wrong thing with Evan. The next day I sprang into action and every time Evan told his bweep story I said things like, "It made you scared, hey?" or "Daddy also got a big fright when that happened," acknowledging his feelings as best I could.

Well, the change in him was almost instantaneous. He calmed down considerably, and soon things were completely back to normal.

Scary Trees

My three-year-old wanted to bring her art supplies upstairs but she refused to go downstairs by herself to get them. I knew I wouldn't be able to convince her to go alone by argument, so I tried the strategy of writing down her fears. The crying stopped as soon as she saw me start the list: *Scary Things Downstairs*. She started telling me, and I wrote them down.

Then I looked at our list. "Okay, so now I understand that you think there are some big, immovable trees by the couch. So, that is a problem. What do you think a solution could be?"

She promptly said, "You come with me and move them!"

I said, "Well I would, except I can't see any trees in our living room so I can't move any trees."

She said, "Okay then, I'll be right back. Wait here." And voilà! She zipped down the stairs. It was like magic. A minute later she was back upstairs with her crayons and scissors.

Fear of Showers

My six-year-old son, Arjun, was afraid of taking a bath or even a shower ever since he had a bad experience in the swimming pool. He had slipped under and swallowed water, which sent him into a panic. I kept telling him that the shower was very different from the swimming pool, and it's very safe. But he still struggled and cried every time I tried to get him in the shower.

After attending your workshop I told him, "It's scary to take a shower after getting hurt in the swimming pool. That was a really upsetting experience." He said, "Yes Mummy, I really don't like taking showers anymore." I said, "Well, the problem is, we need to take showers because otherwise we will stink. What shall we do about this?" Arjun said, "That's okay Mummy, I'll take a shower." He did not cry or complain while taking his shower after that. I was absolutely stunned!

A Dog Day Afternoon (Joanna's story)

I was shopping for garden supplies and had my dog along with me. A family walked by and the young daughter lunged to pet my dog at the same time her older brother lunged away in terror.

I immediately moved away so as not to terrify the boy any further. While the girl happily patted my dog, I chatted with the mom, assuring her that I understood a dog could be very scary-looking to a child, whose face is on level with the dog's teeth!

The mom, seeing an opportunity to help her son overcome his fear, grabbed his arm and started dragging him toward my dog, saying, "This is a nice doggy. You can pet him!" The poor kid was freaking out. She had good intentions, but she was creating a state of panic in her son. I was running out of space to back up so I improvised and asked the boy if he wanted to go stand on the flatbed cart, which was about five feet away. He said yes, and his mom allowed him to scramble up there, where he felt safe.

Then I asked him if he wanted to see some dog tricks. He nodded. I put Kazi through his paces: spin, figure 8, push the cart, shake hands, jump over the leg, take a bow. I asked the boy if he wanted to throw a treat to the dog. Yes, he did. Then his little sister came to pet the dog again. I asked him if he wanted to pet the back of the dog, while I held the head (the toothy end). He did it!

The moral of the story is, don't push your kid! Let them feel safe and take their time. You can't force a child not to be afraid, but you can invite them to face the fearful object from a comfortable distance, and, if they're ready, to approach it at their own pace. The more they can control the experience, the braver they will feel.

REMINDER: FEARS

1. Acknowledge feelings.

"That storm was really scary. The winds were so loud!"

"Dogs can make you nervous. You don't know what they're going to do."

2. Give information.

"It's a good thing we have a basement. We're safe down there."

3. Offer a choice.

"Do you want to hold my hand or do you want to climb up on the cart while you watch the dog?"

4. Put the child in charge.

"Can you choose some snacks and games to bring down to the basement for next time?"

9

Temper Tantrum Hotline
(Julie Coaches a Parent by Phone)

"Can you help me with Ben's tantrums? He's having them daily, and I'm completely worn out by them."

Adina had asked for a phone consultation. She described a recent tantrum.

> Ben asked for a second cup of grape juice at breakfast. All I said was, "No more grape juice. It's too high in sugar. How about some milk?" He screamed, "No! I want grape juice!"
>
> I answered very calmly, "No more grape juice now. And if you yell at me, I'm not giving you any milk, either." That really set him off.
>
> "Yes you will! You WILL give me grape juice. I want grape juice!"
>
> "*I'm* in charge, and I'm telling you that you're not getting any more grape juice. If you don't stop screaming, you're going to your room."
>
> "You're not the boss of me. You're not in charge. *I'm* in charge. You WILL give me grape juice."
>
> "No, Ben, I won't. You can have more tomorrow. *Stop screaming!*"
>
> But he didn't stop, so I dragged him to his room. I had to hold the door shut while he banged on it and screamed. It was pretty ugly. Why does every little thing have to be a crisis?

Life can be frustrating for a three-year-old. Big people make all the rules, and sometimes they don't even seem to make sense.

If Mommy can decide one cup of grape juice is okay, why can't I decide to have another cup?

I reminded Adina about the first tool she had learned in the workshop: acknowledging feelings. "You *really* love grape juice! Why can't it have less sugar? Then you could drink a whole bottle of it!"

Adina agreed to try acknowledging feelings the next time Ben started to have a tantrum.

Two days later she called with the latest meltdown.

We usually eat dinner by six o'clock, but last night Ben and I didn't get home until seven. While I was cooking, Ben picked up my phone to look at photos, and then he dropped it. I told him he could scroll through the photos as long as he left the phone on the table. Well, he picked it up again so he could take pictures of his new mittens and dropped it again. I said, "I know you want to take photos, but I don't want a hundred mitten pictures on my phone. If you pick it up one more time, I'm going to take it away from you."

I went back to cooking dinner, and I heard *click, click, click.* I took the phone away from him, and he started screaming, "I *will* look at the pictures, I *will* hold your phone!"

I put the phone high up on a shelf. He started climbing on my chair to reach it. I said, "You picked it up after I told you not to, and I took it away. I already told you this was going to happen!"

"But I stopped, I stopped, Mommy! I will use your phone!"

He threw himself down on the living room floor, crying and kicking his feet.

I sat down on the floor, too, feeling at my wits end. Finally I remembered about accepting feelings and I said, "You're really angry that I took the phone away. You

193

wanted to use it. You didn't want me to put it away. You're so angry, you're kicking!"

He was kicking blocks and one of them hit me. I said, "You're so angry, you're kicking the blocks. I don't like that. It hurt me." He actually stopped kicking the blocks, which was pretty amazing. But he was still crying and kicking his feet.

I reached for the pad and pencil near the phone and said, "Do you want to show me how you feel?" Ben grabbed the pencil from me and drew zigzag lines all over the page.

I studied the page. "You're not just upset. Know what this paper tells me? You are angry. Very, very angry!"

Ben nodded forcefully.

I said, "Quick, show me again!"

Ben made more wild, slashing lines, and poked holes in the page.

I took the paper from him and held it up to the light. "Look at this . . . and this . . . and this! You're not just angry. You are ripping mad! You are furious!! Quick, show me again!"

Ben paused. He took the pad from me and carefully drew two eyes and a smiling mouth. Then he climbed into my lap and showed me his drawing.

The tantrum was over. We went back to the kitchen and had a lovely meal, except for his table manners, but we can save that issue for another call. Normally he would've stayed mad all the way to bedtime.

I'm happy that I helped him through it, but I wish I could have avoided the whole tantrum in the first place!

One thing that will set a kid off is our well-meaning impulse to warn him of the consequences if he doesn't shape up. "Leave the phone on the table or else . . . !" The problem is that threats provoke defiance.

What Ben needs to hear is: "You really like taking pictures with the phone. You love looking at pictures on the phone. It's fun!" Leave off, "... *but* I don't want more photos on my phone." *But* is infuriating. To him it sounds like, "... *but*, here's why your feelings don't matter."

Instead you can give information, "The problem is, phones are breakable. It has to stay on the table."

"But what if he picks it up again anyway?" Adina asked.

You can take action without insult. "I'm putting the phone away for now. It's too tempting to pick up."

You can help him move on by giving him a choice, "You can play with the blocks or the markers."

Or by putting the child in charge, "What can a person play with that is tough and won't get hurt if it's dropped?"

"Or by being playful," added Adina. "I could have played the restaurant game with him. We pretend that I'm the chef and he's the waiter, and he lays out the napkins and the forks for the customers. I was just too tired to think straight! But next time ... "

Our session was up. A few days later, Adina sent me an email with a subject line that read "Success!"

Two days ago Ben came in after playing outside in the snow. His pants were soaked, and he wanted to sit on the couch. I offered to get him a dry pair of pants but he said "No!"

I said, "We have a problem. I don't want the couch to get wet, and you don't want to change your pants. What should we do? We need a solution."

Ben didn't skip a beat. "Why don't I take off my pants and just wear underwear?"

Normally I would've said, "You're wet, and you're not sitting on the couch." And he would've gone right over to the couch anyway, and I would've screamed at him, "Get off the couch!" This was magical!

I think Ben is starting to see himself as a problem-solver. Yesterday he wanted to wear a red cape so he could be

Superman. I tied a red blanket around his shoulders. I said, "You can wear this anywhere except the kitchen because it drags on the floor, and the kitchen floor is *too dirty*!"

He went to the edge of the kitchen and looked like he was about to step in. I was worried he was going to go into one of his temper tantrums if I insisted he stay out. I said, "This is a problem. It's very tempting to walk through the kitchen with the cape on. And I don't want the blanket getting dirty." He paused, and then picked up the blanket, swung it over his head so it wasn't dragging on the floor, and walked into the kitchen. When he left, he dropped it down again.

I said, "You came up with a solution to the problem! You figured out how to walk through the kitchen without the cape getting dirty."

A couple of days later, Adina sent me another email:

I found an opportunity to be playful! I told Ben to turn off the video and come to dinner. He didn't want to stop watching and I could tell he was about to wind up into a tantrum.

Normally in a situation like this, Ben will start to yell, "I want another video!!" Then I'll tell him, "No, Ben, I told you, that was the last one." And then he'll cry and scream and I'll say, "I told you we were going to stop. Get over it. You're not going to watch another one."

This time I said, with great drama, "Hey! I have a *great idea*! Wanna hear it? Come here and I'll tell you." I was buying myself time, because I didn't actually have an idea yet.

He came over and sat next to me. "Let's pretend we're in a video." I shook my body as if I were transforming myself into a robot and started talking: "I AM A RO-BOT. I AM A RO-BOT. THIS IS HOW I TALK."

Ben started giggling. I kept up my robot voice: "IT IS

TIME TO EAT DIN-NER. LET'S GO TO THE KIT-CHEN. LET'S GO. LET'S GO. LET'S GO." Shuffling robotically to the kitchen, we came across an obstacle on the floor (the red blanket) and I pretended I couldn't move forward.

"THERE IS A CAPE IN MY WAY. STUCK . . . STUCK . . . STUCK . . ."

Ben graciously picked up the blanket so I could move forward.

For the rest of the evening we were very silly and he didn't have a single tantrum. You were right. Even though I thought being playful would take too much energy, *I* was in much better spirits, and not nearly as exhausted as when I've had to deal with his screaming.

In our last phone call, Adina reflected, "Even before I had kids, I babysat, I was a camp counselor. I respect children. But when it comes to my own child, part of me still believes that children should be seen and not heard. That they should do what grown-ups say, obey without question, or suffer the consequences.

"I used to think I didn't have time to consider how Ben feels. It seemed faster just to order him to stop . . . even though, to be honest, ordering takes longer because it doesn't work very well. This approach is still counterintuitive for me. But now I know what you mean when you say, 'The longer way is the shorter way.'"

I felt I should caution Adina not to get her expectations too high. Kids get frustrated. They have a stormy emotional life at this age. There will be more meltdowns! There will be times they are tired, hungry, and beyond their capacity to cope no matter how skillful we are with them. With these tools we can minimize the drama, and reconnect more quickly when the storm has passed.

REMINDER: TEMPER TANTRUMS

1. Acknowledge feelings.

> **Put the feeling into words:** "You are *very* angry. You wanted to use the phone."
> **Use art:** "Here's paper and a pencil. Show me how you feel."

2. Give choices.

> "You can play with the blocks or help me set the table."

3. Be playful.

> "I AM A RO-BOT. IT IS TIME FOR DIN-NER. DIN-NER. DIN-NER."

4. Try problem-solving.

> "I don't want the couch to get wet, and you don't want to change your clothes. What should we do?"

5. Take action without insult.

> "I'm putting the phone away. I'm too worried about it getting dropped."

6. Tend to basic needs: food, sleep, recovery time.

7. Adjust expectations and manage the environment instead of the child. Ask yourself if your expectations match your child's developmental readiness.

Baby Feelings

My son is only nine months old, but I have been trying to learn communication strategies ahead of time.

Usually, when he wails from having something unsafe taken away (as carefully as I try to babyproof, he always finds something!), I would do these things:

Take a comforting tone with him: "Shhhh . . ." and "Noooo, don't cry . . ."

Ignore his wails over something so "trivial"

Quickly hand him other toys

When I'm tired, say "SHH! SHH! Stop! You're fine! Stop!"

These things never work!

So, as silly as it sounds to try to acknowledge the feelings of a tiny baby, I have begun to practice taking his complaints seriously. I match his emotion with my voice, and I say: "ARRRGHH!! MOMMY IS ALWAYS TAKING THINGS AWAY FROM ME! I JUST WANT TO EXPLORE THINGS, AND SHE ALWAYS TAKES STUFF AWAY! I'M. SO. AN-GRYYYYY!"

The first time I tried this, he took a shivery, boogery breath, stopped wailing, and stared. I repeated some of his baby feelings again, in a grumpy (yet less loud) voice.

Now I've been adding other strategies as well. I tell him, "The problem is, this isn't good for putting in your mouth." I act playful and give him silly kisses and raspberries on his belly. Then I give him a new area to explore, or pick him up to see what I'm doing.

It sounds crazy, but I feel like this has helped. His wailing stops sooner, and I feel better because it seems like he doesn't feel alone in his frustration. He feels heard, somehow.

Mommy Do It!

My wife wanted me to get our three-year-old, Dahlia, ready for bed, but she complained that she wanted MOMMY to do it. I tried to stay cheerful and plow ahead, but she got more worked up and was heading for a meltdown.

I know I'm supposed to accept her feelings, but in a case like this I just can't empathize. She seems so irrational; I can't even figure out what the feeling *is*. All I could think of to say was, "You really want Mommy."

Dahlia: Yeah!

Me: You like it when *she* does it.

Dahlia: Because she does it better!

Me: What does Mommy do first? Show me.

Dahlia showed me how Mommy gets her changed into her PJs. It was the first time she let me do it without crying for Mommy.

My wife was THRILLED that she didn't have to change Dahlia herself—huge success!

10

Separation Sadness

Dear J & J,

My son is three years old and he gets really nervous and sad when I leave for work. Once a week he stays with his grandma and he's okay with that (not always but most of the time). However, when he stays with his nanny, he starts crying, shouting, and imploring that I stay home. The nanny says that often when I'm not there he asks for me and gets really sad.

I tried explaining that I go to work because we need to have a roof over our heads, because we need to have food to eat, we want him to be able to go on vacations and discover the world, and furthermore I like working as much as he likes going to school. (I don't want him to grow up thinking that working is difficult and boring. I want him to feel that working is cool and rewarding.) Nothing I said helped.

The same story starts again every week. I would be pleased to get your advice on this.

—Working Mom

Dear Working Mom,

We understand your impulse to explain to your son the reasons why you go to work. They're all such good ones! But no doubt you've noticed that emotions can't be explained away. A sad three-year-old is unlikely to say, "Gee, Mother, now that you've laid out the benefits of employment so logically, I can see that I need to put my personal feelings aside and take a broader perspective."

The most helpful thing you can do for your son is to **acknowledge his feelings**. Not when you're under pressure right before you have to leave for work, of course, but when you can find a peaceful moment to sit down together. Set aside your explanations and logic and focus on his feelings instead.

You might try saying something like:

"I've been thinking, you *really* don't like it when I leave you with the nanny!"

"It makes you so sad, you feel like holding me tight so I won't leave!"

"You wish I didn't have to go to a job."

"You'd rather have me stay home with you *every* day."

Give your son time to reply and encourage him to air all his objections. Reflect what he's saying in your own words so that he knows you understand and accept his feelings.

"Oh, so sometimes the nanny makes you mad! You don't like it when she says you have to finish everything on your plate! You'd rather be the one to say when you're hungry and when you're full."

"Ah, and you don't like having to take a nap. It's boring and you don't feel sleepy. You'd rather watch a show on TV."

It might help to **acknowledge his feelings in writing** by creating a list of his grievances:

> "Wait a minute; let me get a paper and pencil. I want to write down all the things that bother you."

Your son will appreciate hearing his list read aloud, with plenty of emotion! Once he's feeling thoroughly heard, you can **try problem-solving**:

> "I wonder if there's anything we can do to make your time with the nanny more fun, or at least less awful. Let's make another list."

On this new list you can write ideas for how to make things better. Be sure to write everything down, including ideas you find completely unacceptable. (Quit your job! Lock the nanny in a closet!) You can invite your son to think about activities he might enjoy doing with the nanny—make play dough, finger paint, bake cookies, make an obstacle course—as well as his suggestions for what not to do. He may want to keep a photo of you in his pocket. Or perhaps there's some other special keepsake he can hold that will comfort him when you're gone. Afterward, you can go through the list together and check the items you both like. Then you can put your new plan into action.

If you put aside explanations of how important it is for you to work, and instead begin by acknowledging your child's feelings, you may find out that there's a simple problem you can resolve with a simple solution. Or you may find out that the problem is deeper. It's possible that there's something seriously distressing going on during his day with this nanny. One powerful benefit of this approach is that you'll find out more from your child. Accepting feelings isn't just a way to help your child to calm down. It can yield important information!

REMINDER: SEPARATION SADNESS

1. Acknowledge feelings.

"You *really* don't like it when I leave you with the nanny!"

2. Acknowledge feelings in writing.

"Let me get a paper and pencil. I want to write down all the things that bother you."

3. Try problem-solving.

"I wonder if there's anything we can do to make your time with the nanny more fun."

Section IV

Bad Attitudes—Complaining, Whining, Defiance, and Other Unsociable Behaviors

11

Whining

The Sound that Drives You Insane

"Mo-o-om, I'm huuunngry ... It's too ho-o-ot ... I'm bo-o-o-red ... When are we going ho-o-ome ... ?"

Oh that tone, it makes you want to cover your ears and run for the hills. What awful evolutionary error caused kids to develop that maddening singsong? When kids whine, adults counter, "I can't *hear* you when you talk like that," in their own version of the singsong whine. Kids respond by ratcheting up the volume and intensity.

What makes them do it and how can we stop it?

Let's see if we can put *you*, dear reader, in a whiny mood—for the purpose of scientific understanding. Imagine you're in a department store with your partner. You see a forest green shirt that speaks to you. You pluck it off the rack. "Oh no," says your partner, "you just bought clothes last week; you don't need more! We're sticking to the budget, remember? We're here to replace the toaster oven and that's it!"

"But this shirt is my favorite color and it's perfect to go with my new pants. It'll make a whole new outfit I can wear for work. Anyhow, it's on sale. And I *need* it! You're being *unreasonable*." Are you imagining a whine creeping into your voice? You feel frustrated. You're not in charge of your own decisions. You have to convince your partner of your neediness.

Your partner says, "Uh-uh-uh, no whining! I can't *hear* you when you talk like that." (Ahem . . . we'd better stop this fantasy now, before it becomes homicidal!)

Hopefully, this is not a situation you've found yourself in recently. But children are in this position all the time. Kids are nothing if not needy. And they are not in charge. They have to convince us that they really, *really* want that ice cream, need to go home . . . be carried . . . have a turn . . . get to go first . . . stay up late, *pretty please!* It's not easy being so dependent!

One strategy we can use when children whine is to **acknowledge their feelings**, then **offer a choice** to help them move on. Offering a choice gives children an opportunity to figure out how to help themselves, instead of feeling whiny and dependent on us.

When a child moans, "I'm sooo bored," during the endless wait at the pediatrician's office, we want to say, "Just relax. It's only been five minutes." (And probably forty-five to go!)

If that worked, you wouldn't be reading this chapter!

Instead try, "It's so hard to wait and wait . . . and wait! What should we do? Do you want to draw a picture while we're stuck here, or do you want to play 'I spy'? Or should we go out in the hallway so you can see how many hops it takes to get all the way to the end and back?"

When a child complains that "there's nothing to do!" you might give them a more open-ended response. "Sometimes it helps to think about what kind of mood you're in. Are you in an outdoor mood, or an indoor mood?" or "Do you feel like sitting down and making something, or are you in the mood to do something more active?"

Another strategy we can use is to **acknowledge feelings with**

writing. For many children, it's quite satisfying to see their complaints transcribed in black and white. You can write them down and read them out loud with dramatic intensity. "Joey does not like this waiting room. It is smelly. It is boring. It is stupid. It does not have any good toys!" Once the suffering is committed to paper, it's easier to move on to happier feelings.

When shopping with whiny kids, it can help to keep a "wish list" handy and encourage kids to write down what they want. Or take a photo of the desired object with your phone. What you do with that information will vary according to circumstance. A child may want to save up her allowance, or you may use the list as a reference for birthday gift ideas, or it may simply serve as a record of your child's passing passions.

Another way to minimize whining is to find ways to **put the child in charge**. What would that look like?

Let's say your children have sackfuls of Halloween candy that you've responsibly stored out of reach so they won't sicken themselves on sugar. But now you find yourself in the unenviable position of guardian of the treasure, and your kids whine for it many times a day, unimpressed by your lectures on balanced nutrition. You usually make your decision on the fly, based on how much healthy food they've eaten already, and how much energy you have to resist the fussing. This unpredictability makes them all the more persistent. You are deeply regretting the whole trick-or-treating venture.

How can you put children in charge of Halloween candy? Wouldn't that be a "fox guarding the henhouse" type of situation?

Here's how one parent took herself out of the loop and made her kids responsible for regulating their own candy intake:

Sweet Talk

I realized I had actually been training my children to badger me. I wanted to reverse the trend. So I sat down with them and said, "I have a problem I want your help with. We've been having arguments about the Halloween candy every day and I don't like it! I want *you guys* to be in charge of the candy, not me! We know candy is delicious, and we also know it's not healthy to eat too much at a time. I think we need a plan that makes sense to all of us. How many pieces should each person be allowed to eat in a day?"

I started my bargaining low. "Do you think one piece is enough, or should it be two pieces?"

The kids looked concerned. "Some of the candies are really small. If they're small, I think we should get three pieces!"

I allowed as how that seemed very reasonable.

"Where should we keep the bags so they're out of sight and reach? We don't want candy right in front of our faces all day, tempting us."

The cabinet over the refrigerator was universally nominated and approved. I got the bags down each morning and the kids studiously made their picks. No more nagging, no more whining. I was freed!

Transitions can also inspire whining. If we're going to a park or a playdate where we know kids have trouble leaving, we can **put children in charge of time**. It's always nice to have a gadget—a wind-up timer, a sand timer, or if you want to get fancy, look up visual timers for kids.  These are gadgets that help young children understand the abstract concept of passage of time in a more concrete way. We can tell kids we need their help getting out on time, and ask *them* to set the timer and tell *us* when it's time to leave.

For kids who get whiny when they're hungry, we can **put them in charge of food.** For younger children, we can keep some food where they can reach it, instead of whining for us to serve them. Bananas or crackers can occupy a lower pantry shelf. Carrot sticks and peanut butter can sit on the bottom shelf of the fridge. We can transfer some edibles to smaller, more kid-friendly containers. For example, kids can get their own breakfast with minimal mess if we put milk in a small pitcher on the bottom shelf of the fridge, and the cereal in a container that is only as big as the biggest mess you'd be okay with sweeping off the floor or leaving for the dog to "clean up."

In the grocery store, we can **put kids in charge of gathering items** on the shopping list. When children are actively engaged, they're less likely to torment us with their whimpering. Older kids who whine about the dinner menu can be **put in charge of meal prep** by encouraging them to look up recipes that they want to try, adding to the grocery list, and taking a turn cooking for the family every so often.

If we're going to a store where we know that our children are likely to be overcome with acquisitive frenzy, we can **put kids in charge of money.** Remind them ahead of time of the mission—say, getting a birthday present for a friend's birthday— and suggest that they bring their own allowance in case they see something they desperately want for themselves. (You'll have to remember to provide the allowance ahead of time!) It's a great way to start giving kids practice in decision-making, and it frees us from endless whiny arguments about whether or not they *need* another shiny plastic light-up thingamabob.

If you have kids who whine for designer jeans and shirts that are priced beyond your fiscal comfort zone, find a way to put them in charge of figuring out how to clothe themselves within your budget. Let them know how much money you've put aside for new shirts and pants this year, and they can go to work tracking down sales. We're not suggesting you hand over your credit card and go for a stroll. They can submit their purchase plan for your approval. If they want to expand their options, they may even consider earning extra money by advertising their services in the neighborhood for yard work or dog walking.

But what about kids who whine as their default mode of communication? Is there any way to express our desire for a more pleasing tone?

For kids who seem to whine out of habit, we can **describe our own feelings, give information**, and **tell them what they** *can* **do instead of what they** *can't*. "Nico, when I hear that tone, it doesn't make me feel like helping! I like to be asked in a deep voice, like this." Then you can demonstrate by using your most dramatic, gravelly voice. "Mom, can you spread the peanut butter on my bread please?"

If he keeps on whining you can **offer a choice** that will make him feel less dependent: "Nico, you can ask me in your deep voice, or if you're not in the mood for doing that, you can spread it yourself. Here's a plastic knife."

And finally, when you've already said *no* to a request, it's important not to cave in to the whine, or children will quickly learn to persist. If they want candy for breakfast and you've already told them "that's not healthy," you'll have to stand firm, no matter how sonically painful it becomes. You can **acknowledge the feeling, give in fantasy what you cannot** (or will not!) **give in reality**, and **move on with a choice**. "You really, really want candy for breakfast! It would be nice to have a mother who gives you chocolate for every meal instead of this boring old healthy-food mom. Ugh! Well . . . you can have blueberries with yogurt, or a hard-boiled egg. When you decide, let me know."

If your child continues to whine, we give you permission to tell them "I can't listen anymore," and leave the room! Refrain from verbal attacks, don't cave in, and your child will eventually conclude that whining is not an effective strategy.

When you put children in charge, give them choices, and empower them to help themselves, they're less likely to melt into a puddle of moaning misery. We can't promise a completely whine-free child, but these tools will certainly improve the soundscape.

Of course, there will be those moments when no skill works as well as a sandwich and a nap. We've got to **meet basic needs** before demanding social graces. There's no use trying to coax a tired, hungry child to stop acting like a tired, hungry child. You have to know which battles to fight, and which to graciously concede.

Stories from the Front Lines

The Kiwi to Happiness

My son Jacob makes me dread shopping. He whines for everything he sees. This time I told him, "You can pick out something from the produce section for yourself, whatever you want." He took his mission very seriously. He was much too busy studying each fruit to even think about whining. A bag of kiwis won the final honors. It made me realize that it's hard to stand around while someone else makes all the decisions.

Tall Enough

I tried getting Aiden to use his deep voice. He asked for more milk in his usual whiny way. I told him, "It doesn't make me feel like helping when I'm asked that way. I like it when you use your low voice," and I demonstrated.

He said, "But I'm thirrrsteee," in his most helpless moan.

I didn't cave in. I told him, "Maybe you're not in the mood to talk in a deep voice right now. If you want, you can get a drink by yourself instead. You're tall enough to reach the milk!"

I saw a light dawning in his eyes. No, he *wasn't* in the mood for a low voice. He *would* get it himself. A whole new world! I belatedly wished I had put some milk in a smaller container so there would be less to spill, but he poured it very slowly and carefully. He was proud of himself.

Exit Strategy

We were visiting a friend and Maeve started to whine and protest when I told her it was time to leave. I took her aside and said, "Sounds like you're not ready to leave. You haven't done everything you wanted to do."

"Yeah!"

"Here's the problem. I have to pick up your brother from school in half an hour. We can leave now and have plenty of time, or we can spend another five minutes here and be in a rush. We'll have to *rush* to get our shoes and coats on, and *rush* out the door."

"Let's be in a rush!"

"Okay, I'll set my watch to beep in five minutes. You can hold it, and then you'll be in charge of telling me when to start rushing."

Maeve got a kick out of telling *me* that it was time to leave.

Showtimes

One of the big daily conflicts I have with my four-year-old, Tiana, is whether or not she's allowed to watch a video. When I say no, she begs and whines. I realized that to her my decision seemed arbitrary. Sometimes I'd say yes (especially if I was trying to cook dinner or finish an email) and sometimes I'd say no (especially if I was feeling guilty because it was a nice day outside or I'd just read an article about the horrors of too much screen time). Apparently

Tiana had concluded that the best strategy was to whine as often and dramatically as possible in the hope that I'd give in.

I decided to make a schedule with her. I told her she could watch two videos a day. One in the morning if she finishes getting ready to go in time, and one while I'm making dinner. I drew a picture of pants and a shirt (time to get dressed), a bowl of cereal (time for breakfast), a picture of her tablet (time for a video), a car (time to go to daycare), and so on.

I drew a check-box next to each picture and then let her color in the pictures. She got very interested in coloring and making copies of her schedule, and she forgot all about videos for the moment!

Now she loves checking the boxes, and when she asks for a video I can tell her to look at the schedule and tell me if it's video time.

REMINDER: WHINING

1. **Acknowledge feelings**, then **offer a choice.**
   "It's so hard to wait and wait. What should we do? Do you want to draw a picture, or hop down the hallway until the doctor is ready for us?"

2. **Acknowledge feelings with writing.**
   Write down the child's complaints, or make a wish list.

3. **Put the child in charge . . .**

   . . . of time:
   "I need someone to hold the stopwatch and tell us when it's time to leave."

   . . . of food:
   "Take a look at some recipes and let me know what you're interested in making."

   . . . of part of the activity:
   "Here's the shopping list. I could use help finding these four items."

   . . . of money:
   "I'm not buying toys today, but you can use your allowance if there's something you want."

   "This is how much we can spend on your new shirts and pants this year. Do you want to be in charge of finding three of each that fit the budget?"

4. **Describe your feelings, give information,** and **tell them what they *can* do instead of what they *can't*.**

"I like to be asked in a deep voice. That makes me feel like helping." Demonstrate in your most dramatic, gravelly voice, "Mom, can you spread the peanut butter on my bread, please?"

5. **Offer a choice.**

"You can ask me in your deep voice, or if you're not in the mood for doing that, you can spread it yourself."

6. Instead of giving in to the whine, **acknowledge feelings** and **give in fantasy what you cannot give in reality,** then **offer a choice.**

"You really, really want candy for breakfast! It would be nice to have a mother who gives you chocolate for every meal. Well . . . you can have blueberries with yogurt, or a hard-boiled egg. When you decide, let me know."

7. **Meet basic needs.**

Are your children overtired, hungry, at the end of their rope? You may have to provide a nap, food, or comfort without criticism.

Spilled Milk: A Before and After Tale

I used to have frequent episodes like this one with my three-year-old son.

Miles: [Spills milk on the floor intentionally]

Me (angry): What are you *doing*? We *told* you to drink your milk at the table. Now look what happened. You made a mess! Go get a towel and clean it up!

Miles: [Nonchalantly walks out of the room. I follow him, and ten minutes of cajoling, threats, and tears ensue.]
   After reading *How to Talk So Little Kids Will Listen*, we had moments like this:

[Miles spills milk on the floor intentionally.]

Me (concerned voice): "Oh. There's milk on the floor."

[Miles silently walks into kitchen, gets towel, starts cleaning up.]

Me (to self): What black magic is this???

Alienation of Affection

My daughter, Maja, is twelve years old. She used to be very loving and affectionate with me, but for the last year or so she's been acting like I'm toxic. She's always annoyed and rolling her eyes or stomping off to her bedroom to slam the door.

Last week we had a typical encounter that would usually lead to a fight. Maja needed to buy some plants for a project she came up with—making a gecko habitat. She had done a lot of research to figure out the best plants for the terrarium.

I drove her to the garden center, but they did not have a single plant on her list. She got incredibly upset. I wanted to tell her not to make such a big deal about it and encourage her to buy some of the plants that were actually available. But luckily, I was fresh from the workshop.

I said, "It's so frustrating! You put so much thought into picking the perfect plants for the habitat and they don't have a single one! It's ridiculous!"

The first thing I noticed is that she didn't get angry at *me*, which is usually what would happen. I felt connected with her instead of at war with her. She seemed to calm down a bit, so then I asked her, "What should we do?"

She said, "Let's go home and see if we can order them online."

We didn't actually find what she wanted online either, but she took it in stride and didn't get upset. The next day she gave me a big hug out of nowhere. She hasn't done that in such a long time—I can't even remember when the last one was.

12

Sore Losers

The Competition Conundrum

Dear J&J,

Our six-year-old son can't handle losing, even at little helpful games that worked for a while to move daily tasks along. (Who can get dressed first? Who can get buckled in their car seat first?) When he doesn't win, he screams and demands a do-over.

We'd like to play board games as a family, but the screaming, throwing, and sometimes hitting and kicking result in such an unfun time that we're avoiding it more and more. Even losing a single round of cards results in a freak out.

Any suggestions?

—Son Loses It When He Loses

Dear SLIWHL,

We acknowledge that it's tempting to move kids along by pitting them against each other in a race to get dressed, brush teeth, buckle seat belts, etc. Resist the urge! There are too many hazards along that route.

You may have a temporary gain in speed as your kids frantically try to outpace each other, but it won't be worth the price. What you gain in time, you lose in family harmony. The irritation and resentment, not to mention the meltdowns, that follow those contests can poison the atmosphere. You don't want children to feel threatened by each other's accomplishments, to feel like losers if their sibling is a winner, or for that matter to feel like winners if they can beat their siblings. It can be particularly painful for a younger, weaker, or less-coordinated child to lose to a more capable sibling. Competition doesn't have to start in the home. A family works better as a cooperative unit!

If you want to use a playful "race to get ready" approach without the negative fallout, you can do it without casting your kids as opponents. Put them on the same team and see if they can beat you. Who can get to the car and get buckled in first, kids or parents? (We highly suggest letting the kids' team win!) They can work together to buckle each other in before the lumbering parents make it to the car.

Another way to move kids into high gear without causing sibling friction is to encourage them to beat some predetermined time challenge. "How many minutes will it take you to get dressed? . . . Wow, you think you can do it in less than five minutes? That doesn't sound possible. Okay . . . Ready . . . set . . . go! . . . Oh my gosh, you did it in four minutes and thirty seconds! That is unbelievable!"

You probably shouldn't try this approach when your child is still feeling raw from recent competitions with siblings. You'll want to be sure they understand the goal is to beat the clock, not each other.

But what about board games and card games? Don't they teach all kinds of positive things, from simple math skills to good sportsmanship? Shouldn't those kinds of games be a pleasant family activity?

Well, sure! But we need to start by considering the developmental readiness of a child to enjoy an activity that involves "losing." Games are supposed to be fun. To a child who is not ready for win–lose games, it feels like we're asking him to engage in forced failure. Young children are not able to separate the idea of losing a game from being "a loser."

Cherry Contrarian (Joanna's story)

When my first child was almost four years old, I bought him a board game. I was excited. We were about to start a whole new level of interaction. I remembered my childhood game-playing days with fondness. So we opened up Hi Ho! Cherry-O with great anticipation. Dan was happy to put together the spinner and baskets, and to poke the little plastic cherries into the holes in the cardboard trees. Then we started to play.

My goodness, where was the sportsmanship? What was wrong with my child? He insisted on taking endless turns, spinning over and over again until he got the number he wanted. He refused to put cherries back when the spinner landed on "spilled basket." I soldiered on, trying to explain the concept of taking turns, winning and losing, being a good sport. Dan determinedly ignored me and got annoyed when I tried to stop him from playing *his* way. Fortunately, my sluggish brain caught up to reality before meltdown occurred. I gave up my quest, and Hi Ho! Cherry-O became a sort of random performance art activity involving flicking a spinner and arranging little plastic cherries on their cardboard trees, then plucking them into baskets and gleefully counting the loot.

Competitive games, from sports to board games and cards, are not typically terrific activities for young children. Our fond memories of playing board games are probably from later childhood. Little kids cannot comprehend why they should be made to lose, wait for someone else to have a turn, follow the unpleasant demands of a roll of the dice or the flip of a spinner. Parents worry that their children are behaving like spoiled brats. That they won't have the proper social skills they need to have friendships if they can't learn to be gracious losers. Give it time! They're probably not yet developmentally ready for such activities.

For a school-aged child, competitive games often become a regular part of their social interactions with peers. But it can still be very difficult for them to accept the idea of losing without feeling angry and discouraged. Heck, it's difficult for many adults! One of the ways we can teach our kids the fun and satisfaction of game playing is to alter the games just a bit so that the competition factor is lessened. Here are some successful variations that parents and teachers have come up with.

Getting to the End

In my house the board game Candyland is beloved for its depictions of fantasy candy. But my youngest has trouble being a "good sport." During one meltdown I told him, "You shouldn't be mad at us. *You* asked us to play!" causing him to stick his fingers in his ears and scream.

I remembered I was supposed to acknowledge his feelings, so I gave it a try. "Games can be so annoying. You want to play them because it seems like fun, then you get a bad card and you can't get your piece to the end. That's no fun at all!" He took his fingers out of his ears to say, "Yeah!" His brothers agreed enthusiastically. Games were both fun and annoying.

I asked, "I wonder how we could make it fun for everybody?" They came up with one small alteration. The person who gets around the board first is the official "first place winner." But the rest of the players keep on playing until they all get to the end. There are triumphant cries of, "I'm second place winner!" "I'm third place winner!" When I finally got my piece around the board, I modeled for them, acting really happy, "Hey, I'm last but not least! I finally made it!"

Triple Word Score

I love playing Scrabble. But when I tried to introduce it to my children, we had no fun at all. I was crushing the eight- and eleven-year-old competition. Woohoo! Beating little kids! Hey, I don't want to make three-letter words just so they won't feel bad. But after a few drubbings, they wouldn't play with me anymore. So I came up with a new idea. We would try to "beat the game." We had to collectively make 200 points in just ten moves, or the game would win. We added all of our points together. The kids were filled with glee when I made long words on double and triple word scores. I was helping the team. They started to enjoy making more elaborate words of their own. It was a big success.

Daddy Rules (Julie's story)

My husband Don decided to teach our seven-year-old, Asher, to play chess. When they started out, Don stuck to the rules and played to win in order to demonstrate the proper way to play the game. Needless to say, after the first burst of enthusiasm at learning this special game with Daddy, Asher lost interest because he was always trounced.

At my suggestion, Don started making up "special Daddy rules" to even up the playing field. These involved various handicaps so Asher could experience winning, such as playing with fewer pieces, or giving hints when Asher got into a tight spot. Asher was eager to play again. Over time, Don started asking Asher if he wanted him to play full strength or half strength, and Asher would decide how much of a challenge he wanted. Putting Asher in charge let him enjoy the game and learn to

manage his own frustration. He enjoys chess to this day (and does not require his opponents to self-handicap!).

Beat the Clock

My kids love to play racing games. But there are always tears and accusations of cheating when somebody wins and somebody loses. It's an exercise in frustration for the younger siblings to compete with their older brother. Since he's bigger and stronger, they lose every time. The best purchase we made was a big stopwatch. The kids make an obstacle course with tunnels to crawl through, Hula-Hoops to jump through, and various things to climb over and run around. One of them will run while another keeps the time. On the next round, each child tries to beat his own time. They love having a turn to be time-keeper, which involves yelling "Ready, Set, *Go!*" and recording each person's "time to beat" on a chart. I explained that it doesn't matter what anyone else does, because they may be bigger or smaller or have longer or shorter legs, or have practiced more or less than you. I'm amazed at how well this works. You'd think they'd insist on comparing, but they don't. Even the highly competitive neighbor boy, who is infamous for his gloating and tears, happily plays this game with my kids.

Card Drama

When we play the card game Steal the Old Man's Pack I always make a big drama when someone "steals" my cards. "Oh no, I have nothing left! Those cruel thieves have taken everything. What will I eat? I'll starve! Who will invite me for dinner?" Now the kids like to lose cards because they can make up their own little sob story.

Making Change

I always set aside time for games on Fridays with my elementary school resource room students. One of the most popular is Pay the Cashier. Players pick cards that direct them to make various purchases. Paper money and plastic coins are counted out by the "customer" and collected by the "cashier." The player with the most money left at the end wins the game. The kids loved counting out money and making change, but they didn't love losing. They got upset!

These resource room kids already had plenty of experience at failure. That's why they qualified for special services. I figured that gaining the math skills to manage money was more valuable than gaining more experience at losing, so I decided to remove that element. We played the game, making our purchases and talking about what we would do with them, and neglected to count up the money at the end to declare a winner. I thought the kids would challenge me on this alteration. I figured they'd ask, "What's the point of the game if you can't win?" Not a single student ever mentioned it. The point was to play and have fun.

Family Game Night

Once a month, we have family game night with another family that also has three kids. All six kids and the adults have a great time. We play charades, Fictionary, Pictionary, and Scattergories, but we don't make it a competition with winners and losers. We all try to guess what picture the person is drawing, or what title they're acting out, or think of the most ridiculous made-up definition for a word. We have a great time and laugh our heads off. No one seems to miss the point system at all.

To some of our readers it may sound like we're mollycoddling children and not giving them the opportunity to face the competitive challenges that will strengthen their character. We assure you that we have seen our own six children (three each) grow up to enjoy a wide range of competitive activities. Collectively, they've played both team and individual sports (tennis, lacrosse, basketball, soccer, baseball, cross-country, and wrestling), competitive computer games, hackathons, and all manner of card and board games (at least during blackouts and family game nights). They are gracious winners and good losers. They modify their intensity for younger children. They laugh a lot while they play. We believe all that work we did when they were younger, teaching them to focus on the joy and satisfaction of playing rather than the distress of losing, helped build their character and made that possible.

REMINDER: COMPETITION

1. **Adjust expectations.**

   "Let's play this game differently. Instead of trying to beat each other, let's try to beat the game."

2. **Put the child in charge.**

   "Do you want me to play at half strength or full strength?"

3. **Acknowledge feelings.**

   "It's so frustrating when you get a bad card and you can't move your piece to the end."

4. **Be playful.**

   "Oh no, I've lost all my cards. I have nothing . . . NOTHING! What will I do?"

5. **Try problem-solving.**

   "How can we make this game fun for everyone?"

The Locker Solution

I took Rachel, my three-year-old, to the pool. We had planned to visit her cousins afterward, but she was tired and cranky. Here's how the conversation in the locker room went:

Rachel: I don't want to go see my cousins.
Me: You want to go home.
Rachel: I want to go home and sleep in my bed.
Me: You're really tired.

Then I suggested that she could sleep in the car. She did *not* like that idea and she slammed the door to the locker.

Me: That sounded like an angry slam! Do it again!

This was pretty unexpected—I've never done anything like that before, and she was very surprised. I opened the locker door for her, and she slammed it hard, again.

Me: Wow, that was super loud! You are super mad!
She seemed to calm down.
Me: Okay, I'm going to carry you out to the car.
Rachel: I *do* want to go see my cousins.

And we did!

13

Name-Calling and "Bad" Language

"Stupid idiot!"
"You're a poopy-head!"
"Booger brains!"
"Hey, butt-face!"
*"(Curse words that we're not going to write in this book. Use your
imagination!)"*

Kids use forbidden words for different reasons. Sometimes
they're taking joy in the discovery that they can get a rise out of
adults, or make their friends squeal in delight. They intentionally
experiment with words to see if they can get a reaction. What
fun . . . for them.

The problem is, the more stridently we forbid those words,
the more powerful and attractive they become.

One less combative way to respond to young children who
are experimenting with forbidden words is to **describe how you
feel** and **give them information**. You can say, "Hey! I don't like
to hear those words. You can talk that way with your friends, but
not your parents and your teachers." Sometimes that's enough.
But what if they persist?

Another tactic is to give little kids
the response they crave in a **playful**
way. "Whatever you do, don't you dare
call me 'broccoli-toes'!" Then you can
respond with dramatic protestations
when they take the dare. "Oh no, not
'broccoli toes'! I can't stand it. Waaaah!"[1]

But maybe your child isn't using bad

language in a playful, experimental way. Maybe she's using it appropriately, which is to say, inappropriately. For example, she comes home from school and tells you her math teacher is a "B" word (except she actually says the word).

Can't we just tell her that's not a respectful way to talk about her teacher, and that we don't use language like that in this family?

Let's test that strategy on ourselves:

Imagine you have a horrible boss. Today he tried to avoid responsibility for his own error by pinning the blame on you, in front of your coworkers. You arrive home steaming with anger. When your spouse asks you, "What's up?" you explode: "That jerk (except you use a different word) made me look bad in front of the entire department by suggesting I never submitted the proper forms!" Imagine your spouse responds, "Hey, that's not a respectful way to talk about your boss. And we don't use language like that in this family!"

What's your immediate gut reaction?

Did you think: *Well, I'm in this family and I just did use language like that . . . you "jerk!"*

Or maybe you said to yourself, *That's the last time I tell you about my work problems.* And then you suddenly develop a headache when your spouse wants to "cuddle."

So if criticizing how a person expresses anger makes them turn it on you, or shut down, what *can* we do when kids use language that we find objectionable?

We can go back to the basics: start **by acknowledging their feelings**, and then **describe your own feelings**.

"It sounds like you're very angry at your teacher. Something she did really bothered you! My problem is, that 'B word' really bothers me. If we're going to talk about this, we need to find a different word."

And if she persists? **Take action** if necessary, by removing yourself from the conversation.

"I can't talk about this now. That word upsets me so much, I can't focus on the rest of what you're saying."

But what about when kids use bad language to attack *us*?

Yesterday my twins wanted to use the face paints right before bedtime. They'd already had their baths, and I wasn't about to let them start covering themselves in paint. They started to argue, so I told them, "No! End of discussion!" They yelled back, "You're stupid!" "I hate you!"

When kids get very upset, they try to find the most powerful words they can think of to express their frustration. The challenge is to give them language that's strong enough to do the job without being offensive. (Does it help to keep in mind that even offensive language is progress? Your children are no longer hitting, kicking, and biting. They're "using their words"!)

You can **acknowledge how they feel** and let them know **how you feel**: "It sounds like you had your heart set on using the face paints tonight. I don't like being called names!" And then you can **tell them what they *can* say instead of what they *can't***. Give them the words that will help them express their feelings in a more acceptable way. "You can tell me, 'Mom, I'm *really really mad!!* I was looking forward to using the face paint!!'"

That may lead to a civilized discussion. "It sounds like we need to find a time for face paints that will work for all of us. What are our choices? Would after school next year on Tuesday work for you?" (Just kidding! We're giving you in fantasy what you can't have in reality.) "Okay, let's write it down so we don't forget."

Or you may be too upset and insulted to feel like being helpful. In which case, you can tell them, "I don't like being called names. I'm too upset to talk to you about this right now." And then walk off in a huff. You can always revisit the issue and try problem-solving later, after you've cooled down a bit.

> "I was really angry last night. I didn't like being insulted. And you were upset because I didn't let you use the face paints. We don't want that to happen again! Let's see if we can figure out a time for painting that will be good for all of us."

In short, kids use "bad" words for different reasons. But, whatever the reason, forbidding words can make them even more attractive. Taking a playful approach with young children can satisfy their need to experiment while saving our sanity. When children express strong feelings with objectionable language, we can acknowledge those feelings while simultaneously modeling a way to express them in a way that's easier for us to listen to.

Stories from the Front Lines

You're *Rude*!

My eight-year-old daughter frequently talks to me in a disrespectful manner. The other day I was walking her to the bus stop. I had a helicopter moment and grabbed her hand when it seemed like she was about to step out into the intersection. She pulled her hand away and said, "Don't be such a dork!"

I can't stand it when she talks this way. I tend to blame it on American television (her father and I are from England). I always tell her, "You're being rude!" because, frankly, she is! And she needs to know that it's unacceptable to talk to adults that way.

The problem is, she's very strong-willed and usually comes right back at me, "*You're* rude!"

After the workshop, I realized that I was basically calling her a name. "You're rude" isn't that different from "You're a dork." So much for modeling good behavior.

The next time she called me a name, I said, "It hurts my feelings when you talk to me that way."

She immediately said, "I'm sorry Mummy!"

I was flabbergasted. All I had to do to stop her from being rude was to stop calling her "rude"!

A Rose by Any Other Name (Joanna's story)

(Warning: This story contains
an unabbreviated bad word.)

I was twelve years old. I came home from school very upset with my teacher. I remember sitting at the kitchen table ready to get some sympathy from my mom. I told her this teacher was an *asshole*! My mom flinched. "Joanna, that's a terrible word."

"But he *is* an asshole," I insisted.

"Joanna, stop! I can't listen to that word. I'm sure you can find a better way to describe a person you're angry at."

She went to the bookshelf, took out the thesaurus, and thunked it down on the table in front of me. I was intrigued. I looked up the "a" word, and to my delight, there it was in black and white. "Well, that word's not too terrible for the thesaurus," I exulted.

We spent the next ten minutes reading synonyms for the terrible word, laughing over all the quaint, outmoded insults. In the end, even my mom had to agree that there was no perfect substitute. *Unpleasant, disagreeable, half-wit oaf* didn't quite have the same ring. Still, I did learn that my mom felt too uncomfortable with vulgar language for me to use that word in conversation. But at the same time, I felt understood . . . and I learned some great new vocabulary words in the process.

The "S" Word (Julie's story)

We were finishing dinner when Shiriel, age three, announced, "Rashi is stupid!" I told her that could hurt a person's feelings, but this inspired her to start chanting: "Ra-shi is *stu-pid*! Ra-shi is *stu-pid*!"

All my buttons were pushed. I shouted, "Enough! Stop!"

She didn't.

I suggested to six-year-old Rashi that we go to the living room and leave her alone. He actually wasn't upset, and once I got away from her, it occurred to me that she was just playing with the power of words. I suggested to Rashi that he could play our old game, you can call me (blank) just don't call me (blank).

Back we went, and Shiriel immediately started in again with, "Ra-shi is STU-PID!" only this time he responded, "You can call me 'stupid' all you want. Just don't call me 'pomegranate pie!'"

Sure enough, she yelled, "Rashi is pomegranate pie!" He hammed it up, wailing and flailing, and she laughed hysterically. Many repetitions later, they had both collapsed in a heap of giggles.

When I think back on that dinner, I realize that Shiriel probably felt left out because I'd been talking to Rashi about his day. The name-calling was her three-year-old attempt to get in on the action.

REMINDER:
NAME-CALLING AND BAD LANGUAGE

When children use forbidden words to experience their power, you can:

1. Describe how you feel and **give information.**

> "I don't like to hear that kind of language. That's the sort of thing you can say when you're with your friends."

2. Be playful to give children the dramatic reaction they crave.

> "Whatever you do, don't call me 'broccoli toes'!"
> *"Hey, broccoli-toes!"*
> "Waaah!"

When children use forbidden words to express strong feelings, you can:

3. Describe how you feel.

> "I don't like to be called stupid! I'm in no mood to talk about face paints right now."
> "The problem is, that word really upsets me."

4. Acknowledge strong feelings with more acceptable language.

> "It sounds like you're very angry at your teacher. Something she did really bothered you!"

5. **Tell them what they *can* say instead of what they *can't*.**

"You had your heart set on using the face paints tonight. You can tell me, 'Mom, I'm really mad! I was looking forward to using face paints.'"

6. **Take action without insult** by removing yourself from the conversation.

"I can't talk about this now. That word upsets me so much, I can't focus on the rest of what you're saying."

7. If the underlying issue still persists, you can **try problem-solving.**

"I was really angry last night. I didn't like being insulted. And you were upset because I didn't let you use the paints. We don't want that to happen again! Let's see if we can figure out a time for painting that will be good for all of us."

Shoe Squabble

I wanted Maya to get her shoes on. My kids bicker all the time so I used that as inspiration. I picked up her shoes and started "speaking" for them:

"I want to go to school with Maya."

"No, I want to go. It's *my* turn."

"No, it's not! It's *my* turn!"

"No, No, NO! You always get to go."

Maya laughed and said, "Guys, *guys*! I have TWO FEET! You can BOTH go to school with me." And she put her shoes on.

Section V

Conflict Resolution

14

Sharing

Mine, All Mine!

> *If we want to work toward world peace, this is where it starts.*

We want our kids to learn to share. It's an important value, not to mention that without infinite space and an infinite budget, we can't own multiples of *everything*. Which naturally leads parents to ponder the age-old philosophical question:

Why do kids always want to play with the toy that the other kid is playing with, even if they had absolutely no interest in it a moment ago? In other words, why is the best toy in the house the one that's in somebody else's hands?

The answer is . . . because that's how human brains work. It's how our species learns. When children see someone else manipulating an object, they have a drive to imitate. *They* want to put the key in the keyhole and unlock the apartment door, press the buttons on the dishwasher to make it hum and slosh, grab the cell phone to poke at the touchscreen, cut the carrots with the big, sharp knife . . .

And they cry and scream when we don't let them, because

we're thwarting the basic human drive that's encoded in their DNA.[1]

When kids see another child playing with a toy, the same drive kicks in. That is the object they "need" and they need it right now! Which creates a dilemma. We don't want to scold or shame kids for their natural curiosity and urge to learn. But we have to find a way to navigate all the conflicts that ensue. We want them to learn to delay gratification, to resolve disputes with respect for each other's needs, and to *just stop fighting*! So where are the brain scientists when all the kids are grabbing stuff out of each other's hands and screaming? We need to fill in the gap between science and survival.

As you may already suspect, there is no simple one-size-fits-all solution that will put an end to the fuss. It all depends on the ages and developmental stages of the kids, the setting, and the particular nature of the object of desire. It's complicated.

In this chapter you'll find field-tested solutions that have worked to address the eternal challenge of teaching kids to share.

Toddler vs. Baby

Dear J&J,

We have a three-year-old daughter and a nine-month-old son. Now that the baby is crawling, our toddler has become extremely possessive. She grabs everything out of her little brother's hands. If I force her to give it back she goes into total meltdown. She used to be friendly toward her brother, but now she grabs her toys and runs away whenever he crawls near.

With Christmas coming up, I'm worried that gifts given to her specifically might make the possessiveness even worse. Should we consider not putting names on the gifts and allowing them to take turns opening them? Maybe less focus on having her own toys and more practice sharing will help her get used to the idea.

—Mom of a Grabber

Dear MOG,

You raise an interesting question! It would seem that the more we require a young child to share, the better she'll become at it. The key point to consider is, what is this child thinking and feeling while she's "practicing sharing." If she's continually in a frustrated state of mind because the clock is ticking on her turn, and nothing is truly hers anymore, she may become increasingly worried that the new baby is going to get her stuff. We imagine this kind of "practice" might make her feel even *more* possessive and more threatened by the baby.

Consider how you'd feel if some authority declared that you no longer have the right to exclusive ownership of treasured possessions. You used to own your own car, but now it's been decided by your homeowner's association that your next car will be a shared resource. It will belong equally to your new neighbor. (This system will be more environmentally friendly and also keep the streets free of excess traffic, as well as ease the parking shortage.) Your neighbor may come over at any time and grab your keys to go on an errand.

You might not be going somewhere right now, but you're always a bit on edge. You can't count on your car being available. How long will the neighbor keep your car this time? Will you be able to get it back from her when you need it, or will she start to fuss, and you'll have to back off? Will it be returned with scratches on the fender or crumbs in the back seat?

You used to feel pretty relaxed about your car; in fact, on several occasions you freely lent it to a friend whose car was being repaired. But that was your own choice. You felt nice and generous about lending it. Now it's not up to you. You're not "sharing," you're being forced to give up what you used to consider rightfully yours.

Okay, enough about your car. Let's get back to your three-year-old!

It's a balancing act. One goal is to help the older child feel less threatened by the baby grabbing her stuff. The other goal is to protect the rights of the younger child to explore his world

241

and all the marvelous objects in it without being stymied by a tyrannical big sister.

In support of the first goal, it's likely that giving an older child more control, rather than less, will help her relax and practice magnanimity.

Giving your daughter her own gifts will not deprive her of the opportunity to practice sharing. You can approach the sharing dilemma as a problem that the two of you work together to manage. You'll need to start with **acknowledging feelings**.

> "Oh gosh, babies really like to grab all your stuff! Anything they see their big sister playing with is the best thing to them. And then when you try to get it back, they scream and cry. That can be really frustrating!"

Instead of jumping right in with a rule about sharing, look for a way to **put the child in charge**.

> "What should we do? You wanted to play with that teddy bear and your little brother is chewing on its ear. Hmm, if we grab it out of his hands he'll cry. I wonder if you can find something else he'd like. Do you have any stuffed animals you can wiggle in front of him so he'll drop the teddy?"

You can **offer her a choice** about which toys to share:

> "We need a box of toys for little Buzz to play with. Which toys would he like? You decide what to put in the box."

Now you're approaching the problem with compassion for both kids. You understand the older child's need to protect her stuff, and at the same time you're protecting the baby from having toys yanked out of his hands.

You can use **descriptive praise** to let her know how much the baby appreciates it when she brings him something captivating. Instead of, "Good job sharing!" try,

> "Wow, Buzz has a big smile on his face. I think that stuffed tiger is really making him happy!"

When she doesn't want to share, don't label her as selfish. Instead, acknowledge her feelings and keep the door open for future urges to share.

> "You don't feel ready to share your new fuzzy wuzzy *yet*."

This holds open the possibility that at some point she *will* be ready.

It may help to consider that you yourself have some possessions that you freely "share" with your children and other possessions that you do not choose to share.

> "Sure, go ahead and bang on those pots with a wooden spoon. I can see you're having a great time. I'll just pop on these noise-canceling headphones."

> "Nope, you may not use mommy's earring collection on your play dough creatures. I'll just pop that jewelry box up on the top shelf of my closet. Let's get you some pipe cleaners!"

A three-year-old's criteria may seem less rational, but she's just as passionate about her stuff as we are about ours. It's a challenge for a toddler to learn to deal with a newly mobile younger sibling.

But let's not forget the second goal. The baby has rights, too! You probably already have a sense of which objects of contention fall under the category of "special possessions" of the firstborn, and which belong to the broader category of community property. This second category no doubt includes baby toys, older toys that have been kicking around for ages gathering layers of drool and tooth marks, and large play objects that must be shared due to the fact that only one of them will fit in your non-infinite living space, such as a climbing cube or a pop-up tent and tunnel.

You'll have to **take action** to protect the rights of the baby from his not-yet-fully-civilized older sister. If you can manage to do that with compassion (acknowledging feelings, offering choices) rather than scolding, you'll accelerate the learning process for your toddler.

> "I can't let you take the rattle away from Buzz. That's a toy for everyone, and he's allowed to have a turn. It's hard to wait until he's done. Let's find something else to do while you wait! Do you want to help me put away the spoons, or do you want to color with crayons?"

Even if your child wails, you can commiserate. Remember, all feelings can be accepted while some actions must be limited.

> "It's hard! Nobody likes to wait! Grrr!"

> "Even though you haven't used that rattle in a long time, it's still special to you. You have a lot of nice memories of playing with it."

Yes, you'll have to bite your tongue not to say, "That's a baby toy! You're not a baby! You just want to take things away from your little brother and that's not nice!" But it will be worth the sore tongue. Making your toddler feel bad about herself will not help her learn generosity.

Sharing Among Older Kids

But what about when older kids fight over things? Shouldn't there be some kind of rule?

Sure! For purposes of crowd control (and your sanity), whether at school, during playdates, or within a family, you may want to come up with some ground rules about sharing. And then you'll want to **give kids information** about what those rules are. Of course we've got to come up with the rules first . . . and it can be complicated.

Is it a large, single-user item that everyone wants to play with, such as a trampoline, a swing, or a ride-on car? It might make sense to have timed turns. (Or kids may invent another way to share besides timing. Maybe one kid can ride the car while another pushes, or sets up cones for the rider to maneuver around.)

Is it a brand-new toy that one kid just got for his birthday? That child should be given the right to set their own rules for sharing that toy, or be allowed to put it away out of sight.

Is it an old toy that has essentially become community property, and one kid wants it because it's in the hands of another? You won't want to have timed turns for every single object in the house or classroom. Kids need to be able to interact with interesting stuff without being constantly told, "Give it up in five minutes!" Your rule here may be that a child has to ask and then wait until the other child is finished. And by waiting, we don't mean just *waiting*. For a young child, there is no such thing as "waiting patiently." She'll need help. "I *know*! The best toy is the one your brother is playing with! That's the one that looks the most exciting. Let's find something to do while you're waiting. Follow me . . ."

Some playdate battles can be avoided by planning ahead for activities that lend themselves to cooperative or parallel play. Put away the attractive nuisance items such as the remote-control car, the roaring dinosaur, the special doll that pees and cries "Mama." Break out the flour, salt, and water and plan to have kids make play dough, or toss out a basket of balloons for them to bat around, or dump out a bag of blocks—or whatever interlocking brand-name toy is the thrill of the moment—just so long as there are gazillions of interchangeable parts. Or send the kids outside to swarm the climbing structure and roll down the hill. Sure there will be micro-conflicts, but you'll have the energy to deal with them because they'll be fewer and farther between.

In those everyday (and sometimes every minute) battles, there's going to be a range of ever-changing protocols. There's no simple rule that will fit all situations. The best rule to follow is, "Find out what everybody's needs are, and then figure out the best way to satisfy them." Yes, it's complicated, but this is one of the most complicated issues *in the entire world!* This is the stuff that wars are fought over—control of resources! If we can help our kids figure out how to share (and sometimes not share) peacefully, we can be pretty proud of our parenting.

But before you start drafting an updated version of Hammurabi's code, consider this. With kids who are old enough to reason, you can look at competition over toys as an excellent opportunity for them to practice **problem-solving**. It's tempting to institute a rule that seems fair to us, but as the stories below illustrate, children will often come up with their own solutions that work better for them, if only because *they* came up with them.

Flipper Feud

I took seven-year-old Emma and five-year-old Owen to the pool, thinking I was buying myself an entire afternoon of no squabbling. That lasted for about fifteen minutes. We have one pair of flippers (*I know, not ideal!*) and Emma had been using them since we arrived. Owen was tired of waiting for his turn and tried to pull them off her feet.

Two completely contradictory thoughts crossed my mind almost simultaneously. *"Your older sister is using them, you can't just grab them."* and, *"Oh come on, let your little brother have a turn. You've been using them since we got here."*

They were in the middle of a serious tug-of-war. I didn't know which voice to listen to. It struck me that I could try problem-solving, and get *them* to figure it out. Why should I have to be the judge and jury? So I said, "Oh no, this is a problem! We have one pair of flippers and two kids want to use them. Emma's been using them and isn't ready to give them up. And Owen's been waiting a long time and he wants a turn. What should we do? We need ideas!"

Owen said, "I should get them because Emma's been using them for a *really* long time."

Emma said, "I need them for longer because I'm trying to cross the pool underwater."

Owen said, "We should each get one."

I was about to say, "That won't work, you'll end up going in circles." But Emma said, "Okay! You can have *one!*"

They both happily swam off with one flipper each. Certainly not the solution *I* would've come up with. I think this is a very optimistic method. My kids are learning that conflicts can be resolved without force or threat of violence.

T-Bar Trouble (Julie's story)

When Shiriel, Rashi, and Asher were six, nine, and twelve, we got an upside-down T-bar that hung from a hook in the ceiling. It was an immensely popular piece of equipment, and the kids were always vying with each other to hang and spin. I wasn't about to populate the living room with three T-bars, and I needed them to take turns peacefully, so I instituted a five-minute rule.

But this rule did not prevent conflict. I was driving the kids home from school and they were already arguing in the car, anticipating the mad rush to the bar.

"I call the T-bar first!"

"No fair, you can't call it, you were first yesterday!"

"I call youngest first!"

I'd originally been concerned about injuries caused by falling from the bar, but now I realized there was far greater danger in the potential stampede. I envisioned them tumbling from the car before I got to a complete stop, elbowing and trampling each other to get into the house first. I yelled, "HEY!" That got their attention.

"We have a problem! Three kids want to be first on the T-bar, and there's only one T-bar. We need a better rule than 'whoever calls it first gets it first.' Not everyone is happy with that. We need to figure out a system that *everybody* likes before *anybody* gets to use the T-bar."

Major negotiations ensued. The two bones of contention were who gets to be first and how many minutes each person gets. It turned out that Shiriel (the youngest) really cared about being first, and Asher (the oldest) didn't mind waiting but cared much more about getting a long turn. The upshot was that they decided Shiriel would be first and get two minutes, Rashi would be second and get four minutes, and Asher would be last and get six minutes.

They were all very pleased with themselves. I was relieved that I didn't have to practice mob control.

• • •

Sometimes you won't need to have a whole problem-solving session. You can just **put a child in charge** and go enjoy a moment of peace.

Berry Sharing

Blueberries are a big treat for my three kids. I put out a big bowlful on the table, only to see my nine-year-old scooping as many as he could, as quickly as he could, onto his plate. "Alex! Those berries are for all three of you. You took way more than a third!" I removed all the berries from the table, divided them into three smaller bowls, and set them out. I'm sure you know what happened next.

"He has more!"

"No I don't. Yours is up to the rim on that side!"

"No fair, I want the bowl Alex has!"

I sighed. "Everybody wants as many berries as they can possibly get. I don't know what to do. I'm not going to count every berry. I don't have the patience for that."

Alex piped up. "I'll count them! Trevor and Katie can watch me."

We put the berries back in the serving bowl and the two younger siblings watched like hawks as Alex placed a single berry at a time in each small bowl. At the end there were two berries left over and Alex magnanimously gave one to each sibling. Being in charge made him feel generous. Everyone was satisfied.

But what about non-countable treats such as cake, which when cut always results in one piece that's bigger, or more desirable due to the little red part of the frosting from the flower?

We know a few families who successfully employ the "diminishing crumb technique." If all three kids identify one piece as

THE one, then remove a few crumbs from that piece and attach them to the "loser" pieces. Now the loser pieces are bigger? Move half a crumb back. This exercise must be done without sarcastic attitude, in the interests of achieving a mathematical truth. In a

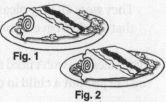

Fig. 1

Fig. 2

WHICH ONE IS **BIGGER** ?

minute or two nobody will be able to tell which is the superior slice, and they'll move on to eating, because those fractional crumbs just don't matter anymore. Eventually the kids will be able to do this all by themselves. You are free to go!

As adults we've learned that an extra berry here, or a missing crumb there, is no big deal. And kids will have to learn that too. We can't always accommodate their desire for perfect fairness. But by acknowledging their feelings and putting them in charge we help them move more quickly toward understanding and accepting the inevitable small inequalities of life.

• • •

Sometimes the best approach to the sharing dilemma is to find ways to avoid it entirely.

Doll Discord

We'd been inviting Hannah's preschool friends to our house to play after school, but it was becoming unpleasant because she never wanted to share her toys. She'd scream or grab anything a friend touched. It was especially embarrassing when the other parent stayed. Hannah was looking like an incredibly selfish, spoiled girl. And I was feeling like a bad mom!

After our workshop session, I started preparing Hannah for playdates by asking her what activities she wanted to do when her friend came over, and which toys she'd like to "show" her friend. I also asked her if there were any special toys that she did *not* want to share, and we put those away on a high shelf in the closet. It's helped a lot that I no longer insist that she has to share all her toys with her friends!

The other day she forgot to put away her favorite doll, Mindy, before her friend Sarah came over. Sure enough Sarah found Mindy and Hannah started to scream, "Give it!" In the old days I would've scolded Hannah and sent her to her room. But this time I told Hannah, "Sarah doesn't know that's your very special doll. You can ask Sarah to give Mindy to you, and offer her one of the other dolls."

I have to admit I was surprised when she quickly stopped screaming and said to Sarah, "Please give me back Mindy. She only likes me to hold her. You can hold Pippi."

I feel like this approach is actually helping Hannah think about sharing in a positive way.

Remote Control Ambivalence (Joanna's story)

When Dan was three, my friend gave him a remote-control truck for his birthday. He was over the moon about it. It was the coolest toy he'd ever owned. It was quite the acrobatic vehicle, with large wheels that enabled it to flip completely upside down and keep on rolling. (It also ate batteries for lunch, but we won't get into that issue here.)

When our next playgroup date came around, Dan was eager to show it off to his friends and he climbed into the car seat with the truck in his arms. I foresaw trouble.

I acknowledged feelings first.

"Dan, I can see that you want to show everyone the remote-control truck. It's really cool."

"Yeah, they'll love it!"

I described the problem.

"I'm thinking that every kid who sees it will want to use it. I know it's your brand-new truck. I don't know how you feel about sharing it so soon."

"I don't want them to break it. I'll just show them how it works and they can watch."

I described the problem again, in different words.

"I'm worried that it'll be very hard for the other kids to watch you play with such a cool toy and not be allowed to have a turn. It could be really frustrating for them."

"Oh . . ."

I put Dan in charge of making the final decision.

"Think about whether you want to bring it and give people turns, or you want to keep it at home because it's new and special."

"I'll leave it home."

Problem solved.

Epilogue: A few weeks later we stopped at the bank before going to story hour at the library. The bank teller gave Dan a lollipop. (She asked me if it was okay *as* she was handing it to him, but let's not get into that issue here!) He was still sucking the lolly as I parked at the library. I found myself kind of hating the teller as I anticipated the fight to extract candy from my kid's mouth before we went in.

I hesitantly said, "I'm worried about bringing the lollipop into the library because the other kids won't have one. They'll see you eating it and want one."

Dan popped it out of his mouth and added, "And then their parents will feel sad, because they don't have lollipops to give to their children. I'll leave it in the car."

We found the wrapper on the floor, dusted it off, and rewrapped the sticky lolly.

I was astonished that not only was he able to think about other children's feelings while experiencing an artificial cherry–flavored sugar rush, but he was empathizing with the *parents*! I think that the remote-control car discussion jump-started his ability to take other people's perspective.

REMINDER: SHARING

1. **Acknowledge feelings with words.**

   "Babies really like to grab your stuff! And then when you try to get it back, they scream and cry. That can be really frustrating!"

2. **Put the child in charge.**

   "You wanted to play with that teddy bear and the baby is chewing on its ear. What should we do? Can you find another stuffed animal to wiggle in front of him so he'll drop the teddy?"

3. **Offer a choice.**

   "Your friend is coming over after school. Which toys do you want to share and which should we put away?"

4. **Praise by describing the effect on others.**

   "Wow, Buzz has a big smile on his face. I think that stuffed tiger is really making him happy!"

5. **Take action without insult.**

   "I can't let you take the rattle away from Buzz. That's a toy for everyone, and he's allowed to have a turn."

6. **Give information.**

   "The rule is . . . no grabbing out of someone's hands . . . everyone gets five minutes on the trampoline . . . you have to wait until the other person is finished . . ."

7. **Try problem-solving.**

   "We have one pair of flippers and two children both want to use them. What should we do? We need ideas!"

15

That Is NOT a Toy

When Kids Want to "Share" *Your* Stuff

It's a funny thing about kids. They want to play with whatever we're playing with. So while we're busy emptying our bank accounts on elaborate toys, they've set their sights on our stuff. Maybe we should be flattered, not annoyed, that our kids have such a drive to emulate us.

But then my stuff isn't there when I need it. It's not just the cost, it's the inconvenience. I don't want to share!

Sometimes it makes sense to **adjust our expectations** and reimagine our definition of "toy." Consider that it's not particularly more wasteful to give a child her own tape dispenser and stack of refills to play with, than it is to buy an expensive arts and crafts kit especially designed (and priced!) for children.

Does this mean we're supposed to get our kids their own personal supply of everything we use? Including the dishwasher, the microwave, and the lawnmower? Because that's what my kid is obsessed with.

We don't subscribe to the slippery slope theory. It doesn't have to be all or nothing. Let's see what we can do to provide the "real stuff" that our kids crave, and then **manage the environment** and provide alternatives when we need to.

We've got to choose our battles. The dishwasher and microwave can't become playthings, but **a child can be put in charge** of pushing the dishwasher button when you're starting up a load, or pushing the microwave button when you're heating up left-overs. You can even **write a note** and attach it to the appliance in contention:

We want to create an environment where we can **tell kids what they *can* do instead of what they *can't*.** The knife drawer may need a child-proof lock, but a drawer with ladles or plastic containers and lids can be left accessible. She can't use your lawn-mower, but she can push her own plastic bubble mower to satisfy her desire to do what Mommy does. You might want to protect your own stash of office supplies, but a few stacks of multicolor sticky notes and an extra box of paper clips could be a good investment. In fact many household items can be repurposed as safe and durable "toys" for children without busting the budget.

Remember, you didn't have kids to make your life neat and easy. You didn't hope for a kid who would have no interest in what her parents do. You wanted that messy, crazy life that comes with children and their intense drive to interact with their environment and to follow in their parents' footsteps, creating little impromptu internships for themselves wherever the opportunity arises.

Stories from the Front Lines

Spice Things Up (Joanna's story)

My husband came home to find me drinking a cup of coffee and reading the newspaper while two-year-old Danny sat happily on the floor, surrounded by spices. "What's going on?" my husband asked in alarm.

"Oh, Danny's playing with the spices," I replied serenely.

My husband objected. "Why does he have to play with the spices? Those are expensive! He has his own toys."

I sighed. I was having a peaceful moment. The spices had utterly engaged my busy two-year-old. I had adjusted *my* expectations. But my man didn't understand.

A few days later I came home to a scene that was a joy to behold. There was Danny surrounded by his spice jars, carefully sniffing and screwing the caps on and off, and there was my husband looking at me guiltily. "What can I say, you were right. It wasn't worth the fight."

Those words were sweet music to my ears! And by the way, at the time of this writing, Danny is all grown up. He still loves spices and he's a creative cook.

The Snappers

Jivan got into the utensil drawer and discovered the tongs. He extracted them and spent the next hour roaming the house exploring what he could pick up with his "snappers." He finally put them to rest in his toy box. I liberated them and returned them to their rightful drawer. He cried. I objected, "The tongs are not a toy." He protested vociferously, "It IS a toy!!"

I realized that I could get another pair of tongs for a few dollars, and that the "snappers" were a lot cheaper than just about any toy he had. So I gave them to him. He was delirious with joy, and his fine motor skills got quite a workout over the next few weeks.

My husband thinks I'm being too indulgent, and that kids need to understand they can't have everything their parents have. But I've realized it's much easier for Jivan to accept limits when I'm not saying "no" *all* the time. Last night Jivan got up on a stool and went for the knife drawer and I didn't even think. I screeched, "Not the knives!!"

He jerked back, and later when his dad came home, he pointed at the drawer and said very seriously, while shaking his head, "Not the knives, Daddy." In the past when I used to be more strict, he was never so easily deterred.

Still, I installed a child safety latch on the knife drawer.

All Taped Up

Soraya lives on tape and cardboard like other people live on air and water. I used to try to restrict her access to the tape, on the grounds that she was being wasteful. After my epiphany in the parenting workshop, I went to the office supply store and bought a jumbo pack of tape. I took a few rolls out for my own supply and gave the rest to Soraya. I filled a crate with empty toilet paper rolls, egg cartons, used Styrofoam trays, and other containers. She loves her new "workshop" and I no longer complain about waste. I was the one who was wasting money on toys that she only used for a few days. Apparently tape is limitless in its possibilities.

REMINDER: THAT IS NOT A TOY!

1. **Put the child in charge.**

   "It's time to turn on the dishwasher. Can you push the start button?"

2. **Adjust expectations and manage the environment** (and remember to choose your battles).

Decide where to draw a firm limit:

> "I'm going to put a lock on this drawer. That way you won't be tempted to play with the sharp knives."

. . . and where you can compromise:

> "You can use the ladles and scoop water in the sink."

3. **Tell them what they *can* do instead of what they *can't*.**

   "These sticky notes and paper clips are for you. You can use them however you want."

4. **Write a note.**

Please Press this Button when Ready to Wash

Muddy Footprints in Eastern Europe

I am from Slovenia and I have three kids—Jurij aged five
and a half, Ana Klara, three, and little David eleven months.
Since Jurij turned two, it's been never-ending tantrums,
stubbornness, yelling, frustration, and questioning ourselves. "OK, so that's it? Being a parent is like that?"

Jurij is a great challenge—he is a very smart and good
boy, but he is a kid of two extremes—his bright side can
all of a sudden turn into the darkest and strongest of the
storms. Since I am a lot like Jurij, it takes a lot of effort
not to start yelling and doing the "blah blah blah" talk when
it comes to a conflict. Especially when I am so tired I can
barely use my brain. (David is not much of a sleeper during
the night.)

I would like to share with you a story of how Jurij and
I solved a problem that in "the old way" would be a lot of
yelling, bad mood, and in the end some punishment (no
bedtime book, for example). This time I tried your tool of
problem-solving.

One afternoon after playing outside he started to come
in with his sneakers all muddy. Of course it was the day that
I did the floor cleaning in the morning. My first reaction was
the "old way": "Get out with those dirty shoes, I did the

cleaning today!" His response was anger because I didn't let him inside to get his slippers. I started the "blah blah blah" of how we cannot go all over the house with dirty shoes, etc. . . . Anger increasing! Then it hit me. OK, we're not getting anywhere, let's try the tools. I sat with him outside with a paper and pen. We started talking about his feelings. I said that I can see how angry he is for me not letting him in. Then I drew a very angry face with lightning bolts going out of the head. He nodded and told me that he was upset because I was expecting him to take off the shoes in front of the door, where his socks would get dirty without the slippers. I could see him relax and the "angry cramp" slide away from his body. He smiled a bit. Then I drew a clean house with a smiley face and another house, full of spots and dirt with a sad face. I asked him for ideas how to keep the house nice and clean. We agreed to the idea that we take dirty shoes off before coming in, and if the slippers are not by the door, he can call me or anyone else and ask to bring them. From that day on he sticks to the solution we agreed on. :-D

Since we are using the "how to talk tools," he comes to hug me more often, and he tells me he loves me several times a day. And I finally have the feeling again that this boy isn't my enemy but my son.

The Haircut

My daughter, Galit, said, "I want to cut my hair."

I repeated what I always tell her, "We don't cut our own hair."

"But I really, *really* want to cut my hair."

My mother was visiting, and she had been very skeptical of the need to take a parenting workshop just to talk to your own children. So I wanted to show off my new skills. "Oh, you really want to cut your hair! Even though you know we don't cut our hair, it's really hard when you want to. How about we draw some hair that you can cut?"

I asked her what color hair she wanted and she said, "Purple!"

"Who should draw the hair?"

"Grandma!"

Grandma drew the hair, and then Galit carefully cut it. She was satisfied—she stopped saying she wanted to cut her hair.

Cut here

16

The Digital Dilemma (Part 1)

Managing Screen Time with Younger Children

What if someone invented a thin, lightweight thingie you could carry with you anywhere that would instantly pacify a child without the use of drugs? That would be fantastically useful to a parent! Maybe you have to hop on a conference call for work and your kids are bashing each other over the head with Barbies. Or you're making dinner in front of a hot stove and your kids are crawling up your leg. Or maybe you're just really, really TIRED and you desperately want your kids to be safely occupied so you can lie down for a *minute*! The screen, in its various incarnations, instantly solves these problems.

And screens don't only entertain children; they can also be educational. No doubt you've discovered all kinds of games designed to help your kid painlessly absorb math skills, foreign language vocabulary, sight words, spatial concepts. And all kinds of shows and movies that expose your child to delightful characters displaying model personality traits of generosity, bravery, and kindness to others. Not to mention the fact that familiarity with computers is necessary for the vast majority of the jobs and careers of the future (and the present, of course).

So what is the problem with screens? Why do we engage in so many battles over our children's love of the technology that we ourselves have introduced to them?

One problem is that we're in uncharted territory. Nobody knows for sure what the outcome will be of raising our children with so much access to screen technology from the time

mush

they're toddlers. We're getting contradictory messages. Some experts warn of the
dire consequences of excessive screen time
while others accuse the first group of overreacting. Many of us worry about children
spending too much time on screens and not
enough "in real life." We want our kids to
have a healthy amount of physical activity,
to have face-to-face relationships, and to develop skills in the
real world from cooking to playing instruments to riding bikes.

So we often end up sending contradictory messages to our
kids. Here's this fantastic, fun, engrossing, educational activity
for you to do . . . *Oh dear, now that you're completely entranced, it's
time to stop! Shut it off, put it away, it's bad for your brain! It's not
healthy for your body!*

We tell kids they shouldn't overdo it when they're using
screens, but how much sense does this make to a kid? Think
about how we usually introduce a new toy or activity. In most
cases, we don't snatch away the toy or end an activity after a
prescribed number of minutes because "it's not good for you."
We don't drag them away in the middle of creating a block city,
or a LEGO spaceship, or tell them *enough is enough* when they're
playing tag, making play dough worms, riding a bike, or reading
a book. Sure, we may need them to stop for dinner, or a bath, or
homework, or bedtime. But we don't tell them the activity *itself*
is harmful, just that we have to do the next thing on our agenda.

Think about how you'd feel if your partner recommended a
very engrossing book to you, and then just as you got to the most
exciting part (will the hero clinging to the cliff in a hurricane
drag herself to safety, or plunge to her death on the jagged rocks
below?) grabbed the book and slammed it shut, saying, *"That's
enough now, too much reading isn't good for your eyes!" "You can
look at it again on the weekend." "Stop complaining, I gave you the
five-minute warning."*

You might have some feelings here! Likewise, it's no surprise that kids get confused and angry and butt heads with us when we try to restrict their access to screens.

We're not suggesting that young children should be allowed to have unlimited screen time. But it's important to realize what it feels like to our kids when we bustle in to announce, "Time's up!"

So now what? Since there's no universally accepted formula to calculate how much screen time is healthy and how much is problematic, we're going to proceed on the premise that each person will make their own determination about what works for their family.

What we can offer is that our communication tools still apply. If we want to resolve conflict around screens, we have to start with acknowledging feelings, and then explore all options: giving information, offering choices, problem-solving, managing the environment instead of the child, and taking action without insult. What does this look like when we apply it to screen skirmishes?

We can **acknowledge feelings** and **give information** tailored to the age of the child. So for a five-year-old, it might sound something like this: "It's annoying when your parents tell you to turn off the tablet. You don't want to stop in the middle of a game! The problem is that people need to take a break and spend time moving their muscles. It's not healthy for your body to sit and stare at a screen for a long time."

If we make screens available at random times during the day, kids can be enormously persistent in begging (and pleading and whining and crying) for them at all hours. You might **offer a choice** about when screen play will be allowed. Think about what might work for you. Are you willing to let your child choose from two different times of day—say, before dinner, or after preschool while the baby naps? When kids know what to expect and they've been involved in the decision-making process, it's easier for them to accept limits.

We're up against a tough challenge. Many computer games and video platforms are specifically designed to be very difficult to turn off. When you need to move your young child away from an engrossing screen activity, it can help to **focus on what they *can* do instead of what they *can't*.** Line up the next activity in advance, so that the end of the video isn't the end of all fun. Instead of saying, "It's time to *stop* watching TV before your brain turns to mush," you can say with enthusiasm, "Hey, it's time to blow soap bubbles and see how high they float before they pop!"

THINGS TO DO
AFTER VIDEO

1. use play doh
2. ride trike
3. blow soap bubbles
4. set up train tracks
5. blocks

Or **try problem-solving.** Sit down with your children when you're not in a moment of conflict. Acknowledge how much they enjoy their screen activities. Briefly describe your concern about too much sitting still, and invite them to brainstorm with you for ideas about how to stop without a battle, and what activities they can do afterward.

And finally, when you want to nudge your children in the direction of non-screen activities, it's enormously helpful to remove temptation. In the face of such alluring (some say addictive) technology, it's unrealistic to expect young children to regulate themselves. We need to **manage the environment instead of the child**, which means putting devices out of reach and, when possible, out of sight, in the same way that we don't leave bags of candy out on the kitchen table all day and then get annoyed with kids when the next dentist bill is shockingly high.

Here are some ways that parents of young children have used these tools to minimize conflict over screen time:

Angry Birds, Angry Boy

My three-year-old son, Oliver, was obsessed with Angry Birds from the moment his uncle put it on my phone. He constantly begged to play it and every time I tried to get him to stop he had a meltdown. I tried having him set a timer, which didn't help. Then we tried putting him in charge of stopping after he completed a level. That didn't help either. He continued to have total meltdowns when we enforced any limits. I finally uninstalled it from my phone. After a few days of withdrawal, he adjusted to the idea that it was really gone. Peace at last!

The One-Hour Rule

I fantasized about getting rid of screens completely. When my kids spend too much time on screens they're always cranky afterward, and difficult to get to bed. But the truth is, I can't give up the one tool I have that keeps them completely occupied. And there's a lot of really great educational content too, not to mention the value of having them grow up computer literate from an early age.

I sat down with the kids and acknowledged how much fun it is to play games and watch shows. Then I explained that too much of it is not healthy for your eyes, your brain, or your body. I told them they could use screens for an hour every day before dinner. (That's *my* most desperate hour of the day!) It was up to them to decide if they wanted to spend the time playing on the computer or watching videos. Or to plan for some of each. (Notice how I gave them a choice.) On weekends we have "movie night" and we suspend the one-hour limit. I know it'll get more complicated as they get older, but for now this is working for us.

Divorced Dad Triumphs Over TV

I have shared custody and I only see my three-year-old daughter two afternoons a week. She always begs to watch television, and I'd been letting her because I didn't want to spend our precious time together fighting. And honestly, I didn't want to do anything to make her cry. What if she told her mom she didn't want to come next time? But then it seemed like I was wasting the little time I had with her, because all we did was stare at the TV.

I bought a bunch of arts and crafts projects. The next time she came over I let her watch one video and then I turned off the TV and told her, "There's something I want to show you!" in an enthusiastic voice. I was expecting tears, but she barely fussed. I said, "Come outside, it's time for fingerpaints!" She loved them. Now we have a new routine together. One video and then . . . art.

The Mud Pie Solution

The daily battles and endless negotiations about screen time with our five-year-old and seven-year-old were sucking up so much of the pleasure from our lives that we decided to put a total ban on screens during the school week. We put them out of reach and out of sight (including the remote controls for the TV). We decided they'd be allowed two hours a day on the weekends. The first week was rough. There was a lot of stomping and complaining. We stuck with acknowledging feelings, "I know! You don't like this!" And occasionally offering a choice of alternative activities, most of which they rejected. After the first week, they stopped begging. The answer was always, "That's not an option," so they found other ways to amuse themselves. It helped that we've become more open to letting them do some messy and noisy activities (baking cookies, having indoor obstacle-course races; we even let them dig a hole in the backyard and fill it with the hose to make mud pies).

Screen Time Screaming

Since we've been locked down because of the coronavirus outbreak, I've been more lenient about letting my five-year-old son, Rijupt, play games on my smartphone when I need to get on a video conference for work. But he started getting extremely upset when I told him it was time to stop. He'd cry for so long it almost wasn't worth it!

I decided to try problem-solving with him. I said, "I know you really, really, *really* like playing Subway Surfers. The problem is that it's hard to *stop* playing! And I don't want to have a fight with you about it every time. We need ideas for how to play and stop playing without a fight. What do you think we should do?"

I suggested that we use a timer, and that he could set it himself. He said he wanted Alexa to tell him to stop. (I think he suspects me of making him stop sooner than the twenty minutes he's allowed. He trusts Alexa more!)

The new routine definitely worked better. He didn't get as upset, but he would still beg for one more minute. We did problem-solving again. This time he came up with the idea that I should give him a special hand signal as a one-minute warning so he wouldn't be in shock when it was time to stop.

Sometimes he's still unhappy after his playing time is over. It helps to tell him how amazed I am that he figured out how to play this game all by himself, and how fast he's getting at dodging the trains. It also helps to tell him about the next activity we're going to do.

REMINDER: MANAGING SCREEN TIME
WITH YOUNGER CHILDREN

1. Acknowledge feelings.

"It's annoying when your parents tell you to turn off the tablet. You don't want to stop in the middle of the game."

2. Give information.

"It's not healthy for your body to sit and stare at a screen for a long time."

3. Offer a choice.

"Do you want to watch a video or play a game?"

4. Tell them what they *can* do, instead of what they *can't*.

"It's time to blow soap bubbles and see how high they float before they pop."

5. Try problem-solving.

"We need ideas for how to play, and how to stop playing without a fight."

6. Manage the environment instead of the child.

Put devices out of reach and out of sight when you don't want children using them.

The Digital Dilemma (Part 2)

Screens and Older Children

Managing screen time becomes vastly more complicated as children get older. Many kids get their own smartphones, and schools may provide them with laptops or tablets. Screens become enmeshed in almost every aspect of their lives, from making social connections, to doing schoolwork, to accessing entertainment, to communicating with parents at the request (or demand) of said parents. They may also be engaged in creative endeavors: using software to compose music or make videos, investigating their interests through discussion boards and tutorials, or even doing their own coding. There is hardly a single activity left that doesn't involve computer screens, with the possible exception of taking a shower (unless, of course, you have a waterproof case). Even when we want to get away from technology and commune with nature, we download a trail map app on our smartphones so we won't get lost in the woods. It's no longer possible to make simple rules about screen use. Any restrictions would be so full of exceptions and loopholes that it would take a team of lawyers months to analyze, and in any case, they would be unenforceable.

But even with all these caveats, most of us aren't comfortable taking a completely hands-off approach. We still want to make sure our kids have balance in their lives. We're aware that digital technology can be powerfully seductive and we want to help our kids learn to manage it.

So what are our options?

You've probably already noticed that nagging your children to go play outside and warning them that their brains will turn to mush doesn't have the intended inspirational effect. When your kids are in the middle of blowing up enemy tanks or checking their likes on social media, they're generally not going to place a high value on your concerns about their cognitive and physical health.

We know some parents who take a very strict approach, even with their older children. They closely monitor every screen-related activity to make sure that screens are only used for homework during the week, and they allow a very short window of free (supervised) activity during the weekend. But this strategy can be problematic for many reasons:

- Older kids spend a lot of time outside of our supervision—at school, at after-school activities, and with friends—which makes inflexible rules difficult to enforce.
- We risk damaging our relationship with our kids if they feel that we're monitoring their every move, not trusting them to begin to navigate independently.
- Sometimes strict controls can backfire by creating an obsession with screen time, just as a child whose diet is closely controlled can become obsessed with the forbidden foods.
- Lack of access to screens can cut kids off from connecting with friends, and from the ability to pursue positive, healthy interests with the aid of the internet.
- Many children can outsmart their elders by circumventing screen controls and creating shadow accounts that their parents can't access.
- When we lay down the law and give ultimatums, we may effectively cut ourselves off from our kids' online

activities and lose our opportunity to influence or protect them.

If you want to have a better chance of helping your child learn to balance screen time with other activities, we suggest starting with something that may seem counterintuitive:

Join Them in Their World

It will be easier to influence your children if you have a strong connection with them. If you start with the premise that what they love to do is a waste of time, and the things they value are all wrong, you're going to have a hard time getting through to them. If you're open to learning about their interests, they'll be more open to considering your point of view.

Ask your young gamer about anti-tank strategies and sit down for a round of blasting. (If you can't abide blasting tanks . . . or zombies . . . or aliens, ask your child to find a game that will appeal to your more "delicate" sensibilities.) Inquire about the memes, picture-sharing websites, or video platforms that are entrancing your social media butterfly. Ask them to teach you how to navigate the latest creative platform they're using. Let them be the teacher and you can be the bumbling student. (Many of us won't have to work very hard to fulfill that role!) Don't just stand behind the screen talking to your kid from the other side. Get on the same side and experience what they're experiencing.

The young adults we've conferred with on this chapter asked us to caution parents to tread lightly here. You can't expect your kids to share posts with you that would cause them to lose the trust of their friends, or that may be innocent but embarrassing, or too hard to explain out of context. Let your kids choose which social media posts they want to share with you. Many of the games kids play are fast-paced and would be almost impossible to pick up quickly. Ask them which game you could play together, or even if you could just watch them play. Don't let "join them in their world" become "barge in on their world." In the same way that it would be intrusive to hang over our older kids and listen in on every real-life social interaction, we need to give them some privacy in their digital social life, barring any indication of serious trouble.

Tell them what they *can* do instead of what they *can't*

Telling a child to *stop* doing something is never going to be as well-received as offering them a chance to *start* doing something else. When we tell kids to stop spending so much time in front of the computer, the message is that something of value is being taken away. If we want kids to expand their repertoire, it will help to present it as an opportunity, not as a loss.

Think about how you would feel in a comparable situation. If your partner was trying to stop you from eating unhealthy food, which approach would make you feel more open to change? "Put down that candy bar immediately! It's going to elevate your blood sugar and cause early onset diabetes!" Or, "Hey I just made some really awesome granola with cashews and apricots. Do you wanna try it?"

Okay, okay, maybe you're not going for the granola. The real question is, how do you figure out what your kid would like to do?

Problem-Solve

As tempting as it is to lecture your children and criticize the way they choose to spend hours (and hours) of their time, you'll get a better response if you start by **acknowledging feelings**, specifically about how much they enjoy their chosen technological activity. Don't start with, "If you keep playing that game you're going to rot your brain, your bones will atrophy, and you'll turn into a slug." Do start by mentioning, for example, something you find intriguing about the multiplayer online game your kid is fascinated with, or how cool it is to share pictures with your friends and keep in contact when you can't see them in person.

Then you can **describe the problem**. You can let your child know you're concerned about the effects of lack of sleep or physical activity, or perhaps the depressing effect of an overdose of social media. Whatever your concern is, find a way to say it briefly and without any attacks on the child's character.

Give your child an opportunity to express his or her point of view. You might find out that he can't "just stop" playing a game when his parents think he's been on the computer for too long, because stopping in the middle of a match ruins the game for all the players and can even get him banned from playing in the future. You might learn that she has friends who get offended if their posts and texts aren't responded to for hours at a time. Listen and continue to acknowledge their perspective. ("Oh, so when I tell you to get off of the computer in the middle of a game, it's like asking you to walk out on your team and leave them one player short in the middle of a soccer match. That puts you in a pretty difficult position!")

You can **give information** by noting that even single-player games are specifically designed to be very difficult to stop. And not just games. The algorithms on other digital media are likewise cleverly designed to draw users to the next . . . and the next . . . and the next un-miss-able thing, so that it's hard to find an endpoint. Or you might share your concern that too much time on social media tends to make people feel inadequate, or left out, or not able to measure up to the images of other "perfect posters."

Then you can **ask for ideas**. Invite your young gamer or social media butterfly to brainstorm with you. What new thing *might* they be interested in trying? Maybe you have a child who's a whiz at online guitar games and is intrigued by the idea of taking actual guitar lessons. Or one who loves dance video games and would consider joining the dance club at school. Perhaps the two of you have an itch to take up running together and compete in the local 5K mud run for charity. Your local community center may offer a theater workshop, a LEGO robotics competition, a remote control airplane club, a rock climbing outing, or a class in photography or pottery. You might not need a formal organized activity. A cooking or carpentry project could provide inspiration. If you have an enterprising youngster, they might want to explore a money-making venture—dog walking, cat sitting, shoveling snow, raking leaves . . .

Consider offering the opportunity to take a class in coding or graphic design so that they can create their own games or websites. If they're going to be fascinated with computer games, then let them be learning and creating. Who knows, they may have a successful career ahead of them (plus, you will enjoy having an on-call technician who can fix your computer when it freezes or blue-screens or fails in all the other myriad ways that computers fail).

You can brainstorm together about how to carve out some screen-free times and places: at the dinner table, after lights out, during Grandma's birthday party. Another question you can tackle with your child is how much time per day is okay to spend sitting in front of a screen. What does your youngster feel he needs in order to get his schoolwork done and also have time for the fun stuff? What do *you* think is reasonable? Can the two of you find a compromise that would be acceptable to all? Who will be in charge of keeping track? How will that work?

We're not suggesting that you'll be able to come up with a strict schedule. Rather that you explore the issue with your child, raise awareness of the digital dilemma, and set goals together.

Sauce for the Goose

My twelve-year-old daughter was spending a *lot* of time on her phone, and especially on social media. My nagging had the effect of motivating her to shut herself in her room for hours at a time. I wasn't having any luck getting her to sit down and talk about it because she was always "busy." So instead I emailed her an article about the downsides of spending hours on social media, along with a note telling her I know it's important to her to use social media to stay in touch with friends, but that I was concerned about some of these negative effects.

The article mentioned a setting on the smartphone that keeps track of how much time you're using the phone, and how much time you're spending on social media. I asked her if she'd consider using that setting. She agreed to keep track, but only if I did it too.

We were both surprised by how often we check our phones. She was surprised by the number of minutes she spends on social media, and I was surprised by how much time I spend looking at the news. We decided to send ourselves alerts so we could cut down. This is having a beneficial effect on both of us, even though when I sent her that article I was not considering changing my own behavior.

The Tomato Solution

My fourteen-year-old son is very bright and he spends a lot of time on the computer. He has actually taught himself how to code and he's always got some complicated project he's working on. So I'm not worried about him rotting his brain! But I do worry about him getting enough exercise. He can spend an entire day in that chair staring at the screen, and it will not occur to him to move his body.

I did a problem-solving session with him. I started by telling him how much I admired the work he was doing, and how he was self-taught and self-motivated. Then I told him I was a little worried that it wasn't good for his body to spend so much time sitting without a break. I showed him a research study about the negative health effects of too much sedentary work and asked him if he could come up with a solution.

Well of course, he researched it on the internet. He found something called the Pomodoro Technique, which gives you intervals for how long to concentrate on a task, and how long to take a break for exercise. He follows his own schedule now, and I feel a lot less worried. I'm so pleased that he's managing it himself instead of me nagging him.

The Digital Dilemma (Part 2)

● ● ●

We apologize for any outdated references in this chapter. The technological landscape is changing so rapidly that by the time you're reading this on your tele-brain extension, you may be chuckling at the quaint references to "screens."

The rapid rate of change is part of what makes this topic so complex. We've only just scratched the surface by addressing time spent in front of screens and leaving all other issues of content, quality, and unforeseen circumstances (such as working from home during a pandemic) by the wayside. It would be easier if we had a formula to calculate how many minutes per day of screen time is appropriate for each stage of a child's development. Or if we could be confident that if we allow kids to self-regulate it will all turn out for the best. Unfortunately, there is no Recommended Daily Amount for screen time the way there is for vitamin C or sodium. Each family is left to figure out what they're comfortable with and what works best for them and for their children.

As a result of all this uncertainty, some of us tend to become alarmed and focus on control rather than communication, and others (sometimes the same people a little farther down the road) throw up their hands because they realize how difficult it is to exert control in this area.

Our intent is to remind you to focus on communication with your child! Treat your child the way you would want to be treated. We're all in this situation together, facing the same challenges that an increasingly digital world presents. It's normal to be struggling to create balance. If you and your child can get on the same team, you'll have a better chance at helping your kids develop skills that they will use as adults . . . and you'll protect your relationship in the process.

REMINDER: SCREENS AND OLDER CHILDREN

1. **Join them in their world.**

   "Can I play this game with you?"

2. **Tell them what they *can* do, instead of what they *can't*.**

   "How would you feel about guitar lessons/taking a dance class/joining the LEGO robotics team/learning to crochet/baking bread from scratch?"

3. **Try problem-solving.**

   "I'm worried it isn't good for your body to spend so much time sitting without a break. Can you come up with a solution?"

18

Does Punishment Prepare Kids for "Real Life"?

Dear J&J,

I've found a lot of your ideas useful, but I can't stomach the idea of no punishment and no consequences. It's just too permissive! How will children learn that their actions have consequences if parents don't punish bad behavior? All they'll learn is that they can get away with anything! How will they function in the real world? They're going to go into shock when they get a ticket for speeding, or fired for coming in late to work!

—Not Drinking the Kool-Aid

Dear Not Drinking,

The idea of raising kids without *giving them consequences* for misbehavior might sound extreme . . . maybe even a little crazy. Kids need to learn to follow rules: at home, in school, on the road, at work. And they need to learn that something happens if they *don't* follow the rules. We agree with you that children who are regularly protected from the natural consequences of their actions will probably have trouble learning to be responsible for their own behavior.

The problem is, when adults think in terms of *giving consequences*, in most cases what they're really doing is trying to come up with a punishment—something just unpleasant enough to motivate a child to change his behavior. These kinds of consequences are actually punishments with a different label.

To briefly review the case against punishment, studies confirm what many parents and teachers learn through experience: punishment is an imperfect tool for many reasons. It fails to address the reason for the misbehavior. It typically leaves kids feeling resentful toward the adult who punished them, or plotting how to avoid getting caught next time. It encourages children to think selfishly—to focus on the repercussions to themselves rather than on fixing the problem or making amends. And kids who are punished are less likely to be able to resolve problems peacefully when they have conflicts with their peers or siblings. The strange, counterintuitive truth is that children learn to regulate their behavior better when we take punishment out of the equation.*

But what if you've tried acknowledging the child's feelings, expressed your own feelings strongly, given the child an opportunity to make amends, tried problem-solving . . . and your child keeps doing that thing you don't want her to do?

Let's think about how we approach conflict with a fellow adult. We usually don't direct our energy toward dreaming up a "consequence." At least not if we value the relationship. We may find it necessary to **take action to protect people or property**. But we try to do it in a respectful way so that the other person will understand our limits without feeling attacked. Here are a few examples to give you a feel for the difference between giving a consequence and taking action without insult.

Giving this "consequence" would probably end a friendship:

> "I can't believe you're asking to borrow money again. You never paid me back the last time! In fact, I should give you a consequence for that. Consider yourself disinvited

---

* For a review of the powerful tools that effectively motivate children to change their behavior and do better in the future, see pages 77–82.

from my end-of-the-summer barbecue. You don't deserve
to go to a party!"

Whereas taking this action would protect your bank account from
future losses and likely preserve the relationship:

> "I don't feel comfortable lending money anymore. I
> don't like having to ask for it back, and I don't want
> it to interfere with our friendship."

A store manager who dreamed up this consequence for customers
would probably lose your business:

> "NOTICE: Shoppers who fail to bring reusable gro-
> cery bags are harming the environment and will
> have their names and photos posted on our Wall
> of Shame!"

Whereas a manager who took this action would preserve the
goodwill of customers while achieving the same ecological
results:

> "NOTICE: We have a new policy to protect the
> environment. We're no longer providing single-use
> plastic bags. You can bring your own reusable bags
> or purchase them here."

This couple may soon be googling divorce lawyers:

> "You're an hour late *again*! You promised to come
> home early to watch the kids so I could get my
> presentation done for tomorrow."

"Whoops, sorry, I lost track of time. And then there was traffic . . ."

"You deserve a consequence for breaking your word. You can forget about going to the game with your pals this weekend. I'm selling your tickets on eBay."

While this couple has a future:

"I'm frustrated! I was expecting you home early to watch the kids so I could get my presentation done for tomorrow."

"Whoops, sorry, I lost track of time. And then there was traffic . . ."

"I can't help out with dinner or the kids' bedtime routine tonight. I need to hole up in my room and finish my work."

When we experience someone's actions as a natural result of our behavior, without the punitive intent that accompanies "giving a consequence," we're more likely to be motivated to change our behavior or make amends because our thinking isn't clouded by anger and resentment.

So how might this sound when we're dealing with children? Here are a few "punishable offenses" to give you a feel for the difference between "giving consequences" and taking action without insult to protect people and property.

Running in the street:

Instead of: "You're a bad boy. Now you've lost the privilege of playing outside."

Take action without insult to protect the child:
"I'm bringing you inside. I can't let children run in the street. I'm too worried about speeding cars."

Leaving a mess:

Instead of: "You can forget about going to the mall with your friends this afternoon. I warned you about cleaning up your mess in the kitchen, and all you did was play video games. You have only yourself to blame."

Take action without insult to protect yourself:
"I'll take you to the mall as soon as the mess in the kitchen is cleaned up. I need the counters cleared before I start dinner, and I'll feel resentful if I get stuck doing it myself."

Too rough with your belongings:

Instead of: "I can't believe you dropped my cell phone after you promised you'd be careful! That's it! You are not touching the phone again. I obviously can't trust you not to run around with it."

Take action without insult to protect property:
"I'm taking back my phone for now. I don't want to risk it getting dropped on the floor and broken."

As you may have noticed, we're not suggesting a permissive approach. Kids are not running wild in the streets dodging vehicles; parents are not mired in servitude to their spoiled offspring; the child doesn't always get what he or she wants at the expense of the parent.

We have our limits. We have to let our children know what those limits are. But it matters what children hear when we set those limits. If they hear, "*You're* getting a consequence..." they're going to feel rebellious. If they hear, "*I've* reached my limit...!" they may not be happy, but they're more likely to reflect and learn from the experience.

But What Happens When Your Kid Grows Up And Finds Out The World Hasn't Read This Book?

What happens when this precious, sheltered child, who's never been punished, is old enough to drive and goes racing down the interstate at 90 mph? The traffic cop isn't going to problem-solve with your little darling.

Children don't need to be punished at home to understand that their actions have consequences in the "real world." In this particular case, the important question is: How can we ensure that our children drive in a way that doesn't endanger themselves or others?

Punishment does not teach this lesson. Studies suggest that while the consequence of a traffic fine helps fund local governments, it doesn't actually encourage a change of behavior. Many drivers who receive speeding tickets are not deterred from repeating the offense. In fact, while they will certainly slow down in the presence of a police officer, they're more than twice as likely as other drivers to receive another speeding ticket in the following months.[1]

As parents, we're not looking to achieve the effect of having our kids behave only when they're in danger of getting caught. What's more, we don't want our kids to fear and avoid us the way most drivers fear and avoid traffic cops. That's not the relationship we're looking for!

If your teenager drives dangerously, you wouldn't depend on a traffic fine to change his behavior. You'd take action by confiscating the car keys. You'd make it clear to him that you aren't doing it to punish him, but rather to protect him, and to protect other drivers sharing the same road. You'd **acknowledge his feelings** and **express your own feelings strongly:**

> "I can see how tempting it is to drive fast and enjoy the power of speed! I can't let you use the car until we figure out a way for you to drive safely. I would never forgive myself if you got hurt . . . or if you hurt someone else."

Then you'd follow up by **problem-solving** until the two of you came up with a plan that you were both comfortable with.

But how about when your coddled kid gets a job and comes in late every day? Won't he be shocked when the boss fires him instead of "problem-solving"?

A person who expects to be punished for misbehavior learns to look for ways to avoid punishment. When faced with the threat of being fired for arriving late, he may look for ways to sneak in without being noticed. Or perhaps he'll focus on polishing up his excuses—his car wouldn't start, the bus got stuck in traffic, he can't walk fast enough because his shoes are pinching his toes.

On the other hand, a person who's been raised to solve problems will look for ways to meet both the employer's needs and his own. Perhaps he'll rig a more effective alarm clock—one that buzzes, flashes, and vibrates while spraying water on his head.

But what if his invention still fails to rouse him from the depths of slumber, and he is late once again? The boss will fire him—not to punish him, but in order to take action to protect the business. This young ex-employee, who has been raised by adults who take action, won't be shocked and disoriented by this outcome. On the contrary, he'll be able to reflect on the fact that he needs to make more of an effort to get to work on time in his next job, because he's learned that employers have their limits and won't tolerate lateness.

But I Was Punished And I Turned Out Just Fine!

Wait! Are you suggesting that kids who are punished will be messed up for life? My parents punished me, and I turned out okay.

We don't doubt that you are an upstanding citizen, a kind person, and a devoted parent!

But it may be that you turned out fine *in spite of* being punished, rather than because of it. If you grew up in the era before car seats and airbags, your survival cannot be credited to a childhood spent bouncing around untethered in a fast-moving vehicle. You just got lucky. Every long-term scientific study suggests that the more often and more harshly children are punished, the more likely they are to have a host of problems.[2]

It's very possible that you turned out well because of other things your parents did, when they *weren't* punishing you. Perhaps they also provided a home where much of the time you felt safe and secure; they listened when you needed a sympathetic ear;

they talked to you when you needed help figuring out what to do in a sticky situation; they modeled caring behavior, encouraged your developing autonomy, and provided moral guidance with love and respect.

Or perhaps you grew up in a chaotic home, but you have a remarkably resilient disposition, and you had at least one person—a teacher, an elderly aunt, a coach—who gave you support and encouragement at the moment you really needed it.

We're not predicting doomsday if you've been using punishment as part of your disciplinary strategy. It's just that there are better strategies available, and it makes sense to try them! If our larger goal is to teach children how to treat others respectfully, abide by rules, fix problems in the present, and avoid them in the future, punishment is not our best tool.

Putting Theory Into Practice With A Preschooler

Annette, a mom in one of our parenting workshops, had a beautiful home and a very destructive three-year-old. Despite numerous punishments, including time-outs and loss of TV privileges, Ivan continued to use black marker on the elegant white couches, scissors on the pillows, and crayons on the walls.

After the session on alternatives to punishment, Annette tried a new approach. She said, "Ivan, I'm very upset that the fringes on this rug were cut! I got this little rug from my grandmother. It means a lot to me. I expect you to fix it." She got out a ruler and held it against the fringes. "This has to be cut very carefully to even it out."

Ivan said, "I'm sorry, Mommy" (he had never before apologized when scolded) and carefully evened out the fringes with the scissors. Then she talked to him about his artwork. "You like making art. And I don't like drawing on the furniture. We need ideas." They decided to create an art box with special supplies just for Ivan to draw with, paint on, and cut.

The next day, Ivan spilled water on the tablecloth. He ran to his mom and said, "There's water on the tablecloth. What should we do to fix it?"

Since the rug incident there have been no more "art attacks" on the house, and more important, there is a new feeling of co-operation instead of opposition between Ivan and his mom.

Putting Theory Into Practice With A Teenager

But what about when kids get older? Don't they need punishment then?

A high school biology teacher reported that he had a student who was constantly disrupting the class. Marco had an inexhaustible supply of energy. As soon as the teen arrived in the classroom, complaints to the teacher would follow in his wake. "Marco touched me . . . tripped me . . . grabbed my pen . . . threw my notebook . . . won't stop humming . . ."

Marco had been thrown out of class again and again. He'd been lectured, sent to the principal, even suspended. Everything had been tried. Every punishment, that is. But none of those punishments made Marco more cooperative.

Finally the teacher decided to try something different. He invited Marco to sit down with him at the end of the day. He started the conversation by trying to see the conflict from Marco's point of view. "I notice you have a lot of energy. You like to move around during class. Sitting still is not for you!" Marco responded enthusiastically. His sullen, sneaky expression evaporated. He told the teacher he didn't care about biology. He wanted to be a welder. The teacher offered to give Marco a few soldering lessons after school to get him started, and to inquire for him about welding programs. He asked Marco to help come up with ideas for what to do with his energy that would not disrupt the class. Marco offered that he could do jumping jacks when he felt like he couldn't sit still. The teacher agreed, as long as he did it in the back of the room.

After this talk the classroom atmosphere improved immensely. No longer was Marco disturbing other students during lessons. Marco and his teacher started a soldering project—connecting copper pipes to create a bugle. The relationship between teacher and student was transformed. Instead of looking to goad the teacher, Marco now sought to impress this man who cared about him and respected his ideas.

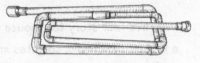

● ● ●

A child doesn't need to be punished at home or at school in order to learn to avoid punishment in the rest of the world.

Children will experience pain of all sorts in the "real world." We don't need to subject them to all sorts of pain just so they are prepared. We don't deliberately scrape their knees to prepare them for the inevitable scrapes at the playground. We don't bully them to prepare them for the taunts of their classmates or coworkers.

Perhaps you're still thinking, "But sometimes in the real world, misbehavior *does* result in punishment." You're right! But that doesn't mean it works. We know that adults who are punished, by fines or imprisonment, tend to be recidivists.[3]

The reality is that punishment teaches the wrong lessons. What's more, it's not even an effective deterrent, so why bring it into our homes and schools?

When we take action to protect people and property and then encourage children to make amends and problem-solve, we are truly modeling the attitude we want our kids to take toward conflict in their lives. Not, "Who should be punished, and what should the punishment be?" Not, "How can I get away with breaking the rules?" But rather, "How can I fix my mistake?" "What should I do differently next time?"

Teaching children how to make amends and solve problems will help them behave better in the present and become grown-ups who know how to resolve conflicts peacefully in the future.

Gatekeepers

I live in a four story townhouse with steep wooden staircases. I have a fifteen-month-old, so gates are a very important safety tool! The trouble is that my older kids, ages four and five, can open the gates and freely navigate the steps. We've had more than one scary moment where I didn't realize that one of the kids left the gate open, and Baby made a beeline for the stairs.

In the past I've scolded, "You left the gate open!" and lectured in a frustrated tone about "what could have happened!" My lectures have way too many words for a four-year-old. They make her feel like a failure and a bad big sister, but she doesn't "learn her lesson." She always does it again.

I was determined to try to handle it differently because I know that four-year-olds are forgetful and to expect her to be totally reliable here isn't even developmentally appropriate.

Of course, the next time it happened I forgot my plan and yelled, "You left the gate open!" Then I saw the look of sadness on her face and caught myself. So instead of following up with the usual lecture, I said, "Hmmm. It's so important for us to close these gates so the baby doesn't get hurt. But it's hard to remember all the time. We need ideas!"

Her five-year-old brother ran over, and before I knew it the two of them were smiling and making signs out of construction paper to hang on every gate. Big brother wrote, "Close me!" They got a kick out of imagining the gate as a living thing wanting to be closed. Little sister drew smiley faces so it would be a "friendly reminder." They scurried around taping them to all the gates. I almost can't believe it, but nobody has forgotten to shut a gate in the two weeks since!

Section VI

Bedtime & Bathroom Battles

19

Toothbrushing

The Most Terrible Torture

What is it with kids and brushing teeth? The way some kids fuss, you'd think we were trying to pull the teeth out instead of trying to clean them. For some folks, it's a wrestling match every night. Short of giving up altogether (and if you've done that, you're not alone), what's a parent to do?

Let's look at this ritual from a kid's perspective first. Brushing teeth can involve so many potentially unpleasant sensations. The taste of the toothpaste, the feeling of the brush scraping on teeth, the feeling of gagging when the brush gets too close to the throat. Even just having to sit with your head back and your mouth open can be very uncomfortable. Not to mention that you have to stop whatever fun thing you're doing in order to start this torture.

And the payoff is pretty dubious for a kid. All you really get is a lack of negative outcome. If you brush your teeth every day, you might not have a cavity at some distant point in the future.

With such a miserable activity, we're more likely to have success if we add some silliness.

Here are the results of a brainstorm from one of our parenting groups on how to **be playful** when it's toothbrushing time:

Ease transitions by bringing the play into the bathroom: "Let's give your teddy bear a ride to the bathroom so he can watch you brush your teeth . . . Come on, Bear—do you want Jake to brush your teeth, too?"

Pretend to discover interesting stuff in her teeth. "Oh, here's a corn flake from breakfast . . . and here's a little bit of blueberry from snack time. Gee, I don't remember serving red crayon for dinner . . . and here's that tennis ball you were looking for."

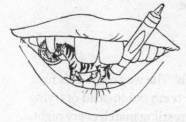

Pretend the animals from the zoo are on the loose, and no one can find them. Do a thorough search, with the toothbrush. "Oh, look, I think I found the kangaroo! No, no, wait, it's not a kangaroo, it's a hippopotamus! Oh my goodness, there's Grandma Molly next to some penguins! Would you like a little brushing up, Granny?"

Make the toothbrush talk:

Army officer voice: "TEN HUT! Teeth, forward march, present for inspection!"
Robot voice: "Must - clean - in-ci-sor - beep!"
Mouse voice: "Whatcha got hiding behind that tooth? Ooh a tasty bit of peanut butter. Yum!"

Pretend you're a wacky dentist and your child has come to your office for a visit. Ask him to knock on the door. Say, "Welcome to my special dental chair" (toilet, with seat cover down). Act like you're confused about how to use the toothbrush: "Oh my, what's this thing for? Does it go in your ear? Wait, which end do I put the toothpaste on?"

Make it a race. Set a timer for two minutes: "Ready . . . set . . . go! Here we are at the first tooth. Okay, that one's scrubbed. On to the second, and the third. This one's a doozy. Lots of granola stuck in there. The clock is ticking. Will the green toothbrush make it to the lower level before the time runs out?"

Play is a very good start, but we may want to grab some other tools as well. Take a look at the reminder page at the end of the chapter to see more ideas our group came up with.

Stories from the Front Lines

Thumbs Up

I'm ashamed to admit that I haven't brushed Anton's teeth in a long time. I tried brute force but I don't have enough hands. I'd need two to hold him down, one to pry his mouth open, and another to brush his teeth while he screams.

I already tried putting the child in charge by taking him on a shopping trip so he could pick out three different flavors of toothpaste. That was a failure. He hated all of them. It turns out, it's common for kids on the spectrum to be sensitive to strong tastes, which is probably the main reason he hates brushing so much. I called the dentist to ask for advice. He told me that toothpaste is not that important; he can brush with plain water. What a relief!

After the workshop, I had a talk with Anton. I started by acknowledging his feelings. "You really don't like having your teeth brushed."

He said the toothpaste was disgusting, and he felt like choking when I stuck the toothbrush in the back of his mouth. I told him that sounded pretty awful. Then I said, "Guess what? I just talked to the dentist and he said you can brush with NO TOOTHPASTE!" and I stuck the toothpaste in the cabinet and slammed the door on it. I could tell Anton was pretty pleased with that.

I was on a roll so I went on to the next issue. "But we still need a signal so when you feel like you're choking I'll know to stop. Do you want to squeeze my hand, or put up your thumb?" He chose the thumb.

For the next part you need to know that we have a cleaning woman named Philomena. I asked him if he wanted "Philoteetha" to clean upstairs first, or downstairs first. He chose "upstairs" and I carefully brushed his top teeth. He gave me the thumb signal once. I stopped and waited till he put his thumb back down, then I did the bottom teeth. Then I yelled, "We did it! You are a boy with clean teeth!" It was a triumph.

Talkative Toothbrush

Last night I really didn't have the energy to be playful, but I knew it was my last chance to do my workshop assignment, and Aliya still hadn't brushed her teeth. So I half-heartedly told her, "Listen, I hear something." Then I covered my mouth, and in a funny voice I pretended to be her toothbrush calling, "Aliya, I miss you! I miss your teeth!"

She laughed and went straight to the bathroom, so I picked up the toothbrush and made it talk to Aliya: "Hi! I'm so glad you're here! Can I see what you brought for me to snack on tonight?"

She said "Sure!" and opened her mouth up really wide.

I started brushing her teeth saying, "Oh look, you saved me a piece of toast from breakfast. Delicious—thank you! Oh boy, here's a piece of apple. What else did you bring me?"

She said, "Look for the chicken!" and then opened her mouth again. She loved it! I have to admit, this was less exhausting than the usual battle.

KNOCK KNOCK. CAN I COME IN?

Toothbrushing School for Dolls

Yesterday Riley didn't want to brush her teeth. Usually I say, "I'm sorry, but you *have* to brush your teeth." It's always a battle.

This time I said, "Let's teach your doll how to brush her teeth." She said, "Let's teach two!" and then she brought in *three* dolls. We had a little workshop. First we demonstrated to the dolls how it's done by brushing Riley's teeth. Then she put the first doll on the stool and said, "Open your mouth really wide."

She brushed her dolls' teeth (without toothpaste) while I busied myself cleaning up the bathroom and occasionally made admiring comments about how well the dolls were cooperating with her.

REMINDER: TOOTHBRUSHING

1. Acknowledge feelings.

"You're not in the mood to brush your teeth."

"It's annoying to have to hold your mouth open to get your teeth cleaned."

2. Give wishes in fantasy.

"It would be nice if you could take your teeth out at night, and we could clean them in the dishwasher. You could just pop them back in when you wake up in the morning."

"I wish we could be like sharks. They don't need to brush their teeth, they just keep growing new ones."

3. Be playful!

"Look what I found in your teeth—the mitten you lost last winter."

"What do we have to brush—your elbow?"

4. Put the child in charge.

Play "Stop and Go": Child has a special signal to use when she needs a break—a finger pointing up, or squeezing your arm.

Give her a turn. Let the child go first, and then a parent goes in for the final "spiffing up."

5. Offer a choice.

"Which toothpaste would you like to use tonight—the mint or the strawberry?"

"Do you want to brush your teeth in the kitchen sink or the bathroom?"

"Do you want to sit on the toilet or stand at the sink while we brush?"

6. **Give information.**

Use disclosing tablets* to show your child which teeth need more brushing.

Have the dentist explain to your child why brushing is important. (Kids are more likely to pay attention to information from anyone who is not their own parent!)

7. **Write a note.**

"You're invited to a toothbrushing party after dinner. Love, Your Toothbrush"

"Tonight's agenda:
1. Eat dinner.
2. Brush teeth.
3. PJs.
4. Read dog book."

8. **Adjust expectations: manage the environment instead of the child.**

Some children don't like the sensation of using a manual toothbrush and do better with an electric toothbrush.

---

* Disclosing tablets produce a pink dye that reacts with plaque so children can see which teeth aren't clean yet. We are told that they can also stain bathroom surfaces, so consider yourself forewarned!

Flood Evacuation—A Bath Time Tale from India

My boys, ages seven and five, had just returned sweaty and tired from outdoor play and needed a shower. A couple of gentle reminders didn't help.

A quirky idea popped into my head and I announced in an official voice that there was a flood in the bathroom and that ducky, froggy, and turtle need to be rescued. And we need brave rescue workers to help.

My boys ran into the bathroom, showered themselves and their bath toys, and came out. I gave them each a badge (those received as party favours from endless birthday parties they get invited to) to honour their efforts.

They love this pretend play and I've used it many times since then.

Three Special Steps—A Bedtime Battle

Last night my kid was having an epic bedtime tantrum. He was in and out of bed and crying. I was just trying to get him to put. his. freaking. head. on. the. pillow. Finally, instead of negotiating, asking, threatening, etc., I remembered how he loves this show where they break everything down into "Three Special Steps." So I said, "Okay. There are three special steps for going to sleep. Step One: Put your head on the pillow. Step two: Pull up the covers. What's step three? Take a spaceship to the moon?" He immediately got under the covers with his head on the pillow and started giggling. It was like a switch had flipped. We spent a minute or two talking about ridiculous suggestions for what Step Three could be: eating breakfast, walking on the ceiling, going to the library, etc., and then he calmly settled down for bed. MAGIC! Or no, just being playful.

Hungry Hairbrush in Slovenia

I had a big problem with my three-year-old daughter, Ana Klara. Doing her hair was a nightmare because she has knotty hair and the whole thing was screaming and crying. I was already exhausted even before I picked up the hair-brush because I knew what would follow. But then, out of the blue I had an idea. I took the brush and played silly. The brush claimed to be hungry and in order to fill her tummy she had to eat hair knots. While brushing the hair, I was doing "Mnom, mnom, mnom . . . how many tasty knots, but I am still very hungry, I want more!" Since that day brushing her hair in the morning became a funny game. Now that she is almost six we don't do that anymore, but from time to time she still says, "Mum, do the hungry hairbrush!" :-)

20

Potty Power Struggles

Dear J&J,

My five-year-old daughter, Molly, is the oldest of three children. Ever since she's been toilet trained, she's had problems with pooping in her pants. We've ruled out all medical issues (after a full year of testing). It's obvious that when she's motivated to go, she can. However, there is little that will consistently motivate her. She reverts to her standard method, which is to crouch down and do the deed while denying that she needs to go to the bathroom.

I've tried everything! Natural consequences (after pooping I tell her we can't go to the park because you need to bathe instead, and then I put her in PJs). Telling her she smells bad. Not giving her positive attention after she poops in her pants (I make her go clean up the mess and take a bath by herself. She cries for me to come in). A reward chart with stickers (that worked for two days). Not scolding her for two weeks straight (it didn't help).

I try to be patient with her, but by the third or fourth (or fifth!) time in a day, I just lose it. The situation stinks (excuse the pun) and is embarrassing when it happens in public places, and costly because sometimes I have to throw the underwear in the trash because the stains won't come out.

Please help!

—Mom of a Pooper

Dear MOAP,

What a frustrating situation! It sounds like both of you are feeling bad.

Let's start by changing the mood. Most five-year-olds respond well to a playful attitude, and as you've noticed they can shut down when they're subjected to our strong disapproval.

Next time she poops in her underwear, try telling her, "That poop is very sneaky! Even though we want it to go in the toilet, it sneaks out and ends up in your underwear."

If she's sitting on the toilet with no success, you can sympathize, "Oh, that stubborn poop doesn't want to come out!"

When she does get it in the toilet, even just a little bit, that should be cause for celebration, dancing, and singing. "Oh the poop is in the toilet, yes indeed! Hurray, hurray, it's a poopiful day!" (Feel free to substitute your own lyrics.) Don't tell her she's a "good girl," which implies that if she has an accident she's a "bad girl." Instead describe her accomplishment, with pleasure. "You did it! You got the sneaky poop to go in the toilet!"

For now, suspend all attempts to get her to clean herself up, and don't withdraw your attention or give her any consequences for mistakes. In fact, it will be helpful if you can go out of your way to find opportunities to give her positive attention. Do what you can to strengthen her sense of connection to you—read stories, play games that she likes, cuddle. You'll be satisfying a basic need and mending some of the bad feelings that have come up around this issue. It's going to be hard not to show your annoyance, but keep in mind that the old methods aren't working, and tell yourself you're just going to try this new approach for a week.

You might also want to try problem-solving, but that should come after this week of your new role as poop whisperer. Let's start by taking away the sting of disapproval and shame.

Good luck and please let us know how it all "comes out"!

—J&J

Dear J&J,

It's been a few weeks since I started the new approach, and I'm excited to report that we've had tremendous improvement in the poop department. At first, Molly was still mostly pooping in her underpants, but she seemed very happy to have me help her clean up, and she laughed when I told her about the "sneaky poop." The couple of times she got a tiny bit of poop in the toilet we had a grand celebration in the bathroom (singing and dancing).

We did try problem-solving, and she came up with a few ideas:

- Molly will sit on the toilet while Mom counts to ten.
- Molly will sit on the toilet for ten minutes to try to get the poop in the toilet.
- We got a higher step stool for the toilet because she said that it "hurt" to sit up there with her legs hanging down.
- If Mommy suspects the poop is trying to come out, she'll say the code word: "SNEAKY!"

The first two ideas didn't really work, but I think she liked problem-solving because she got to spend the time with me. A couple of times I saw her crouch and said "SNEAKY!" and she ran to the toilet. The first time she just pooped a tiny bit. We celebrated. She got off the toilet, and a few minutes later, said, "I think the poop is trying to sneak out again!" and she climbed back on the toilet. She made a big poop! She was very proud of herself!

Since then she's been going without any reminders, but she still runs to tell me and I make a big deal about it every time.

Then last week she came home from school with diarrhea! I was worried that all our progress would be lost. I told her, "Diarrhea is even sneakier than regular poop. It's VERY hard to get in the toilet. If you feel like it wants to come out, you have to run *fast* to the toilet." I was doubtful, but she actually managed to get to the toilet several times that afternoon and had NO ACCIDENTS! Turns out the diarrhea gave her advanced-level practice.

Molly has always been very sensitive to my moods. On the mornings when she pooped in her pants and I got mad at her, she'd have a bad day at school. The teachers were concerned because she was refusing to finish her work and seemed shut down. The principal had asked me to come in for a meeting with the staff. But since this progress with the toilet training, Molly is doing much better. She is doing her work and seems much happier at school and at home.

In fact, just yesterday I was feeling really burnt out and I let my temper show. I was overtired and the kids were being really loud and messy all day. In the past, Molly used to get very upset and melt down whenever I showed my irritation, but this time she took it in stride and was able to listen to me, help me clean up, and still be cheerful afterward.

My guess is that she has more reserves from all that positive attention I've been showing her.

REMINDER: POTTY POWER STRUGGLES

1. **Be playful.**

   "That poop is very sneaky!"

   Talk to inanimate objects.

   "Hey Poop, you're supposed to go in the toilet, not Molly's underwear!"

   Sing a silly song.

   "Hurray, hurray, it's a poopiful day!"

2. **Describe what you see.**

   "You did it! You got the sneaky poop to go in the toilet!"

3. **Take time to reconnect.**

   Read, play, draw, cuddle, wrestle, dance, sing . . .

4. **Try problem-solving.**

   "It's not easy to get poop in the toilet. We need ideas!"

Potato Head Needs to Pee

We were visiting a friend's house, and Kacey, age two, was crossing her legs and wiggling, clearly needing to pee, but refusing to go to the bathroom. I was very worried that she'd pee on the carpet at my friend's house! But I couldn't convince her to go to the bathroom. She was playing with Mr. Potato Head. I told her, "I think Mr. Potato Head needs to go to the bathroom." She took Mr. PH to the bathroom. She was wiggling and wiggling, and then pulled down her pants and peed in the toilet!

Playing Your Cards Right—Four-Minute Bedtime Routine

The bedtime routine with Simon, age two and a half, has been dragging out longer and longer. I'm short on patience by that time of the night. I'm writing to share my success with being playful.

I made a getting-ready-for-bed game, complete with laminated pieces with Velcro on the back. I had my dad, who is an artist, do the illustrations: bath, PJs, brush teeth, potty, find favorite stuffed animal, read books.

We start with the pictures in a pile like this:

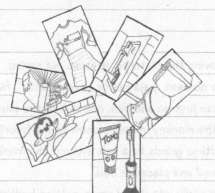

Simon gets to determine the order of events, so long as it all gets done. He puts one picture on the board at a time, after he's completed each task.

Once the pictures are stuck on the board, it looks like this:

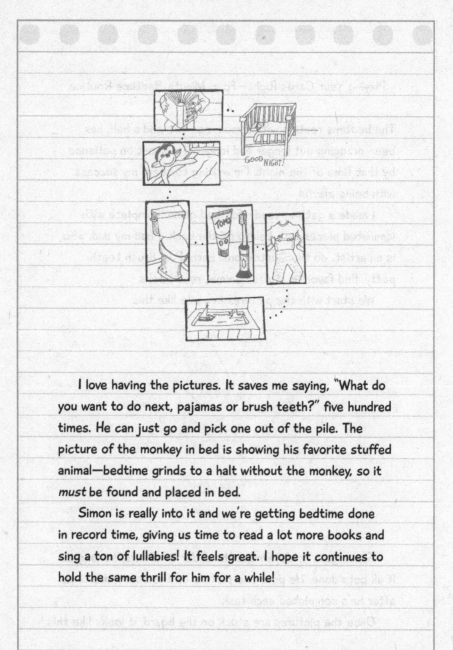

I love having the pictures. It saves me saying, "What do you want to do next, pajamas or brush teeth?" five hundred times. He can just go and pick one out of the pile. The picture of the monkey in bed is showing his favorite stuffed animal—bedtime grinds to a halt without the monkey, so it *must* be found and placed in bed.

Simon is really into it and we're getting bedtime done in record time, giving us time to read a lot more books and sing a ton of lullabies! It feels great. I hope it continues to hold the same thrill for him for a while!

Section VII

Touchy Topics

21

Divorce

Helping Children Cope with Change and Loss

Nobody going through a divorce needs to be reminded that it can be immensely stressful for everyone in the family. Kids will probably regress or act out in all kinds of ways, and parents, who are experiencing their own pain and loss, may not be in the best shape to provide patient, loving support. So consider the following advice aspirational! If you are in "no mood" then go easy on yourself and try again later.

In rough times, it can be helpful to review a few of the basic skills that tend to be the first to fly out the door (in the whoosh of air as you slam it behind your ex).

Your main goal is to resist the powerful impulse to minimize or dismiss your child's feeling of loss. We desperately want to explain to our children why this overturning of their known world is "not so bad." Our kids just as desperately need to have their feelings heard. *It will actually be more comforting to your child if you can bring yourself to accept the hard feelings.*

Acknowledging Feelings

Let's take a look at some of the common conversations about divorce that parents have with children and compare what we want to say with what is helpful for kids to hear.

1. Parent: Daddy and I are going to live in separate houses from now on. We'll take turns taking care of you.

Child (starts to cry): I don't want to go to a different house!

Instead of:

> "I know, honey, but this really will be better. Come on, you don't like it when Mommy and Daddy fight, right? Everyone's going to be so much happier this way. It'll be fine, you'll see. I'll let you decorate your new room however you want."

Acknowledge feelings:

> "You really don't like the idea of moving."

> "You'll miss this house."

> "It can make a person feel really sad to move."

Give in fantasy what you cannot give in reality:

> "You don't like having your parents live in different houses. You wish it could go back to the way it was."

> "You wish we could stay all together in this house and never move."

"Wouldn't it be cool if you could just push a button and be in Daddy's house, and then push a button and be in this house, so you could go back and forth whenever you wanted?"

Acknowledge feelings with art:

"We both feel sad. I'm going to draw a picture of how sad I feel. Do you want to make one too?"

"Even though I'll see you on weekends, it will be sad not to see each other every day. I'm going to give you a photo of me, and I'll put your photo near my bed."

2. The day of the move is fast approaching. You take your child to see the new house and visit her new school. She starts to cry and says, "I don't want to go to a new school. I like my old school."

Instead of:

"Oh honey, this new school is great. The teacher is so nice. I'm sure you'll make lots of new friends. Don't you think the playground looks like fun?"

Acknowledge feelings:

"This is hard, thinking about going to a new school, with a new teacher and new students. It doesn't feel comfortable and familiar like your old school. You miss your teacher and your friends."

Give in fantasy what you cannot give in reality:

"I wish we could bring them with us!"

3. You and your ex are now living apart and sharing custody, and it's time for you to bring your child to your house.

Child: I don't *like* your house. I'm not going.

Instead of:

> "Yes you do *so* like it. Remember how much you cried when Mommy picked you up on Sunday? She had a hard time dragging you out of there."

Acknowledge feelings:

> "It's hard to have to pack up and move."

> "You're not in the mood to change houses again. You like to stay in the same place for a while, not change every week."

Give in fantasy what you cannot give in reality:

> "It would be nice if Mommy and I lived right next door to each other, so you could run back and forth whenever you wanted."

> "I wish I had a magic wand so I could go *ZOOP* and make a double of everything you have, so you'd never have to pack."

4. Your child complains, "But Daddy lets me eat candy before dinner!"

Instead of:

> "Well Daddy doesn't seem to care if your teeth rot. And I guess he's not planning to help out with the dental bills either. You know what, I don't want to hear what Daddy does or does not let you do. When you're in my house, you live by my rules. End of story!"

Acknowledge feelings:

"It's hard to live in two homes with two different sets of rules. It doesn't seem fair to you."

Give in fantasy what you cannot give in reality:

"It would be nice if candy was really good for you, and your mom always said, 'Don't forget to eat your candy so your teeth stay strong!'"

Try Problem-Solving

This may not be the end of the discussion. You might find yourself problem-solving about what times of day are acceptable to both of you for eating sweets, and what kinds of foods you can shop for together that would satisfy both a child with a hankering for a treat, and a parent who is trying to provide a nutritious diet.

We're not suggesting you need to change your rules or compromise your values because your ex has a different lifestyle. There are likely many issues on which you and your ex come down differently: bedtimes, homework routines, chores, screen time, to list a few popular battlegrounds. The key will be to accept your child's feelings and then help them manage the challenge of adjusting to two different sets of rules. If you can involve a child in finding acceptable alternatives, it will be easier for them to accept your limits.

Here's an example of how problem-solving might play out in a conflict about watching television during dinner:

If your child complains, "Why do I have to sit at the table? Mommy lets me watch TV when I eat dinner."

Resist saying, "Listen kid, my house my rules!"

Instead start by acknowledging feelings:

"It doesn't seem fair to you to have different rules in different houses . . . You like eating while you watch TV . . .

It's frustrating/disappointing/makes you mad . . . You enjoy eating and watching at the same time." (Allow time for your child to respond and elaborate on the unfairness of it all!)

Then **describe your own feelings:**

"The problem is, I don't like crumbs and spills on the sofa and the carpet. I don't even like having to worry about it. Also, I really like to eat at the table and have a chance to talk to you, since I don't get to see you the rest of the week."

Brainstorm for a mutually agreeable solution:

"I wonder if we can find a solution that will work for both of us. I don't want dinner in front of the TV, but how about we pick a snack that has no crumbs and watch a show together after dinner? Do you want to make a list of foods that would be good for TV watching?"

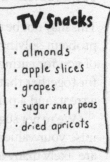

TV Snacks
- almonds
- apple slices
- grapes
- sugar snap peas
- dried apricots

After a discussion like this, we're betting that a child will feel much happier and chattier at the dinner table. Maybe the two of you will have a pleasant mealtime conversation discussing the best snacks to eat while watching *SpongeBob*. Problem-solving can become a way to connect, or reconnect, with your child.

Engaging Cooperation

When you're in the middle of a stressful custody hand-off, you're probably not thinking about all kinds of delightful ways to engage your child's cooperation. You just want to get it over with and get out of there. But a quick review of the tools can help with that goal.

Let's say you're trying to get your toddler into your car and she's resisting. Your ex isn't helping. To be fair, her lawyer told her not to get involved.

Instead of: "Let's go, you need to get in my car *now*! No, you can't stay with Mommy. There's no choice. This is a court-ordered custody arrangement!"

Try offering a choice:

> "Do you want to climb in the regular way, or should I open up the tailgate so you can climb through the back?"

> "Do you want to walk to the car or do you want a piggy-back ride?"

Try being playful:

> "Your teddy bear is jumping around in my car. He won't let me buckle him in. He wants *you* to do it. I need your help—he's being too wild."

> "Let's take the train to the car. Do you want to be the engine or the caboose? (Link arms.) Chugga-chugga chugga-chugga CHOO-CHOO!"

● ● ●

Custody hand-offs, dessert negotiations, and adjusting to life in two households may go swimmingly with all your skillful moves. But chances are things will still fall apart at some point. Then what? **When in doubt, go back to acknowledging feelings.**

Sometimes you won't know why your kid is upset. *They* may not even know why they're upset. Children often regress or act out when their parents divorce. They may start wetting the bed. They may become short-tempered, easily frustrated, whiny—or all of the above! You may have to take a guess and try to express their feelings for them.

Kid Goes Bananas (Chips)

My ex-husband and I changed our custody schedule a week ago, and it's been hard on Javier. Recently, when he doesn't get his way, he goes from slightly frustrated to complete meltdown in less than a minute. Last weekend he wanted some banana chips and demanded that I give him the whole container. I offered him a reasonable amount in a bowl and he immediately flipped out. I told him, "You can have *some*. Not *all*!" He started screaming and picked up a truck to throw at me.

I grabbed him to stop him from throwing the truck. Then I got the idea to *speak for him*. "I am *so* frustrated! I don't understand why I can't have the whole container! I don't want the banana chips in a bowl . . . and I don't like that sometimes Mommy isn't here . . . I don't like that sometimes Daddy isn't here . . . I don't like that sometimes Mommy and Daddy are *both* not here . . . I don't like not knowing who's going to be here!" I went on like this for a while. "Is that what's going on, buddy?" He nodded his head, his whole body relaxed, and he snuggled into my lap.

His meltdown over the chips wasn't just about the chips. I had been spending extra time playing with him, thinking that would help. But I guess he really needed me to put into words what he's been feeling. He hasn't had another meltdown so far this week.

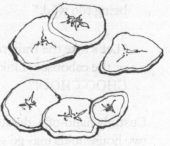

REMINDER: DIVORCE

1. Acknowledge feelings with words.

"You really don't like the idea of moving."

2. Give in fantasy what you cannot give in reality.

"You don't like having your parents live in different houses. You wish it could go back to the way it was."

3. Acknowledge feelings with art.

"We both feel sad. I'm going to draw a picture of how sad I feel. Do you want to make one too?"

4. Try problem-solving.

"It doesn't seem fair to you to have different rules in different houses . . . You like eating while you watch TV . . ."
"The problem is, I don't like crumbs and spills on the sofa."
"I wonder if we can find a solution that will work for both of us."

5. Offer a choice.

"Do you want to climb into the car the regular way, or should I open up the tailgate so you can climb through the back?"

6. Be playful.

"Your teddy bear is jumping around in my car. He won't let me buckle him in. He wants *you* to do it. I need your help—he's being too wild."

 TIP When in doubt, go back to acknowledging feelings.

22

Protecting Kids from Problematic People

With so many stories in the news about kids getting molested, it's impossible for parents not to worry. Lectures about "good touch" and "bad touch" can be confusing to young children, especially since we don't want to explain exactly what we actually mean. What do kids make of these deliberately vague warnings? After all, many predators start with touch that feels good: hugging, back rubs, hair stroking. Those bathing suit–covered areas may not be involved until much further down the line. And then sometimes it *is* okay for doctors to touch those bathing suit areas . . . You can see where this would be hard for a child to understand.

Should we be issuing more explicit instructions? "By the way, if you're competing on a gymnastics team and the doctor who's treating you for a twisted ankle tries to touch your vagina, be sure to say 'No.'" But then, to be thorough, we'd have to warn against every variation on the theme. By the time we finished the litany of horrible things that could happen, the kid would be a basket case.

The first thing we need to do is to **adjust our expectations**. We won't guarantee kids' safety by terrifying them with scary warnings. We need to rely on adult supervision to keep little kids safe.

Beyond direct supervision, a powerful way to protect our children is to **acknowledge and accept our children's feelings**, *even when those feelings are negative or make us uncomfortable.* (This may sound familiar if you've read chapter one.) When we help children recognize and value their own feelings, we also make it more likely that they'll communicate with trusted adults about something that makes them uneasy.

In an ideal world, our children would always tell us about the truly important problems, and they wouldn't bother us with petty complaints. Unfortunately, children are not always able to make that distinction. And a lifetime of training that "bad feelings" are unacceptable has a cumulative impact. Consider the effect of these familiar phrases:

"Stop crying, there's nothing to be scared of."

"Enough whining, it's only a scratch."

"Don't say you hate Grandma! I never want to hear those words coming out of your mouth again."

The safest kid on the block is not the one whose zealous parents have filled her head with nightmare scenarios of predatory adults, but rather the child whose parents give her the everyday gift of accepting feelings. The one whose parents say:

"Fireworks can be scary. They're so loud."

"Even a little scratch can hurt! Do you need a kiss? Or a Band-Aid?"

"It sounds like you're pretty annoyed with Grandma right now. Something she did really bothered you!"

Take another look at that last example. Think about the child who feels secure enough to come to a parent saying, "I hate Grandma!" Or "... the teacher." Or "... the coach." Think about the parent who responds, "Sounds like you're very upset with the coach. Something he did really bothered you!" instead of, "How dare you talk that way about your coach! That's very disrespectful. He works hard to help you kids."

The child whose parent accepts negative feelings is less likely to be convinced to keep quiet about a situation that makes her uneasy. That child knows that her feelings matter and her parents will listen, even when she says something unpleasant about a respected adult or family member.

We also want to convey to children that they have a right to control their own bodies, and we want them to know they can talk to us if they feel "uncomfortable." But unless we expand that to include their everyday experiences, we are undermining our message.

If Aunt Irma wants to hug your five-year-old and he tries to squirm away, don't tell him, "Don't be rude, give your aunt a nice hug. She loves you!" To your child, that hug is *uncomfortable* touch. Instead, you can tell Aunt Irma, "Bucky isn't in the mood for hugs. He'd like to wave hello instead."

One parent reports that she gave her three-year-old daughter very specific language to use when strangers would touch the girl's blonde, curly hair without her consent, which happened frequently. When an older woman approached at a restaurant and began to pet those apparently irresistible curls, the little girl said firmly, as she had practiced, "Please don't touch my hair!" The woman was shocked, and looked to the mother to correct this "rude response." Mom backed up her daughter. "She doesn't like strangers touching her hair." The woman walked off in a huff.

These are the common, everyday experiences that give children the confidence that they have a right to control their own bodies.

What's more, if we don't protect children from physical discipline—spanking, slapping, rapping knuckles, soap in the mouth—we are clearly sending the message that "bad touch" is okay. It's difficult to teach children that adults are not allowed to touch them in ways that make them feel uncomfortable, while simultaneously signaling that it is acceptable for adults to hurt them.

Of course there will be times when our kids do have to put up with physical discomfort. It's not necessarily a bad skill to develop. In those cases, we can still respect a child's feelings and do whatever we can to help them feel in control.

For instance, if a child needs a blood draw and he's hiding in the corner screaming, "Get away!" we're not going to say, "Oh well, I guess we'll just skip it and have ice cream instead." But we can **acknowledge his strong feelings**. Instead of saying, "Don't be such a baby, it'll be over before you know it," we can say, "It's scary to have a needle stuck in your arm. I wish you didn't need it." We can **offer him a choice**: "What's the best way to get through it? Do you want to squeeze my hand? Or would it help to distract yourself with a video game?"

Or for example, if your child is in the back seat of the car, vociferously complaining that his brother's elbow is touching him, you're not going to ditch that small sedan by the side of the road and call for an immediate upgrade. But instead of scolding, "He's barely touching you. I don't want to hear another word of complaint for the rest of this ride!" we can demonstrate respect for his feelings: "Ugh, it's not easy to be squeezed together for a long car ride." (Even if it's short, it's long!) You might even **give in fantasy what you cannot give in reality**. "It would be nice if we had a stretch limo. We'd have plenty of room back there. Enough to lie down or play catch. Enough for a swimming pool! What else would we have?"

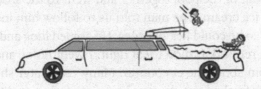

Thirty-five years ago Joanna's mother, Adele Faber, made the case for the powerful protective effect of accepting children's negative feelings in her first book, *Liberated Parents, Liberated Children.*

> If we deny a child his perception, we dull his ability to sense danger, and make him vulnerable to the influence of those who do not have his welfare at heart. . . . When we tell a child that he doesn't feel what he is feeling, we strip him of his natural protection. Not only that. We confuse him,

desensitize him. We force him to construct a false world of words and defense mechanisms that have nothing to do with his inner reality. We separate him from who he is.[1]

You may wonder if Adele ever had an opportunity to put theory to the test in the case of a real-life predator. Well (since you asked), we'll tell you a story from our childhood.

Creepy Encounter at the Pool
(Joanna's story, and Julie is in it too)

When Julie and I were eight years old, we used to go to the town pool together. In those days, it was normal for kids that age to get on their bikes and go adventuring without adult supervision. One day, a young man started playing with us, tossing us around in the pool. I thought he must be a friend of Julie's family, and I later found out that Julie thought he was a friend of my family. We were both delighted to be getting attention from this fun guy. At one point, we all got out of the pool together and went to the snack bar to buy ice cream. The man told us to follow him into the woods so he could lick our toes. He argued long and hard, but we refused. It didn't feel right. I went home and told my mom about the encounter. Many years later she told me how freaked out she was by my story, but at the time she just said, "You trusted your feelings, and they told you what to do!"

When children are old enough to be on their own, whether walking to school or playing at the park, we can **give information** that will enable them to begin to take responsibility for their own safety. This information needs to be calibrated to the individual child. We want to empower them without frightening or confusing them.

We know children who have experienced crippling anxiety after being warned about strangers who want to harm them.

Keep in mind that stranger abductions in the United States are rarer than the likelihood of being struck by lightning,[2] so we need to balance our children's physical safety with their emotional well-being.

Keep it Simple, Not Scary

I have this childhood memory of walking home from school after our teacher warned us about adults in cars who would lure us with candy and then kidnap us. I clearly remember my heart hammering as each car passed, thinking this may be the one that slows down and grabs me. My family lived in a suburban area with very little crime, so in retrospect I'm sure that the risk was infinitesimal,* but I didn't understand that then. It took a long time for the terror to ease its grip. Even sleep wasn't safe. I had nightmares for years about cars following me, and not being able to move my legs to run away.

So when my daughter's elementary school announced a special assembly about "stranger danger," I decided to keep her home. My friend was critical. She warned me that my daughter would be at risk if I didn't teach her not to talk to strangers. But that rule never made sense to me. I mean, we talk to strangers all the time—the librarian, the bus driver, the mail carrier. I don't want my kids to be scared of every person they don't know, the way I was when I was a kid. What if they fall off their bike and skin their knee and need help, or they have to ask for directions, or talk to a store clerk?

* ". . . children taken by strangers or slight acquaintances represent only one-hundredth of 1 percent of all missing children. Far more common are children who have run away, have gotten lost or injured, have been taken by a family member (usually in a custody dispute) or simply aren't where they're expected to be because of a miscommunication."[3]

But I was worried that my friend was right—I should say *something* to my daughter.

Here's what I came up with: "Now that you're old enough to play outside with your friends without me watching you, I need to teach you a *very* important safety rule: *Never go with anybody without asking Daddy or me first.* If a person asks you to get in their car, or go to their house, or go look for their puppy . . . you have to ask us first. Even if Grandma asks you to go with her to get ice cream, you have to ask first! If anybody ever invites you to go with them without waiting for you to ask me first, that is a person you should not trust! You can say, 'Wait, I have to ask my mom or dad before I can go with you.'"

My daughter seemed to take it in stride. It made sense to her. "Because you wouldn't know where I was!"

I agreed. "I'd be looking all over for you. I'd be worried!"

I felt like I had managed to walk the fine line between giving her some information that could help keep her safe without freaking her out.

• • •

Of course each parent will have to make their own decision about the level of supervision and the kind of information that's appropriate to share with their child, depending on the maturity of the child and the relative risk of the environment. There is no single script, no one-size-fits-all solution, that will keep kids physically safe and emotionally secure.

Here's a story from a parent who figured out how to give information that would be helpful to her teenager without scaring or confusing her:

Confident Tap Dancer

When Amanda was a teenager, she got an opportunity to perform in a one-week tap dance festival. She would need to take the train into New York City every day by herself. I trusted her to be responsible, but at the same time I was worried—a teenage girl traveling alone could become a target. I gave the usual warnings about keeping your wallet out of sight, and handing over the money without a fight if someone tries to mug you. Then I reminded her that if she ever needed help, whether she was lost or someone was making her uneasy, she could duck into a store and talk to an employee. But if that wasn't an option, she should look for a mother with young children, because that's likely to be a safe person to go to for help. She rolled her eyes at me, but I figured she got the message.

The first two days went smoothly, but on her third trip to the city, she was sitting alone on the train when a man sat down next to her and started harassing her, demanding that she talk to him and crowding her in the seat. She tried to ignore him but he wouldn't leave her alone, and she was really scared. No one on the train seemed to be paying attention, and the conductor was nowhere in sight. She got up and walked down the aisle until she found a mother and her two young children and squeezed in next to them. The man didn't follow her.

As she told me this story, a long-forgotten memory came to me. I was taking a bus to Texas to visit a relative when I was seventeen. A man sat down next to me and started touching my legs under cover of darkness. I spent an hour in fear, carefully nudging his hands away, too scared to ask any of the strangers on the bus for help. At one point he asked me how old I was and when I told him, he grunted, "Jail bait," and moved away.

In retrospect, that safety talk I had with my daughter was worth a few eye rolls. I was glad I had been able to empower her to take action to protect herself.

● ● ●

And then we release them into the world. Are they ready?

Confident College Student (email from a dad)

I took a workshop with you five years ago, and I wanted to share this story.

It was the first day of college. I was helping my daughter move into her dorm room. It was a coed dorm. The halls were a madhouse. At one point, a small throng of young men stuck their heads into the room and said to my daughter, "We're going to the pub, come with us!"

My daughter replied, "Thanks for the invitation, but I'm pretty busy unpacking here."

One of the guys said, "Oh come on, don't be a party pooper! You're ruining the fun."

My daughter looked completely unruffled. Without missing a beat, she replied cheerfully, "Well, I'm not here for your entertainment, but have a good time."

I feel like the whole approach I learned in the workshop helped me give her the confidence to become this young woman who can hold her own so effortlessly.

REMINDER: PROBLEMATIC PEOPLE

1. **Adjust expectations:** We can't guarantee kids' safety by terrifying them with scary warnings. For young children, we need to rely on adult supervision to keep them safe.

2. **Acknowledge feelings** even when they're negative or make us uncomfortable.

   "It sounds like you're pretty annoyed with your coach. Something he did really bothered you!"

   "You can tell Aunt Irma you don't want to hug. You like to high-five instead."

3. **Give information** calibrated to your child.

   "If somebody is making you uncomfortable, you could duck into a store and talk to an employee. You can also look for a mother with young children. That's likely to be a safe person to go to for help."

23

Sex

It's Only a Three-Letter Word

One subject that often causes profound discomfort among parents of prepubescent children is *sex*.

"My daughter is only six years old, and the kids in her class are talking about how babies are made. Isn't that too young??!!"

"My son is in second grade. The other day in the carpool his friends were giggling and whispering in the back seat about 'being gay.' I felt like I should say something, but I didn't know what."

"My son is in fifth grade. Last week they had a special presentation on drugs and sex. The school sent home a notice saying that we should take a look at the materials and have a talk with our kids now so as to 'strike while the iron is hot.' I tried to talk to him about it and he completely freaked out. He was screaming at me and crying. He said he was going to run away from home. All this information really upset him. I feel like the school took away his innocence."

There is no popular consensus on when kids should learn the facts of life. Some parents want to preserve the "innocence of childhood" for as long as possible. Others embrace the philosophy of "the earlier the better."

Our experience has been that pubescent children are often acutely self-conscious talking with their parents about the mysteries of procreation. They can find conversations about sexuality painfully embarrassing. On the other hand, younger children tend to see the whole process as just another fascinating set of facts about the endlessly strange world they live in.

An additional benefit of starting the conversation about procreation with younger kids is that they'll know they can come to us with questions as they get older and start to hear about sex from the rest of the world. If we don't talk to kids about sex when they're younger, the message they get from us is that sex is a taboo topic. Our opportunity for input is lost. Research confirms that talking about sex with younger children encourages responsible behavior and does not result in kids having sex earlier.[1]

If you're having trouble broaching the topic of sex and reproduction with children, here are some stories from parents to inspire you:

Baby Book

When I got pregnant with my second child, Christopher was just three years old. I decided not to tell him made-up stories like my parents told me. I bought a book called *A Child Is Born*, by Lennart Nilsson, that shows pictures of the sperm fertilizing the egg and the development of the embryo and the fetus at every stage. Each month we'd look at the next picture and talk about the baby growing inside me. Christopher never had any discomfort about it. It was science—his favorite subject!

The Incredible Journey (Julie's story)

Asher was five when my husband and I told him I was pregnant. Asher had already learned about eggs and sperm and he immediately asked, "How did the sperm get from Daddy into you?" Before I had a chance to respond, he suggested his own explanation: "I know! When you hold hands, the sperm goes from Daddy's hand to Mommy's hand, and then it finds the egg." It was very tempting to say, "Oh yes, something like that!" But a friend had recently coached me on how to have this talk, so I was prepared. "No, that's not what happens. Daddy put his penis into my vagina, and the sperm came out of his penis and traveled up into my uterus to find the egg."

I can understand why all those myths about storks got started. It felt pretty weird to talk to my five-year-old about his dad and me having sex. I thought he might be shocked, but he just said, "Oh," and asked when the baby would be born.

Lesson in the Mall Stall (Joanna's story)

I was in the mall with my three-and-a-half-year-old, Zach, and my friend Lynda. We made a bathroom stop and while I was in the stall I heard Zach ask Lynda, "What are those?" He must have been pointing to the tampon machine because then I heard Lynda say, "That's called a tampon. Every month a woman's body makes a tiny little egg. That egg can grow into a baby. But if it doesn't, the egg comes out from between the woman's legs. There's also some extra blood in there for the baby, and that blood comes out, too, when there's no baby, because it isn't needed. The woman tucks a tampon between her legs to absorb the extra blood."

I was really impressed with how easily and simply my friend answered that question. I would've had no idea where to start! Zach didn't seem at all worried about it, but he must have been giving it some thought. About a month later he walked in on me in the bathroom and saw some blood in the toilet. He looked a little alarmed, but then he said to me, "Mom, your body probably made a little egg, but it didn't turn into a baby. So the extra blood had to come out. Don't worry." He gave my arm a comforting pat.

I never would have thought to bring up the topic of menstruation with a three-year-old boy. But in hindsight, I think it's good for kids to learn about both male and female bodies, especially when they're young enough to think of it as a simple fact of life.

Thanksgiving Miracle

When my son was in second grade, he picked out a film from our local library called *The Miracle of Life*. It had a picture of a baby on the cover and it was filed under educational films. I checked it out without giving it a second thought. The whole family sat down to watch, including my kindergartener and my two-year-old. Well it turned out that *everything* was in that movie. They used this amazing fiber optic technology to show the eggs being released from the fallopian tubes, the sperm being released and wiggling their way up the vaginal canal, bumping against the egg to get in, the embryo developing, and the actual emergence of the baby.

Dylan was fascinated. He hit rewind and replayed the birth scene many times. Then he asked how the sperm got from the man into the woman. I gave my husband a look like, "You're the man, you should tell him this." He shot me a look right back like, "*You* brought home the movie. You deal with it." I gulped and said, "Well, the man puts his penis into the woman's vagina, so that the sperm can go into her body and find the egg." Dylan was wide-eyed. "*You* did *that*?"

Now my husband pipes up, "Three times!"

Then Dylan asked, "When I want to have a baby, how will I know when to do that?"

Wow, I was so not prepared to have this conversation with a seven-year-old! But I rallied. "It's a feeling you get that I can't explain to you, because your body's not grown up enough to make sperm yet. But you'll get to know what it feels like when you're older."

Dylan was content with that explanation. He was excited about his new knowledge. He was ready to run out and enlighten the world. It was just before Thanksgiving and he had an assignment from school to write, "What I Am Thankful For." Dylan wrote, "I am thankful for the sperm and the egg, because without those things I would not exist." He proceeded to write the longest essay he had ever produced in his entire young life—two inspired pages explaining all that he had learned about fertilization and birth.

I had to dissuade Dylan from immediately running next door to share this information with our next-door neighbors' kids. I told him that some parents don't want their kids to know about it until they're older, and would be upset if they found out.

I'm glad I brought home that movie, even though it seemed like a mistake at the time. Dylan and his brothers added to their store of knowledge about sex bit by bit as they grew up, instead of having it dumped on them in one shocking blow. I was grateful that they learned about sex in a positive way before the school started their education program about STDs and date rape drugs.

One of these incremental bits of knowledge came when Dylan was twelve, and his health class did a unit on sex education. He asked me why people need condoms. "If they don't want a baby, why don't they just not have sex?" I realized that just because he knew about the mechanics of procreation didn't mean he knew the whole story! I explained that nature designed sex to feel good so that creatures would reproduce. If it didn't feel good, species would not survive. This was a lot for him to absorb. He walked out of the room and the conversation ended there. As he matured, the topic of sex came up every once in a while, from a discussion of a newspaper article or movie, to conversations about politics, adding incrementally to his understanding of sexuality. It's a big topic.

Where Little Trucks Come From

I was riding in the car with my friend and her very articulate two-and-a-half-year-old son. We saw a tow truck hauling a pickup by its front wheels. "Look Mommy!" the little boy squealed happily. "Those two trucks are mating!"

I guess she taught him about sex pretty early. He still has more to learn, though.

The Birds and the Bees (and the Chickens)

My six-year-old learned about sex when an adult friend asked me how my chickens can lay eggs without a rooster. I explained to her that chickens lay eggs with or without a rooster. If there's a rooster to fertilize the eggs, they'll hatch. If there's no rooster, then you get an unfertilized egg. My friend was quite amazed. I guess she didn't grow up on a farm. But my son was confused. After my friend went home (with a dozen eggs), I explained fertilization to him. I told him that the rooster gets on top of the hen and puts his penis inside her body and then sperm comes out of the rooster and goes into the hen. The sperm fertilizes the egg when it's still inside the hen's body, before the egg has a shell. Then, when the egg comes out, it has a tiny embryo that grows into a baby chick and hatches.

He's seen this happen because for a short time we had a rooster who was mounting the hens . . . and also crowing at four a.m. You can imagine how popular we were with the neighbors!

At another point, he got to watch eggs hatching. He treated my explanation as just one more piece of the puzzle. I have to admit, it was a lot easier for me to talk about chickens than about humans. I can see why someone came up with the idea of explaining sex with "the birds and the bees." Eventually I'm sure he's going to ask about humans, but at least I've gotten a start on the subject.

Kissing Trouble

When my son was in first grade, he kissed another boy's hand on a dare in school. The kids had been saying that kissing was disgusting, but my son, always up for a challenge, said he would do it anyway! The other kids started calling him "gay." Then kids in other classes started asking him if he was gay. They would shove him or hit him and run away and he would chase them. He came home and told me he didn't really know what gay meant, but that he was pretty sure he was gay, because that's what everybody said. I talked to the teacher, and she said it was best to ignore the problem and let it blow over.

I didn't feel like I could ignore it. It was awful! Nobody wanted to sit next to my son or play with him. So I sat him down for a talk. "You know how when a man and woman fall in love they want to hug and kiss, and sometimes live together, get married, have kids? Well, sometimes a man and a *man*, or a woman and a *woman* fall in love. That's called being gay. When you kissed a boy it made them think about two boys being in love, so that's why they called you gay." Then I explained that some people think being gay is wrong, and that's why kids were being mean to him. But *I* don't think it's wrong for people to love each other—whether it's a man and a woman, or a man and a man, or a woman and a woman. People should love whoever they want to love! I told him that he didn't have to figure out whether he was gay or not gay because he's only six years old.

My son was satisfied with this explanation. He was like, "Ohhh, so *that's* what they're talking about." I also suggested that he not chase the kids when they tease him, because that makes them more excited to keep doing it.

He went back to school armed with new knowledge and confidence, which put an end to the harassment. I feel good about giving him all the information he needed at the time, and inoculating him against prejudice that he might encounter, or develop, in the future.

No More Secrets!

When my son was seven years old, I still hadn't told him the story of his birth. It seemed too complicated and it was never just the right moment. I mentioned this to my friend, who looked a little alarmed and urged me to tell him as soon as possible.

She was so persuasive that my husband and I had "the talk" with our son the very next day. I told him, "Dad and I want to tell you the story of where you came from before you were born."

"Why? Are you pregnant?"

"No, don't worry."

"I wasn't worried. I'd like that!"

Before we got too far off topic, I reminded him about when he and his dad had talked about eggs and sperm. Then I said, "Before you were born, we really wanted a baby but I couldn't get pregnant. So Daddy and I asked another woman to help us have a baby. Daddy gave his sperm to this woman, and the baby grew inside of her. We were there when you were born and then we brought you home."

He said, "I don't get it. It's like I was adopted?"

"No."

"But you're not really my parents?"

"We *are* your parents. You have a birth certificate that has our names on it. It says we are your parents."

"Just because you have a paper that says you're my parents, doesn't mean you're really my parents. You don't have my genes and I didn't grow inside you." (He's heard about genes because his dad is a science teacher.)

"You have Daddy's genes, and I took care of you from the moment you were born."

"Oh . . . I'm tired." He curled into me and fell asleep.

Over the next few weeks, questions continued to bubble up:

"Is the woman who was pregnant with me still alive?" ("Yes, I'm in touch with her.")

"What about Ryan? He just has moms. Where did *they* get sperm from?" ("They got a man to help them by giving them sperm.")

"I'm not normal. Trevor is the only one of my friends who's normal because he has regular parents. Devon was adopted and Ryan has two moms and they had to get a sperm from a man. And you had to get somebody to be pregnant with me." ("There are so many different ways families are made. This is how ours was made.")

I wish I *had* told him when he was younger. For more than a year afterward, he was very angry that I kept this secret from him. He'd often say things like, "It's not fair that parents can have secrets and kids can't. You didn't tell me that I didn't come from your egg!" I feel like he had formed a certain understanding of himself and his world, and this really shook it up.

It's been two years since the talk, and he still refers to "those years when you kept secrets from me." The secrecy was so much more troubling to him than the thing itself. The surrogacy has finally become okay and a fact of life. He recently shared it with his good friend Ryan and with Ryan's mother. He likes to talk about how much he's like his dad because they share genes, but he also talks about how much he's like me, even though we don't share genes. He's got the whole "nature-nurture debate" figured out at the age of nine.

Not Like the Old Days

When my daughter was a preteen I was determined not to make her feel uncomfortable about the topic of sex and reproduction. I remember my own mother telling me that I could ask her anything, but I somehow knew that sex was a bit of a taboo topic. Those conversations felt secretive. They always happened when my brother and father weren't around and I sensed my mother's discomfort. I certainly didn't want to pass that along to my daughter. But I wasn't sure I could pull it off!

I decided that honesty was the best policy, so I told her, "When I was a girl, most people didn't talk about sex. It was something that was supposed to be private, and people got really embarrassed if the subject came up.

"I think parents *should* talk to their kids about sex. But I still sometimes feel uncomfortable about it, because that's how I grew up. So now you know why! But I'm still going to talk about it, even if it makes me feel a little embarrassed."

That confession helped me relax because I didn't feel so much pressure to present the perfect attitude. My daughter found it interesting. I think she figured I must have grown up in prehistoric days. She's much more comfortable with the topic than I ever was. A few years later she had no problem letting her family know (including her brothers and father) when she had cramps because she was "on her period." I never could have conceived of talking that way around the males in my family!

Movie Syllabus

My thirteen-year-old son wanted to rent a movie that, from the trailer, seemed to be about a handsome, charismatic man who has mastered the art of romancing women in order to get into their beds. The predictable twist is that he will end up falling in love with a woman who treats *him* the way he's treated all those previous women, and he has to work very hard to win her heart.

I wasn't too happy about this movie choice because I assumed that the majority of the movie would be modeling poor behavior. Even though I knew there would be the "lesson" at the end, I didn't think that lesson would outweigh the preceding hour and a half or so, depicting a glamorous lifestyle that would include lots of objectification of women.

Then it struck me that this was my golden opportunity to sneak in a lecture about dating and relationships. I told him we could watch the movie (it was rated PG-13 after all), but it would have to be after his brothers went to bed, because they were too young.

He asked why. I tried to make it short. "Because the main guy in the movie treats women badly. He acts like dating is a competitive sport, and in order to win points, you have to convince the woman to sleep with you. When that happens, you dump her and go on to date a new woman. I don't want you and your brothers to think that's a good way to treat people—to trick them into having sex with you so that you can get a notch on your belt." (And then I had to explain *that* expression.) "*You're* old enough to understand that it's just a movie and they're trying to make a funny story. I'm pretty sure the main character *eventually* learns the lesson that you should love and care about someone you have sex with."

My son seemed interested, and we actually ended up having a discussion about dating. He told me some things about kids who were dating in middle school, and he asked some questions about my first date with his dad (where I spent the entire outing calling him by the wrong name and he never corrected me). I recall thinking that I wouldn't have had such an open and positive response if I'd just started lecturing him out of the blue about how to treat girls. That would have been awkward and painful. By talking about a movie script, it gave the subject some comfortable distance.

• • •

So there you have it, folks. Talk to your kids about sex before it becomes the monster in the closet. Mention it tangentially, when the topic comes up in relation to movies or advertisements or animals (or trucks). Keep it simple and developmentally appropriate. Just because a five-year-old wonders how babies are made doesn't mean he needs a lecture about STDs and date rape. We don't want to overwhelm children with more than they can handle. In our experience young kids *can* handle the facts of life, related in a simple and positive way. In fact, they usually handle it better than an older child.

REMINDER: SEX

1. Give information.

"The sperm swam up into my uterus to find the egg."

2. Describe how you feel.

"I still sometimes feel uncomfortable talking about it, because that's how I grew up."

3. Acknowledge feelings.

"You didn't like that it was a secret. You like to know where you came from!"

24

Too Much Hugging

When Affection Is Nonconsensual

Dear J&J,

My six-year-old loves to hug and kiss his friends. The problem is he doesn't know when to stop hugging, even when they loudly object.

I've tried talking to him about how important it is to respect other people's bodies. He acts like he understands what I'm saying, but he still can't seem to help himself. I've tried giving him a consequence by taking away his tablet. That didn't help either. It just made him mad.

The only solution that has worked so far is to physically pry him away (gently) from the other child. Which works fine when I'm around, but I can't do that when he's at school. His teacher says this is something he should have learned at home. Obviously he hasn't, and how can I control him when I'm not there?

It seems like it would be simpler if he were hitting other children. We teach our kids that it is NEVER okay to hit, period! But hugging and kissing are a lot more complicated. How do you teach a six-year-old how much physical affection is okay? And how can we teach him to back off when the other person has had enough?

—In a Tight Squeeze

Dear Squeeze,

You're on the right track! Punishment and restricting privileges will not help your son learn to control himself. It sounds like you're trying to do some **problem-solving,** but you're missing the all-important first step.

Step One: **Acknowledge your child's feelings.**

We cannot emphasize this enough! Spend a generous amount of time talking about how nice it is to hug and kiss. How much he loves to do it—in the morning, in the afternoon, at bedtime, with his parents, with his teachers, with his friends. A good squeeze is the best! Once you get started, you really don't want to stop, even when the other person says "Enough!" It feels too good to stop!

Step Two: **Describe the problem.**

Then, and only then, can you talk about other people's feelings. "The problem is that sometimes other people are not in the mood to be squeezed. They can get upset. What can a person do when he loves to hug but the other person doesn't want to be hugged so much?"

Step Three: **Ask for ideas.**

Maybe your son can come up with some of his own ideas. Here are a few to start you off:

1. Would he like a big stuffed animal or cushion that he can hug to his heart's content?
2. When he feels the urge to hug, can he hug himself, wrapping his arms around his own shoulders and kissing his inner elbows while doing so?
3. Could he ask a person if they'd like a hug? If they say yes, the hug is on!

4. Can he come up with a special word that friends or teachers can use to signal him when they want him to stop hugging?

5. Perhaps the two of you can play a hugging game, so he can practice starting and stopping. You hug him nice and tight and he can say "more" or "stop." As soon as he says stop, fling your arms away dramatically and say something like, "Hug OVER!" (or "Break free!" or "Blast off!" to make it more fun to stop hugging). Then let him do the same to you. Let him practice on other family members as well, and get some stuffed animals to boot. They can talk to him in their own cute little stuffed animal voices.

Write down all your ideas. Choose the ones you both like. Talk to his teachers about the solutions to get them on board. When he manages to use a solution, **use descriptive praise:**

"You felt like hugging, but you knew Amy didn't want to, so you hugged your own self. You did it!"

If he doesn't use his solutions, **take action** by gently extricating the "victim" without scolding your son. Just repeat, "Amy's not in the mood to be squeezed right now. Let's find something else to squeeze!"

Finally, it may be helpful to find a way to **tend to his basic needs** by giving him the experience he seeks. Some kids crave deep pressure, especially those who are on the autism spectrum

or have sensory processing differences. A playful way to meet this need is to pretend your child is a hot dog (or a tofu dog, for vegetarians). Wrap him tightly in a blanket (the bun) and then put "condiments" on him. "Ketchup" gets spread on with long firm strokes. "Sauerkraut" is added by chopping up and down his back with the edges of the palms, mustard is pounded on with gentle fists, salt and pepper are sprinkled with little fingernail touches, and then the whole thing is eaten up, yum-yum-yum. (Feel free to substitute your own favorite toppings!)

REMINDER: TOO MUCH HUGGING

1. Acknowledge feelings.

"Hugging feels good. It's hard to stop."

2. Try problem-solving.

"The problem is, sometimes other people are not in the mood to be hugged. We need ideas."

3. Use descriptive praise.

"You knew Amy didn't want to be hugged, so you hugged your own self. You did it!"

4. Take action without insult.

"Let's find something else to squeeze!"

5. Tend to basic needs: provide the sensory input your child craves.

"I'm going to wrap you up like a hot dog in a bun."

Section VIII

Troubleshooting

25

The Trouble with *YOU*!

Dear J&J,

Whenever I try to empathize with my daughter she gets angry. I tell her things like, "I can see how frustrating this is for you," or "You must be so scared," or "It's okay to be sad," and she screams at me, "Don't say that!" or "No I'm not!"

I like the idea of acknowledging and accepting feelings, but it just doesn't work with my child. It's like pouring gas on a fire.

—Feeling Failure

Dear FF,

To understand the reaction your daughter is having, let's take the statements from your email and try them out on ourselves.

Imagine that you're struggling to learn how to enter income and expenses for your new home business using an online spreadsheet. You've never used this program before and it's not going well. You exclaim to your spouse, "Ugh, this program isn't working! I hate this!!"

Your spouse responds, "Oh, I can see that this program is frustrating for you."

Would you feel better? Or would you feel a little bit patronized? Like maybe your spouse is analyzing your deficiencies?

That final "for you" sprinkles salt in the wound. It implies that computer spreadsheets may be easy for most people to figure out, but *for you* (with your feeble mind) they're a terrible struggle.

It would be much more comforting if your partner dropped the "for you" and simply exclaimed, "Oh, those programs can be so frustrating!"

Now she's describing the program, not *your* inability to cope. It feels more like she's putting herself in your shoes and truly empathizing, rather than judging you.

Let's try the next statement in your email. This time imagine that you're scared of speaking in public and you have to give a presentation to a large group at work. Your boss notices your shaky hands and grim expression and says, "You must be so scared!"

Was that comforting? Or did you feel like he was being presumptuous and perhaps a bit self-congratulatory for identifying your miserable state of mind? Who appointed him your psychologist? Last you checked you weren't paying him to tell you how you feel!

What if instead, your boss, noticing your signs of nervousness, said to you, "It's scary to talk in front of the entire company. Especially the first time."

You might feel a little less nervous, knowing that your boss understands how stressful this assignment is. He isn't analyzing *you*, he's describing the situation. It feels like he's on your side.

You may have noticed the common thread in these conversations. In both cases that little word "you" can sabotage an attempt at empathy.

Of course you can't strike the word "*you*" from your vocabulary. There will be plenty of times when it performs its normal, highly useful function without giving offense. The challenge is to be aware of its potential to irritate. Avoid "you" if it makes your response sound like you're judging or analyzing the child. Instead of telling a child how they're feeling, you can describe the situation or the experience, and name the feeling that might go along with it. The idea is to empathize with the universal experience of feeling scared, sad, frustrated, angry . . .

Here is a handy conversion chart for YOU:

Instead of:	Try:
You look really scared.	Thunder can be scary. It's so loud!
I can see how frustrating that is for *you*.	Long division can be frustrating! There are so many steps to remember.
You must be so upset! It's okay to cry.	It's upsetting to be left out of a friend's party.
I understand that *you're* very disappointed about not getting the job.	Oh no, how disappointing!

Notice that several of these statements are even more irritating because the speaker says "I *understand* . . ." and "I *can see* . . . ," firmly putting the emphasis on his own perceptiveness at being able to identify your emotions. When people are in distress they want their feelings acknowledged, not analyzed. If they're children, it may cause them to scream and run away. If they're adults, they may just steam silently to themselves, and days later, snap at you "for no reason."

We're not trying to cancel all *"you's"*! We do realize that there will be plenty of times you'll need to use *"you"* in order to form a coherent sentence! And plenty of times that *"you"* is completely inoffensive, even in the context of acknowledging feelings. Here are some examples:

> "You sound really angry at your sister. She must have done something that bothered you a lot."

"It sounds like you feel ambivalent about joining the team. Part of you wants to, and part of you is not so sure . . ."

"You were really looking forward to visiting your grandparents. It stinks that you can't go just because you have a fever."

How will you know when "*you*" is a problem? Accepting feelings is definitely an art, not a science. Your child (or partner, or coworker, or friend) will give you a clue by how they react. If in doubt, try it out on yourself and see how it feels.

It can also help to imagine what you would say if you were empathizing with an adult friend. If your friend complained about a rough day stuck inside with the kids, you wouldn't say, "Oh, I can see that parenting is frustrating for you. You must feel so overwhelmed. It's okay to get angry with your children sometimes. That's perfectly normal."

You'd no doubt be better received if you ditched the "*you's*" and instead put yourself in your friend's shoes. "Rainy days are the worst! The kids always end up fighting and there's no escape!"

• • •

Some readers may be thinking, "*Why are these authors trying to micromanage every little word that comes out of people's mouths? How annoying of them!*"

Many of you don't have to worry at all about this topic. Plenty of kids appreciate a sympathetic statement even if it isn't a perfectly sculpted work of art. But if your attempts at accepting feelings are being met with outrage or rejection, it may help to fine-tune your responses.

26

The Trouble with *BUT*

Dear J&J,

Acknowledging feelings didn't work with my five-year-old son. He loves to color, and I've been printing out a different animal for him to color every day. Yesterday he asked for a cheetah, but the printer jammed and I couldn't get it working again. He started to cry. I tried acknowledging his feelings and giving him a choice.

"I know how much you wanted to color in a cheetah, but the printer's broken. You can pick out any of these other animals that are already printed."

He went into a full-on tantrum.

Maybe this method doesn't work with some kids. Or do I have to keep practicing until he gets used to it?

—In a Jam

Dear Jam,

When acknowledging feelings, it's very tempting to follow up with a "but," and then top it off with some helpful advice.

"That sounds very upsetting, *but* you still can't skip school! Why don't you play with somebody else at recess?"

"It's so frustrating! *But* you can't just sit around complaining. You need to either do something about it or let it go."

"I know, you really wanted to color a cheetah, *but* the printer's broken. You can color a tiger instead. It's almost the same—just stripes instead of spots."

We feel it's our duty to immediately point out the reality that our child must learn to accept! And we'd like them to move on quickly and accept a perfectly reasonable alternative. The problem is, a child in distress isn't ready to consider choices or advice. And as soon as we inject the "but" we cancel out any good feelings that flow from our previous empathic response. It can be experienced less like sympathy and more like a scolding. It's as if we're telling the child, I understand how you feel, and now I'm going to tell you why you shouldn't feel that way.

Let's try it out on ourselves, and see how it feels to be "butted" when we're feeling low.

"Getting up for a crying baby multiple times a night is exhausting, *but* you have to understand that's what you signed up for when you decided to be a parent. You can either learn to nap when the baby naps, or accept more help from your mother-in-law."

"It's so disappointing to have the play canceled because of the coronavirus, *but* it would be selfish not to cancel. You have to consider the welfare of others."

"It's awful to have your best friend move to another city, *but* you'll make new friends. You just need to put yourself out there."

Think about how much nicer all of these responses would be if we simply chopped off the second halves of the sentences!

"Getting up for a crying baby multiple times a night is exhausting!"

350

"It's so disappointing to have the play canceled because of the coronavirus!"

"It's awful to have your best friend move to another city!"

Doesn't that feel better? Maybe you'll share more about what you're going through. Maybe once you feel heard, you'll be open to thinking about a plan to make the situation better. Or maybe you'll just feel comforted, knowing that someone understands.

The next time your printer jams, the dialogue could go something like this:

"Oh no! You were looking forward to coloring a cheetah, and the printer won't print!"

"No fair!"

"It's so disappointing!"

"Yeah!"

"You jammed-up printer, why won't you work when we tell you to work?"

"This printer is bad!"

"What should we do? Should we find another animal, or should we make our own cheetah? Or do something else?"

If your child persists in demanding the cheetah printout and doesn't seem to understand the limitations of your technological expertise, you might be hard pressed to bite back the "*but.*" Here are two handy phrases you can substitute:

How to Talk When Kids Won't Listen

1) *The problem is . . .*

> "Oh no, you were really looking forward to coloring
> a cheetah! It's so disappointing! *The problem is*, the
> printer is broken."

> *The problem is . . .* suggests that there's a problem that
> could be solved if you put your heads together. Maybe
> the two of you can google fixes for "jammed printer." Or
> perhaps lay a paper over the computer screen and trace
> a cheetah. The emphasis is not on dismissing the feeling,
> but rather on fixing the problem.

2) *Even though you know . . .*

> "It's annoying when you expect to color a chee-
> tah, and there's no cheetah to color! *Even though
> you know* that the printer is broken, it's still really
> frustrating!

> *Even though you know . . .* gives the child credit for un-
> derstanding the situation, while still acknowledging his
> strong feelings.

27

The Trouble with "Say You're Sorry"

Dear J&J,

I always make my kids say "I'm sorry" when they hurt someone. But sometimes it makes things worse.

Here's a typical scenario: Jared is racing through the house and crashes into his younger sister. Haylie falls down and cries.

Me: Jared, no running in the hallway. You hurt Haylie. Say you're sorry!

Jared (rolls his eyes): Okay, okay, sor-REE!

Haylie (tries to kick him): I hate you!

So this whole "say you're sorry" thing isn't working for me. I understand that when we force them to apologize, it's probably not going to be sincere. But what are you supposed to do when your kid body slams his sister? Just let him wander off as if nothing happened? Make him repeat the apology until it sounds sincere, while his sister is kicking him? There doesn't seem to be a good solution.

—In a Sorry State

Dear ISS,

It does seem like teaching kids to say "*I'm sorry*" is part of our job as parents. But as you've already noticed, the command to "*say you're sorry*" often elicits no more than sullen compliance on behalf of the aggressor. When forced to produce those words, some kids will say them sarcastically, while others use "*I'm sorry*" as a get-out-of-jail-free card, repeating the words robotically, with no actual regret.

Then there's the kid who refuses to say the words, and laughs or runs away instead, making us wonder if we're raising a little sociopath. (Please cross that worry off your list! Inappropriate laughter or running away are often signs of embarrassment or fear, rather than heartlessness. A crying sibling and an angry parent is a lot to face for a young child.)

You've also noticed that the words "*I'm sorry*" often do not serve their intended function to soothe the injured party. Which makes one wonder why we work so hard to pry an "*I'm sorry*" from a child's lips. Could there be a more effective way to teach children what to do when they unintentionally (or intentionally) cause harm?

We'd like to suggest that the phrase "*I'm sorry*" be saved for minor accidents, such as when you bump into someone's cart at the grocery store. It's a nice, polite shorthand to let a person know you didn't mean any harm.

But when you've actually hurt someone or damaged something, those words alone can be unsatisfying. We expect people to make an effort to make amends, or at the very least to assure us they intend to do better in the future. Otherwise an apology will be experienced as insincere, or simply as a plea that the injured party stop being mad. So maybe we're focusing too much on the words alone, and not enough on the actions that should accompany them. Consider these scenarios:

When a dinner guest spills the milk, would you rather he apologize profusely, "I'm very sorry! I'm such a klutz!" . . . or that he say, "Oh dear," and grab a sponge?

If your sister borrows your car and gets in a fender bender, which would you rather hear?

The Trouble with "Say You're Sorry"

A tearful, "I am so, so sorry! Can you ever forgive me?"

... or, "I wish that hadn't happened. I'll take your car to the body shop and get the bumper replaced tomorrow."

If your neighbor's dog digs up your prize petunias, which response would appease your wrath?

"Okay okay, I'm sorry! I already told you *I'm sorry* like ten times!"

... or, "Oh no, your beautiful flowers! I'm going to buy you a new flat of petunias, and with your permission I'd like to plant them for you. But first, I'm going to fix the latch on the gate so Digger won't be able to get free anymore."

Any one of the above responses could include the words "*I'm sorry*," but those words are not the most important part of the apology. The key is to offer to **make amends**, either by making things better in the present or by communicating your intention to make things better for the future . . . or both!

Focusing on *these* elements of an apology will help our children learn what to do when they hurt or upset somebody. The same child who infuriates us by laughing or running away when confronted with an angry "*Say you're sorry!*" will often do a complete about-face when they're given a chance to redeem themselves in some concrete manner. It's a relief to see that our kids can behave in a caring way when we give them the opportunity.

So how can we help a child do the right thing when an apology is called for? We can start by briefly **describing the feelings** of the injured party and then find an age-appropriate way for the child to make amends. This might take the form of a physical offering. Here are some examples:

"Idris is crying. That rough play hurt his knee. We need a Band-Aid! Can you get one for him from the medicine cabinet?"

"Camila is upset that her balloon got popped. Can you find something else for her to play with?"

"Bart's lip got bruised in that pile up! You can bring him an ice pop to suck on to make it feel better."

Once kids have the hang of it, we can ask *them* to think about what to do.

"Jack looks pretty upset. What would make him feel better?"

You may notice that we try to avoid the accusatory word *"you."* If we say, *"You* deliberately popped Camila's balloon. That was so mean," we'll probably get a defensive reaction. "No I didn't!" or "She tried to pop mine first!"

• • •

But what if in spite of all your inspired promptings, your kid, who has just bashed his playmate over the head with his toy bulldozer, refuses to make amends of any kind? Should you then insist that your child, at the very least, produce the traditional *"I'm sorry"* before going back to his earth-moving endeavors?

We would argue that an insincere apology can be worse than no apology at all. It's meaningless to the apologizer, and insulting to the apologizee. You're better off modeling the appropriate behavior and **taking action** so your child can cause no further harm. It might go something like this:

"Oh no, Whimper got hurt by Whomper's bulldozer. I'm so sorry, Whimper. Let's get you an ice cube for your head."
"Whomper, I'm taking the bulldozer and putting it away for now! I can't let children get hit in the head with it!"
If Whomper is in a ferocious mood and continues to attack with alternative vehicles, it's either time to end the

playdate, or to find out what's bothering Whomper to see if the problem can be solved.

● ● ●

If the words "*I'm sorry*" flow easily from your child's lips, but are unaccompanied by a change in behavior, refrain from snapping at them, "*Sorry's* not enough!" That will just confuse them. (*Isn't that what I'm supposed to say?*) Instead you can give them a nudge in the direction of making amends and planning for the future.

"Okay, I hear that you're *sorry* you bopped Whimper on the head. Now, what should we do to make him feel better?"
"What should we do next time? We need a way to let your friend know you're angry that doesn't include hitting!"

Stories from the Front Lines

Finger Squeezer

Five-year-old Alex is always cast in the role of the rough kid in our family. Of course he's rougher—his little sister is only eighteen months old. But we fall into the trap of thinking of him as this insensitive brute. Yesterday he squeezed her fingers when she reached for his LEGO. She started wailing. I resisted the urge to scold him. ("You're being too rough again!") Instead I said, "Abby's fingers got hurt! We need to find a way to make her feel better. What can you do?" Alex said, "I'll kiss her fingers!" He started kissing each finger, just like we do for him when he gets hurt, and she started giggling. This approach really brings out his good side!

Halloween in July (Joanna's story)

Five-year-old Sammy came in from playing outside with his brothers. He was crying and ran into his room and slammed the door. Seven-year-old Dan came in looking happy and oblivious.

I must admit I had to bite back the urge to accuse. (*What did you do to your brother?*) With great restraint, I stuck to describing what I saw. "Dan, something happened out there that really upset Sammy. He's crying in his room."

Dan looked crestfallen. "Oh . . . he was bothering us when we were trying to play. He always wants it to be his turn. I kicked the ball away from him and he fell down, but I didn't know he was crying."

"I guess it's not easy playing with a five-year-old. How can we make him feel better?" Again I resisted criticizing Dan's behavior so as to leave his mind free to feel regret!

"I know what to do," said Dan. "Can I use the little knife?"

With my permission Dan took an apple and cut out a little jack-o'-lantern face. He then poured a cup of juice and brought his peace offering to Sam in the bedroom. Sam was pleased. Harmony was restored . . . for now.

• • •

It can help to acknowledge that your child didn't have bad intentions. If we talk to a child as if he's basically a well-meaning person, he's more likely to act like one. So instead of saying, "Look what you did!" when your child accidentally hurts someone or breaks something, we might say, "Oh no, you didn't want *that* to happen. That was not the plan." Such a sympathetic response makes it easier for a kid to feel regret, make amends, and plan to do better in the future.

Pool Panic

Our friends invited us over to swim in their pool. My son, Mikey, jumped in too close to their son, Kyle, and Kyle swallowed water. The poor kid was gagging and crying. His parents were looking at me, waiting for me to make Mikey apologize . . . which is what I normally would have done, even though I knew it would ruin the rest of the playdate. When I try to get Mikey to say "*I'm sorry*," he often gets upset and runs away. He never says it graciously.

So I tried your advice word for word. I said, "Oh no! Kyle got hurt! You didn't want *that* to happen. That was *not* in the plan!" Mikey looked so relieved. He repeated it, "THAT was NOT in the plan!" Then he said, "Sorry Kyle," really sweetly and Kyle said, "I'm okay," and they went back to playing.

● ● ●

When your child offends an adult, be it a teacher, a bus driver, a coach, or a neighbor, it can be difficult for them to face that grown-up and offer a gracious apology. It's scary! This is a great opportunity to teach them how to write an apology note. Notes are generally well-received by adults, who appreciate the effort.

Fidgety Chorister

My son came home from elementary school in tears.

"Mr. Singer said I'm out of the chorus concert!"

"Oh no, that's upsetting!"

"Just because I was jumping off the risers when we were practicing."

"Oh! It sounds like that made him really mad."

"But it's hard to stand still for such a long time. It makes my legs hurt."

"Oh, so it isn't easy to stand still for so long. Maybe you could ask him to sit down when you need a break?"

"No, I could stand. But it's too late. He said, that's it, no more chances."

"Well it sounds to me like Mr. Singer is getting nervous about the concert going well, and having kids jump around during rehearsal is really upsetting him. He's usually a pretty friendly guy. I think if you wrote him a note he might change his mind. You could explain that you were jumping around because your legs hurt when you stand still for so long, but you really want to be in the concert and you'll be sure to stand still for the rest of the rehearsals. Do you want me to help you write it?"

"YES!"

We wrote the note. The teacher was impressed. My son sang proudly in the concert. Also, he learned the power of the written apology, which he put to good use several times during the rest of his school career.

• • •

When we're teaching a young child how to apologize, we focus on helping them take a simple action to fix the problem or help the person feel better.

Of course a more complex and nuanced "mature" apology includes acknowledging the feelings of the injured party, in addition to making amends.

This advanced skill is best taught by modeling. When we hurt a child's feelings, we should refrain from demanding forgiveness.

Not: "I'm sorry. Can you forgive me? Come here and give Mommy a kiss!"

Instead we can let them know we understand how they feel: "I'm really sorry I embarrassed you in front of your friends by reminding you to take your inhaler. Next time I need to tell you something like that, I'll do it in private."

If we want to coach a child through this process, we can let them know explicitly what words would help us feel better: "It would help me to hear that you understand how worried I was when you came home late and didn't call to let me know where you were! And *then* we can talk about what to do next time."

It's very likely that a child will be more receptive to this message if he's heard you model the same kind of understanding to him.

Recycle Debacle

In the last few months, we've amassed a lot of mess in the form of cardboard, paper, clay, and Scotch Tape creations. They've been gathering dust and the house has been feeling very cluttered.

With the kids home all day because of COVID-19, there hasn't been an opportunity to discreetly get rid of stuff. So yesterday, while they were playing, I quickly dumped a pile of cardboard creations into the recycling bin. I was sneaking outside with it when I was caught red-handed!

My eight-year-old daughter, Sahana, was clearly upset and she demanded to know what I was doing. She started digging through the bin, pulling stuff out. I explained that we hadn't used these things in a while, they had been left lying around, and it was time to clean up.

Tears welled up in her eyes. She ran upstairs with one of her rescued creations and shut the door. I felt really bad.

Lately, we've been writing notes to each other when we have disagreements, so I wrote her a note of apology and sent it upstairs with her brother. Funny enough, she had been writing a note to me at the same time!

> Dear Mommy,
> I am upset because it makes me sad to see that your throwing away some of the things that are special to me without asking. How would you feel.
> Love,
> Sahana

How to Talk When Kids Won't Listen

Hi Sahana,
    I am sorry that I started throwing out your stuff without asking. I would feel really angry if someone threw out my stuff without asking me first. How can I make it better?

                        Love, Mommy

Dear Mommy,
    Can we take some of the things out of the trash?
I forgive you! We are freinds!
Love,
Sahana :)

Dear Sahana,
    If we take stuff out of the trash, will you put it away? I am also worried that you will not be able to say bye to things that you and your brother have not used in over a year.

                        Love, Mommy

    Mabey we will only Save a few things That Have the most memorys
Nex time still ask though.
Love,
Sahana

Sounds like a good plan. :)
    Thanks for understanding. I am ready to go through the trash and recycling whenever you are.

                        <3, Mommy

Egged On

I got a call from the physics teacher. My fifteen-year-old son Drew had been disrespectful to him. He had refused to clean up his broken egg from the "egg drop" lab. The teacher said that Drew was usually a good kid and he didn't want to report this to the principal, but he wanted me to talk to my son because his behavior was unacceptable. When Drew got home I told him about the phone call. Drew looked embarrassed. He explained that they had done the egg drop lab, dropping raw eggs down the stairwell, to see if they would break or land safely in the student-designed landing pads. Drew had been very excited about this lab, and he had worked all weekend on his project, staying up late to test different materials and designs.

To his great disappointment, his egg missed the landing pad completely and smashed on the floor. It *would* have worked if it was aimed correctly! Drew wanted a second chance. He had put so much effort into his contraption and had been very eager to go to school that morning. But the teacher just snapped at him, "No second chances. Go clean it up!" Drew was so upset he stalked off in a huff without doing the clean-up.

I allowed as how that must have been really disappointing. And how unfair it was not to get a second chance after all that work. And how cool his impact-absorbing invention had been. And so on. But at the end I said, "I'm worried that your teacher is very upset with you. I know you like that class, and I'd hate to think of you spending the rest of the year with the teacher feeling like you're a disrespectful kid."

Drew said, "Don't worry Mom, I'll apologize to him. I don't need help." He went to the computer and tapped out this letter, which he gave to the teacher the following day:

Dear Mr. L,
I am sorry for being rude to you yesterday. I must have missed the fact that everyone else had cleaned up their

eggs, and so it seemed like a direct poke at me when you told me to clean up my egg. Also, and I hate to say it, but I think I have a slight "authority problem," because when anyone orders me to do something, a message goes off in my brain saying, "don't do it just because he/she told you to!" This is such that even if I am on the verge of doing whatever it was anyway, something tells me not to.

Obviously this is not good, so I am trying to fix it. I sincerely apologize for the way I acted yesterday, and since I don't know how to make up the clean-up to you as of now, here are some eggs from our own chickens that I hope you will enjoy.

Sincerely, Drew

Needless to say, the letter was received warmly and the relationship was repaired.

REMINDER: THE TROUBLE WITH
"SAY YOU'RE SORRY"

Instead of demanding that your child say "I'm sorry":

1. **Describe your feelings** (or those of the injured party) without being accusatory.

   "Oh no, Melissa's fingers got caught in the door! That's very painful!"

2. Give your child an opportunity to **make amends** by . . .

   a. **making things better in the present**

   "We need a Band-Aid. Can you get one from the bathroom cabinet?"

   "Can you find something to make her feel better?"

   b. **making things better for the future**

   "We need a way to remind everyone not to slam the door. Would a big sign on the door help? We have cardboard and crayons . . ."

3. Let your child know how to **acknowledge *your* feelings**.

   "It would help me to hear that you understand how worried I was when you came home late and didn't call to let me know where you were!"

*When the opportunity presents itself, you can **model the behavior you want to see:***

4. **Acknowledge the feelings** of the injured party, and **offer to make amends.**

> "I'm really sorry I embarrassed you in front of your friends by reminding you to take your inhaler. Next time I need to tell you something like that I'll do it in private."

The Old Way

I've been trying to change how I talk to my kids. So when my nine-year-old, Miley, complained about something, instead of correcting her, I acknowledged her feelings. She looked a little startled and suspicious.

Miley: You're just saying that because you're reading that book.

Me: You're right. It's different from the way I usually talk. Do you like the old way better?

Miley: *No!*

Final Words
Until We Meet Again

Who could do this stuff all the time? All this advice is exhausting.

You don't have to be a "perfect parent." Nobody is! Be as kind, patient, and forgiving with yourself as you strive to be with your children. We give our children a thousand chances and then one more. Let's do the same for ourselves.

Dr. Haim Ginott, the esteemed child psychologist and forefather of this approach to child-rearing, used to say, "You don't have to be orthodox. You can be reform. We aim for 70% . . . some days 50% is all we can manage . . . and even 10% can make a real difference in the relationship."

Then why go to all this trouble? Does it really make that *much of a difference?*

We have two reasons for making the effort: the present and the future.

When we use these communication tools, our life with children in the present becomes more pleasant. Kids become more cooperative, they fight less with us and with each other, and our relationships become stronger.

As for the future, consider the qualities you'd most like your children to have when they're grown. Parents and teachers tell us they want kids to be kind, considerate, responsible, and respectful; to be independent problem-solvers who can understand another person's perspective.

If we want our children to go out into the world caring about other people's feelings, we have to start by caring about *their* feelings. If we want kids to grow up to be independent thinkers and responsible problem-solvers who can consider the perspectives of others, we have to consider *their* perspective and give them practice making decisions, taking responsibility, and solving problems.

Imagine a world full of kind, respectful, problem-solvers. If we can populate the planet with adults like this, it could be worth the effort!

Reminder Index

SECTION VII: TOUCHY TOPICS

SECTION VIII: TROUBLESHOOTING

We are very grateful to . . .

Our husbands, Andrew Manning and Don Abramson, who believed in us and provided vital services from cheerleading, to proofreading, to in-house art support.

Our children, Dan, Sam, and Zachary Faber Manning, and Asher, Rashi, and Shiriel King Abramson, who offered thoughtful feedback, tech support, and the occasional hot meal. An extra thanks to Dan for designing the font we used to re-create children's handwritten notes in some of the stories.

Our parents, Adele and Leslie Faber, and Pat and Ed King, for their unwavering love, support, and collective wisdom.

Our artist, Emily Wimberly, for her whimsy, creativity, and good cheer, who was able to capture complex emotions with a simple squiggle of the pen.

Our editor, Kara Watson, and **our agent,** Margaret Riley King, for their invaluable feedback and suggestions, from their dual perspectives as both professionals and parents.

Workshop participants and readers from all over the world who shared their stories, asked us questions, and trusted us with the details of their lives.

Adele Faber and Elaine Mazlish, our founding mothers and our inspiration. We're proud to carry on their work.

(And to Kazi, Joanna's Belgian Shepherd, for the dog stories and for warming her cold toes with his nose while she typed.)

Endnotes

PART ONE

Chapter One

1 Carole Hooven, John Mordechai Gottman, and Lynn Fainsilber Katz, "Parental Meta-emotion structure predicts family and child outcomes," *Cognition and Emotion*, 1995, 9: 229–264.

Chapter Two-and-a-Half

1 https://www.consumeraffairs.com/news/reading-scores-higher-for-children-who-eat-lunch-021419.html; https://www.ncbi.nlm.nih.gov/pmc/articles/PMC4824552/#:~:text=Although%20not%20all%20studies%20found,school%20start%20times%20on%20academics; https://www.npr.org/programs/ted-radio-hour/564577402/simple-solutions.

2 Alfie Kohn, *Punished by Rewards: The Trouble with Gold Stars, Incentive Plans, A's, Praise, and Other Bribes* (Boston: Houghton Mifflin Company, 1993).

Chapter Three

1 Alfie Kohn, *Unconditional Parenting* (New York: Atria Books, 2005), 63–73; https://www.alfiekohn.org/parenting/punishment.htm.

2 https://www.aappublications.org/news/2018/11/05/discipline110518.

3 https://www.nytimes.com/2018/11/05/health/spanking-harm
ful-study-pediatricians.html.

4 https://www.ncbi.nlm.nih.gov/pmc/articles/PMC3447048/.

Chapter Four

1 Carol Dweck, *Mindset: The New Psychology of Success* (New
York: Random House, 2006).

2 Alfie Kohn, *Punished by Rewards*.

PART TWO

Chapter 3

1 "... the mean correlation between time spent on homework
and achievement was not significantly different from zero
for elementary school students." Cooper, Harris, Jorgianne
Civey Robinson, and Erika A. Patall, "Does Homework Improve Academic Achievement? A Synthesis of Research,
1987–2003," *Review of Educational Research* 76 (2006):
43. Available here: https://www.almendron.com/tribuna
/wp-content/uploads/2016/02/Does-Homework-Im
prove-Academic-Achievement.pdf. For a detailed analysis
of the research on homework, see Alfie Kohn, *The Homework Myth*.

2 John J. Ratey, M.D., *Spark: The Revolutionary New Science
of Exercise and the Brain* (New York: Little Brown, 2014),
ch 6: 10.

Chapter 6

1 Daniel Kahneman, *Thinking Fast and Slow* (New York: Farrar, Straus and Giroux, 2011), 41–42. "A Series of surprising experiments by the psychologist Roy Baumeister and his colleagues has shown conclusively that all variants of voluntary effort—cognitive, emotional or physical—draw at least partly on a shared pool of mental energy. . . . [They] have repeatedly found that an effort of self-control is tiring; if you have had to force yourself to do something, you are less willing or less able to exert self-control when the next challenge comes around. The phenomenon has been named *ego depletion*."

Chapter 7

1 https://drsophiayin.com/blog/entry/dog_bite_prevention _how_kids_and_adults_should_greet_dogs_safely/.

Chapter 13

1 This game comes from Lawrence J. Cohen, *Playful Parenting* (New York: Ballantine, 2002), 83.

Chapter 14

1 *Hidden Brain* (podcast), "The Monkey Marketplace," Oct. 21, 2019.

Chapter 18

1 https://www.ncbi.nlm.nih.gov/pubmed/17366333.

2 See endnotes 2, 3, and 4 for Chapter Three: The Problem with Punishment.

3 https://www.nij.gov/topics/corrections/recidivism/Pages
/welcome.aspx.

Chapter 22

1 Adele Faber and Elaine Mazlish, *Liberated Parents, Liberated Children* (New York: Avon Books, 1974, 1990), 39.

2 Lightning Injures About 1,000 People In The U.S. Each Year. https://web.archive.org/web/20051029004621/http://www .lightningsafety.noaa.gov/resources/Ltg%20Safety-Facts .pdf. "During the study year [2002], there were an esti- mated 115 stereotypical kidnappings, defined as abductions perpetrated by a stranger or slight acquaintance." http:// www.unh.edu/ccrc/pdf/MC19.pdf.

3 https://www.washingtonpost.com/opinions/five-myths -about-missing-children/2013/05/10/efee398c-b8b4-11e2 -aa9e-a02b765ffoea_story.html.

Chapter 23

1 https://jamanetwork.com/journals/jamapediatrics/article-ab stract/2740229?guestAccessKey=f4c21d39-7699-4bee-94d c-8255e4faf7bf&utm_source=For_The_Media&utm_medi um=referral&utm_campaign=ftm_links&utm_content= tfl&utm_term=072919.

Index

Index

Index

Index

Index

Index

sharing *(cont.)*
  reminder list for, 253
  rules on, 245
  taking action on, 244
sleep, *see* bedtime routine;
  tiredness

temper tantrums, 192–198
  reminder list for, 198
  strategies for, 195
threats and warnings, 29, 30,
  172
time, putting child in charge of,
  210
tiredness
  cooperation and, 51–53
  homework and, 125
  whining and, 213
  wound-up child and, 141
toothbrushing, 291–97
  playfulness and, 291–93
  reminder list for, 296–97
toys, children using non-toy
  items as, 254–58
  and managing environment,
  254
  and putting child in charge
  of household tasks,
  254–55
  and reimagining definition of
  "toy," 254
  reminder list for, 258
  and telling children what they
  can do, instead of what they
  can't, 255

toys, sharing, *see* sharing
train game, 138–39

unreasonableness, 101–10
  and acknowledging child's
  feelings, 102–5
  reminder list for, 110

warnings and threats, 29, 30, 172
whining, 207–17
  basic needs and, 213
  child's feelings and, 208–9,
  212
  choice and, 208, 212
  and giving in fantasy what
  you cannot give in reality,
  212
  and giving information,
  212
  putting the child in charge,
  209–12
  reminder list for, 216–17
  stories about, 210, 213–15
  telling child what he can do,
  instead of what he can't,
  212
words
  acknowledging feelings with,
  11
  bad, *see* name-calling and bad
  language
  "but," 349–52
  single, in eliciting cooperation,
  35
  "you," 345–48

386

Index